Whose India?

Whose India?

The Independence Struggle in

British and Indian Fiction and History

Teresa Hubel   *Duke University Press Durham & London 1996*

© 1996 Duke University Press

All rights reserved

Printed in the United States of America on

acid-free paper ∞

Typeset in Sabon by Tseng Information Systems, Inc.

Library of Congress Cataloging-in-Publication Data

appear on the last printed page of this book.

Cover photo: Photographer unknown, *The
Royal Bath,* Delhi, 1890s. © *The Last Empire:
Photography in British India, 1855–1911,*
Aperture, New York, 1976.

For Mom, Bob, Karen, Dave,

Holly, Terry, Jess, Em, Conor,

Calam, and Caesie,

And for my father, Dale Hubel,

who would have been proud,

And for you, beloved

Contents

Acknowledgments

Researching and writing this book has been a predominantly joyful, occasionally trying, and always intense experience. So many people have helped to make it happen. I must thank Balachandra Rajan, whose life and work and presence have been and remain an inspiration to me. I am grateful as well to Carole Farber for pointing me in the right directions and for generously sharing with me her ideas about India. My dance teacher, Lakshmi Ranganathan, without whom this book would not have existed, deserves a special mention, as does my buddy Liza Rumjahn, who has always brought herself and Canada to India just when I needed them both.

The Social Sciences and Humanities Research Council of Canada, the Faculty of Graduate Studies at the University of Western Ontario, and the Ruse Travel Service gave me the funding I needed to complete this study and to visit India for two months in 1990 to conduct some research. I must also acknowledge the assistance of the library staff at the Nehru Memorial Museum and Library in New Delhi and the National Library in Calcutta, and of the people at the Shastri Indo-Canadian Institute, who made a huge difference while I was in India. The faculty and the staff in the English department at the University of Western Ontario have been wonderfully supportive and interested throughout the project.

The Marty Memorial Scholarship, which I received from Queen's University in 1991–92, enabled a significant amount of work. And my colleagues in the English department at Saint Mary's University, where I taught for two years, helped me to hone many of my intellectual tools. My thanks to both institutions and to the people there.

This book had four anonymous reviewers, all of whom provided sage advice. I am grateful for their interest and their assistance in getting this book published.

A very great debt I owe to Tom Tausky, initially my thesis supervisor and now my good friend. It is difficult to express gratitude to a person who has made such a profound contribution to my life. His guidance, his example, his never-failing encouragement and affection leave me humbled.

Three of my muses for this book were Wendy Hayton Russell, Therese Khimasia, and Saloni Mathur. Our passionate discussions over wine, food, and cigarettes have been and continue to be among the best things that the Canadian academy has given me. I could not have begun my theorizing about class without Wendy's brilliant impetus, and I am supremely grateful for her continued presence in my life and my work.

Thanks also to the following friends for constantly making me rethink my ideas: Ellen Broughton, Russell Perkin, Sian Echard, Brian Bartlett, Ken Snyder, Elizabeth Harvey, Wendy Katz, Sukeshi Kamra, Elizabeth Stephen, Richard Green, Eric Fergusson, David Kinahan, Gillian Thomas, Ann Mayer, Fredericka Maclean, Elizabeth Sauer, Mark Cheetham, Monika Lee, Madine Vander Plaat, Mary Arseneau, Sandra Bell, Carolyn Quick, James Miller, John Leonard, Karen Dahl, David Bentley, Darcy Terrel, Claire Fyfe, Joanne Buckley, and Terry Whalen. And I must name Clare and Len Patton as well as Chris, Max, and Benjamin Wall, who regularly give me fresh approaches to my academic world and lots of love and laughter.

My family is the foundation of everything I do and think. They are Joyce Hubel, Bob Hennessy, Karen Campbell, David White, Holly Gilmour, Terry Gilmour, Jessica Campbell, Emily Campbell, and Conor White. Much of my intellectual life is simply working my way back to them. My father, Dale Franklin Hubel, died in 1979, but he would have known that this book could not have been written without him.

And finally there is the incomparable Brian Patton, whose take on things is always different from everyone else's and who keeps me joyful everyday.

Introduction

Who owns India? If India existed solely as a territorial possession, a piece of property, the answer to this question might be simple. Whoever rules India, owns it. Prior to 1947, when the administrative machinery of the British Empire was still intact, the ruler/owner was England. The English controlled its central and provincial governments, dictated its politics and economics, and mapped out its boundaries. Insofar as one country can own another, then, England owned India. But India is more than a geographical entity. If it were not more, how could Salman Rushdie describe it as a "new myth—a collective fiction" (112); how could V. S. Naipaul call it "a wounded civilization"; how could Edwin Arnold assert, "I declare myself not so much her friend as her lover" (324)? Clearly India's reality extends beyond its geographical presence. It has also an imaginative dimension. The imperialist connotations traditionally implicit in the word 'own' are hardly erased by this broadening of the epistemic boundaries of India. On the contrary, the potential for appropriating India increases when it is recognized as a property of the imagination.

Within the context of this expanded conception of India, then, the issue of its ownership becomes much more complex. Whoever defines India, whoever speaks to and for its people, and whoever imagines its destiny with the hope of determining its future can be said to have a part in it. Depending on one's focus, India is a cultural, spiritual, political, social, or emotional construct, and as such it belongs to whichever individuals or groups are able to constitute its formation in discourse and, additionally, assert their right to claim it. These two programs are usually simultaneous. Rudyard Kipling and Jawaharlal Nehru, for instance, stake their claim to the ownership of India by the very act of writing about it.

This study assumes that writing can possess exactly this kind of power, the power to establish ownership, and that some writing works to this end. Indeed it treats British imperialism and Indian nationalism in India *as if* ownership and its implicit authority were the dominant themes underlying this history. The texts I examine in the following chapters all seem intensely concerned with acquiring India. In the cross-cultural confrontation that occurred between the Indians and the English from the seventeenth to the twentieth century, the opportunity to stake one's claim to a construct-cum-place was enormously empowering. Nehru knew this, and the title of one of his books, *The Discovery of India*, not only alludes to the idea of India as a possession but also to his efforts to procure it by discovering, through writing, his latent ownership of it.

Understandably, the issue of appropriation figures prominently in this analysis of British and Indian texts. Whenever there is a statement of ownership, inevitably there is a contestation of it. In the long history of the British colonization of India, one or another group of Indians has always resisted the usurpation of their culture by foreign imperialists. Similarly, from the inception of the Indian movement for independence, the charge of appropriation has been leveled against the movement's leaders by those communities and individuals whose lives, identities, and sufferings have been sacrificed to the cause of nationalism. Ownership and resistance to that ownership emerge in these pages as mutually constructing categories. Each engenders the other.

My study explores this notion of India as a property of the imagination within the specific historical parameters of the Indian nationalist movement. I have chosen this particular perspective on modern Indian history for a number of reasons. First, the era of nationalism in India created a political moment when the cultures of India and Britain publicly collided. Though Indian resistance to British imperialism has always existed, in the second half of the nineteenth and the first half of the twentieth centuries that resistance became organized and, consequently, began to represent a profound threat to the British government and to British life in India. What this in turn produced was an intensified articulation on the part of the British of their role in India. Patrick Brantlinger and Francis Hutchins have both noted that in the late Victorian and Edwardian years, British imperialism grew increasingly aggressive and outspoken, and Jan Morris has written an entire book on the dazzle and din that accompanied what she calls the "climax of an empire."[1] I suggest that this new enthusiasm for empire, evident in so many texts written during the age of nationalism, was partially a justification of England's imperialist designs in the face of a movement that questioned those designs.

Second, the British/Indian confrontation over India's independence brought to the fore contending constructs of India, and these constructs were emotionally charged and therefore capable of producing powerful changes in the social and political structures of a colonized country. While there is much debate in historical scholarship about the extent and nature of these changes, especially as those changes affected exploited groups,[2] a basic assumption of the majority of texts written during the century of nationalism is that this era was indeed a time when an image or construct had the capacity to effect transformations in the status quo. I have chosen the Indian nationalist movement, then, as the thematic and historical frame for this book because it was a period of change and contention. Moreover, it represents a moment of trauma in the history of both the British and Indian cultures. The Indian struggle for political independence and its corollary, the demise of the British Empire, constitute traumatic events on the ground that their meaning remains, in the words of Hayden White, "problematical or overdetermined in the significance that they still have for current life" (87). One has only to call to mind the enormous number of books—fiction *and* history—published in the last forty-five years or so that remember and reconstruct the Raj and the nationalist movement, to recognize the importance of this historical period for late twentieth century English and Indian societies. The recent popularity of British films about the Empire and the nationalist period (David Lean's *A Passage to India* and Richard Attenborough's *Gandhi,* to name two) and of the television serialization of Paul Scott's *Raj Quartet,* under the title of *The Jewel and the Crown,* is, I think, indicative of the depth of the trauma. It is clearly not confined to the realms of academic scholarship and literature alone.

History and historiography are major concerns of mine. I choose to read history critically, emphasizing its textuality and applying many of the same analytical tools and strategies to it that I use in examining fiction. I also locate the fiction I discuss in this book very decidedly in its historical context. With a few exceptions—and these are histories written predominantly by Indian authors—the historiography surrounding the period of Indian nationalism is not self-consciously written, so as to make apparent the ideologies on which it rests. The numerous history texts which document the events that followed the 1857 revolt and that eventually led to the transfer of power from a British government to an Indian one in 1947, usually purport, either implicitly or explicitly, to describe and analyze objectively the Indian movement for political independence. For example, in the foreword to their 1942 volume *India Today: The Background of Indian Nationalism*, authors W. E. Duffett, A. R. Hicks, and G. R. Parkin state that they "have refrained throughout from expressing any opinions of their own, preferring to present what in their judgment appear to be the elementary, significant facts of the Indian political situation . . ." (Duffett 9). As I read the book, however, it became increasingly obvious that Duffett, Hicks, and Parkin had a hidden agenda (hidden even from themselves, I think) and, furthermore, that their history has a metahistory, which consists of the various ethical and aesthetic decisions the authors made in the course of writing their narrative. In the case of Duffett, Hicks, and Parkin, it is clear throughout the text that they do not entirely approve of the cause of Indian nationalism, since they consistently refute nationalist accusations against the British government in India. But *India Today* is hardly unique in its dubious claims to objectivity; the bias is equally detectable in some texts that implicitly support Indian aspirations for self-government. The point is, as White reminds us in *Tropics of Discourse,* that describing an object and actually constructing it amount to much the same thing. So-called 'objectivity,' or relying on "facts" instead of "opinions," is simply the means by which a writer of history conceals his/her own subjectivity and the constitutive nature of his/her narrative.

White observes that in the scholarly disciplines of history and literary criticism "there has been a reluctance to consider historical narratives as what they most manifestly are: verbal fictions, the contents of which are as much *invented* as *found* and the forms of which have more in common with their counterparts in literature than they have with those in the sciences" (82). The collapsing boundaries between history and literature make it pointless to use history texts as a means of verifying the accuracy of literary creations. The historiography of Indian nationalism is, therefore, not the yardstick against which we might measure such works as the Indian fiction of Kipling, Sara Jeannette Duncan, E. M. Forster, and Philip Mason or the novels of Swarnakumari Devi, Mulk Raj Anand, and Bhabani Bhattacharya. Nevertheless, this historiography does mediate our reading of these works and vice versa. Our current perception of this age of nationalism in India is, moreover, a product of both discourses. For this reason, I balance each section of my analysis of the literary texts with an examination of some principal historical claims concerning the two major periods of the nationalist movement in India: 1885–1909 and 1909–1947. My intention is to explore the constitutive nature of these claims in order to understand the ways in which British and Indian fiction work with other public texts in the construction of Indian history.

The scope of this study is necessarily wide. I am curious about the multiplicity of perspectives about India which the British/Indian encounter generated. What this means in practice is that I move from an examination of the fiction and history of the rulers to the counter-discourse produced by the ruled, and then further to the writing of disadvantaged groups within the subject population: specifically high-caste Hindu women and untouchables, whose contributions to the dialogue on India are frequently elided in literary and historical studies of this period. Their voices call into question implicit assumptions in mainstream histories and fiction that British imperialism created a battleground on which only the ruling British and the ruling Indians meet. In addition to this panorama of the British versus the Indians, the following chapters sketch other pictures. I argue that both national groups were far from homogeneous, as the panoramic view suggests. Consequently, Britons often confronted each other about the issues of imperialism in India, and the possibility of political independence did not mean the same thing or carry the same importance for all Indians. The conception of Indian nationalism in which India simply squared off against Britain loses the complexity of the events and erases too many disputes and alliances. Class and gender categories invariably get subsumed into the larger dichotomy. But the examination of class and gender has the potential to disturb and complicate standard views of this colonial confrontation.

In the interests of retrieving that multiplicity, I have also chosen in this work to study canonical texts alongside non-canonical ones. Little-read histories of modern India, even those not intended for or well received by an audience of scholars, help to shape a nation's view of itself and generate its international reputation. Furthermore, sometimes non-canonical texts articulate attitudes that are more widely held by members of either the colonized or the colonizing population. These texts must, consequently, be considered products of their historical moments and their premises need to be analyzed in terms of their contributions to those moments.

In literature, the separate canons of Indian fiction in English and modern British fiction both preserve the uncomplicated image of imperialism as the confrontation between the two ruling classes of India and Britain. The result is that in the two unquestionably canonical texts I examine in the following pages, namely, *A Passage to India* and *Untouchable,* potentially subversive details such as the participation of Indian women and untouchables in the nationalist movement (or their dissatisfactions with it) are elided. Furthermore, British women whose approaches to imperialism and nationalism are significantly different from those of British men are left out of the story altogether. Forster's novel reiterates the typical version of the memsahib (a white woman in India from the British upper or middle classes) with her ultraconservative attitudes and her isolationist stance, a version which was popular in many nonfictional accounts of Anglo-Indian life written in the late nineteenth and early twentieth centuries. Examining non-canonical texts in this study opens up new vistas, one of which is the view that there *were* memsahibs who had something interesting to offer the British discourse on imperialism, something that their men had not already said.

The idea of the canon, however, is a thorny one in this examination of Anglo-Indian and Indo-Anglian fiction,[3] since the status of these literatures in western universities is precarious. Anglo-Indian authors tend to be excluded from university courses on Victorian and modernist literature, although Kipling is occasionally incorporated. I contend that the fact that Anglo-Indian writers are avowed imperialists has everything to do with their placement outside the recognized canons of English literature or on their margins. English and American scholars, literary critics, and authors, who have in the past helped to determine which works of English literature are studied and which are not, seem to have been hostile to imperialist voices. Indeed, imperialist elements even in the opus of canonized authors are invariably excoriated or downplayed.[4] During the modernist era, when many of the period canons western scholars now use were constructed, the wave of anti-imperialism which swept through English and American academic institutions ensured that authors who were admittedly imperialist would be dismissed outright by canon-builders.

As Barbara Herrnstein Smith and Edward Said have demonstrated, canons are not constructed in vacuums. Like the texts they valorize, they are part of the historical, social, and cultural reality from which they draw their values and impetus. Literary scholar Arnold Krupat observes that *the* canon of English literature, which contemporary students study in western universities, is, "like all cultural production . . . never an innocent selection of the best that has been thought and said; rather, it is the institutionalization of those particular verbal artifacts that appear best to convey and sustain the dominant social order" (310). To some extent, canons disseminate codes of thought and conduct, which contain political messages about values and morality, specifically those values and that morality deemed acceptable by the dominant group in a culture. During the age of modernism in the West, there occurred a general repudiation of imperialist politics by liberal and Marxist intellectuals, and the canons created at the time, specifically the Victorian and the modernist ones, contained little knowledge of western imperialism. This was the age that rendered Kipling's relationship to the English canons so uncertain. Indeed, the modernist disavowal of imperialism was so pronounced that its exclusions and blind spots still permeate contemporary scholarship. A 1984 article by modernist scholar Hugh Kenner attests to the continued existence of this denial. Entitled "The Making of the Modernist Canon," the article acknowledges the canon's debt to an enormous variety of distinctly twentieth-century activities, from the Russian ballet to the discovery of the electron, but it neglects to mention that England was engaged in a massive defense of its Empire throughout the years that saw "the making of the modernist canon." So thoroughly was the fact of imperialism repressed by modernist scholars and authors that Kenner can write an article decades later which applauds London as the center of "International Modernism," while ignoring that it was also the center of British imperialism.

What this seeming rejection of imperialist aspirations and activities disguises, however, is how all canons share the very structure of imperialism. It is the imperialism of the modernist canon, for example, that keeps Anand's *Untouchable* and virtually every other piece of Indo-Anglian fiction from finding a place among the so-called 'great' texts of modern English literature. Having said this, I should also add that Anand's texts have undergone a similarly troubling canonization in India, where they are, along with the works of R. K. Narayan and Raja Rao, privileged in comparison to other Indian novels in English. Swarnakumari Devi's novel,

An Unfinished Song, and Bhattacharya's *So Many Hungers!* are no longer in print in India, although Anand's *Untouchable* was available in every bookstore I visited in New Delhi in 1990.

This book, then, foregrounds issues such as canonization and gender in its efforts to confront head-on the politics of imperialism and nationalism in India. Its organization is primarily chronological, but it does proceed along developing thematic lines as well. After the first chapter, which analyzes the orthodox conception of the British/Indian encounter, it questions that orthodoxy from the perspective of various groups whose experiences have been underrepresented or completely erased by mainstream histories and literary canons. The last chapter reexamines the traditional paradigm of India versus Britain once again, but by this stage that paradigm has been challenged, which allows for a much more critical reading of it.

The first chapter focuses on two of Kipling's short stories and their contribution to the British understanding of the early nationalist movement. It argues that one of these stories, "The Enlightenments of Pagett, M.P.," serves to comfort Kipling's Anglo-Indian community by dispelling the threat of nationalism, while the other, "On the City Wall," makes the same attempt but does not succeed. In the second story, the narrator, who is supposed to provide the comfort by using his knowledge of India to contain Indian nationalism, ends up inadvertently participating in a nationalist bid to overthrow the British government because of his immense attraction to an India he feminizes. Sara Jeannette Duncan articulates a similar feminization of India in her novel *The Burnt Offering,* the subject of the second chapter. However, she complicates this construction of femininity by undermining its patriarchal origin. Though her novel finally upholds the doctrines of British imperialism, it also introduces the image of the politicized Indian woman and lends support to the picture of an increasingly politicized India. The images of women and narrative point of view in Duncan's work begin the process of subverting the traditional British/Indian historical paradigm, which histories of Indian nationalism by authors from both countries usually construct.

The third chapter examines Forster's *A Passage to India* as a vehicle for the liberal myth of imperialism, a way of seeing India which not only appropriates its nationalist movement but also neutralizes its alterity. In *A Passage to India* all things feminine, including India, are emptied of their otherness in the interests of an ideal that exalts the cross-cultural connections between men. This chapter also combines a reading of subaltern maleness in Forster's novel with an analysis of the Subaltern Studies series edited by Ranajit Guha, which incorporates the dissident practices of India's subordinate classes within a new understanding of nationalist history.

The fourth chapter marks the moment of internal transition in this study when the emphasis shifts from British to Indian literary texts. At this stage I temporarily disturb the chronological sequence and return to the late nineteenth and early twentieth century for a discussion of the construction of the high-caste Hindu woman in nationalist and imperialist writing. Although I refer to two nonfictional books written by English women, this chapter is principally concerned with writing by Indian women of the colonial period. I therefore juxtapose Pandita Ramabai Saraswati's *The High-Caste Hindu Woman*, a treatise on the status of the nineteenth-century Hindu woman, with Swarnakumari Devi's little-known but fascinating novel in English, *An Unfinished Song*. This chapter charts the double subordination of high-caste women in India and scrutinizes the extent of their protest against imperialism and indigenous patriarchy.

While the fourth chapter endeavors to locate female voices with Indian nationalist aspirations, since such aspirations are usually depicted as belonging almost exclusively to Indian men, chapter 5 looks to another group which was exploited during the struggle for independence, India's untouchables. Using Anand's famous *Untouchable* as the basis for discussion, I delineate two opposing views on untouchability current in India throughout the 1930s and 40s: namely, Gandhi's ideas of trusteeship and upper-caste reparation and the belief of untouchable leader B. R. Ambedkar that the members of his community needed to experience empowerment personally and not through the efforts of those who had traditionally oppressed them. Both attitudes are present in Anand's work. The novel, nevertheless, ends up supporting Gandhi's ideal of upper-caste leadership.

My final chapter investigates the nostalgia that erupted on each side of the discursive border in 1947, when India and Britain were on the verge of parting political ways forever. I contend that nostalgia is frequently a feature of Indian and British fiction and nonfiction about the Empire, particularly during the last few years of the nationalist movement. I therefore argue in this chapter for the existence of nostalgia in two novels, one each of Anglo-Indian and Indo-Anglian origin, both published in 1947. Philip Mason's *The Wild Sweet Witch* is a lament for Britain's lost power in India. Bhabani Bhattacharya's novel *So Many Hungers!*, though on the surface less nostalgic than Mason's, is nostalgic nevertheless when placed in its historical context. What I finally suggest is that the nostalgia in both texts is dependent on the exclusion of certain problematic issues.

At this point I feel obliged to say something about myself and the place from which I speak and read, insofar as I am able to articulate that place. Since I began work on this book, I have been grappling with Spivak's idea about being aware of one's assigned subject position. It seems to me to be a necessary though difficult thing to delineate, and I have rarely seen it done well. What it appears to consist of is an attempt to make clear to one's readers the connective tissue between oneself and one's subject matter. In practice it is often simply a confession of one's race. Surely that confession should constitute only a beginning.

Aijaz Ahmad's book *In Theory* takes this question one step further. Bringing a Marxist epistemology to the reading of various postcolonial and colonial discourse theories and texts, Ahmad criticizes some post-modern and postcolonial scholarship for its suppression of the question of human agency:

> A difficult but also pressing question for theory, one would have thought, would consist of the proper specification of the dialectic between objective determination and individual agency in the theorist's own production. This would be an especially pressing issue—not so much in the form of censorship as of self-censorship and spontaneous refashioning—as the radical theorist takes up the role of the professional academic in the metropolitan university, with no accountable relation with classes and class-fractions outside the culture industry. The characteristic feature of contemporary literary radicalism is that it rarely addresses the question of its own determination by the conditions of its production and the class location of its agents. (6)

Ahmad's criticism is a significant intervention in postcolonial theory. For it points to the need for those of us who have an investment in scholarship to lay our cards on the table, to describe and theorize our specific allegiances and placements, both of which circumscribe our work and, in part, prescribe what we will say and see. Here are my cards.

You should know that I am neither British nor Indian. I am a white, Canadian woman from Ontario's Anglo working classes. So what does this mean? To begin with, being white in Canada marks me as a beneficiary of certain racist/colonialist structures that privilege whiteness by normalizing it. Because one of the repercussions of whiteness in a society dominated by white people is its invisibility—white people can escape being cognizant of their race—reconfiguring whiteness as both a place of dominance and of seeming normality goes some of the way toward dismantling those structures. As Ruth Frankenberg writes in her contemporary book on the subject, "Naming 'whiteness' displaces it from the unmarked, unnamed status that is itself an effect of its dominance" (6). But naming whiteness is not enough. Recognizing that whiteness can be a site of resistance is also necessary. As a white postcolonialist—someone who has inherited a system of racism but who questions it—I think it is important to develop strategies to combat my own race privilege. Writing a book that uncovers and challenges the racism implicit in British imperialism is one of those strategies. Questioning a canon that encourages scholars to study predominantly the literature of white people is another.

As difficult as race is to theorize, class, for me, is even more vexed. Coming from a working-class background and ending up in the Canadian academy, whose deepest cultural connections are to the middle and upper classes, has left me straddling two worlds. This would not be so vexing a position if its viability were not so undermined by certain North American myths about class, particularly the myth about the possibility and desirability of upward mobility. Among the Canadian middle classes this myth has become so entrenched it has achieved the status of truth. But, like many of the women who contributed essays to the anthology *Working-Class Women in the Academy*, I resent myths that tell us that an individual is able to move around the class system, because these myths perpetuate the fallacy that class has no effects, no restrictions, and produces no solidarity. They therefore blind us to the implications of class status in our theories and our interpretations. The result of this screening out of class issues is the paucity of good class analyses in Canadian and American postcolonial scholarship. The idea that one's values, experiences, and "standpoint" is partly determined by one's gender and race is a foundational axiom in postcolonial studies and feminist theory. But that class also contributes to the influences that make up our perspectives and those of the authors we study has hardly been addressed.

As a postcolonialist and a feminist, I am committed to the theoretical position that experience is a way to knowledge and that it structures our various standpoints. I am consequently confident that my working-classness is a gift rather than a liability (as it is often conceived of in the academy), because it has made me suspicious of middle-class ideas and ideals that pretend to speak for whole nations.

The position I have constructed for myself—in regard to this study and to other scholarly work surrounding it—has made me conscious of my privilege as a white woman in a Canadian academic institution that has powerful ties to the middle class and its class authority. I am also conscious of the fact that the people and the place about which and whom I have chosen to write are marginalized within my academic context, and I am speaking here not only of the Indians and India but of the Anglo-Indians too. I envision my interpretative role as operating somewhere between the center I, at least in part, represent and in which I participate as a white person in a middle-class academy and the periphery I study and also—because of my gender and class grounding—at least in part represent. Specifically, I wish to make the center more aware of this periphery, because to ignore it or continue to relegate it to edges alone is to repeat the illusions of imperialism and nationalism.

"To tell the history of another is to be pressed against the limits of one's own . . ." (Suleri, *Rhetoric* 2). Personal and political identity, though initially generated from agreement and affiliation, is also, I think, created out of difference. For me, India has been one of those differences.

1 Containing Indian Nationalism:

Kipling's Struggle

Indian nationalism, most twentieth-century historians tend to agree, was not always an issue in India. It did not become an issue until the last three decades of the nineteenth century when various Indian associations were founded—among them the Indian National Congress in 1885—which sought to change the political make-up of the Indian government. That is not to say that Indians did not repeatedly struggle to throw off British political domination prior to the twentieth century. A number of Indian historians, writing in the last twenty years or so, tell us that the Maratha wars and uprisings of the late-eighteenth and early-nineteenth centuries and the great revolt of 1857—or the Indian Mutiny, as some British texts still prefer to call it—were attempts to eliminate the threat of British hegemony in India.[1] But even the ardent nationalist Jawaharlal Nehru does not, in his writing and reclamation of Indian history, endeavor to recoup these events for the cause of nationalism. In *The Discovery of India,* written in the early 1940s while he was in prison, Nehru places the 1857 revolt outside of the nationalist historical moment. Although he does recognize the anti-foreign sentiments that ignited this violent retaliation against the absolute power of the British East India Company, he distinguishes between these emotions and those that would later enter the Indian political arena:

> It is clear . . . that there was a lack of nationalist feeling which might have bound the people of India together. Nationalism of the modern type was yet to come; India had still to go through much sorrow and travail before she learned the lesson which would give her real freedom. (237–38)

The "lesson" that would free India, according to Nehru, involved the pursuit of another cause—not the "lost cause, the feudal order" (238), which he believes Indians were trying to recover in 1857, but a new cause with a new vision, a nationalist vision through which India would find the unity and strength to overcome British rule once and for all.

Charles H. Heimsath, an American historian whose well-known book *Indian Nationalism and Hindu Social Reform* was published in 1964, broadly defines nationalism as "an attitude of mind, or set of beliefs, that is shared by a group of people large enough to be influential, and that embodies ideas of the nation and the nation's goals, elevates those ideas to a prime position over other public values, and compels the assertion of the identity and the aims of the nation" (133). Although Heimsath finds this definition adequate to describe the all-India independence movement that won Indians world-wide admiration and attention in the 1920s, 30s, and 40s, he does not believe that it can be applied to nationalism of the nineteenth century; the reason for its inappropriateness lies, I think, as much in the definition itself—in what it leaves out—as in the state of Indian politics at that time. Heimsath's notion of nationalism cannot properly accommodate the situation in India prior to Indian Independence in 1947, for it does not take into account the existence of imperialism. That imperialism was a social, cultural, and political structure in India for at least one hundred years and an economic one for even longer, and that the effects of this circumstance were undoubtedly instrumental in the public construction of a nationalist belief system, are details that Heimsath and many other western writers of India's history simply elide.

Heimsath and conservative British historians such as Percival Spear regard Indian nationalism, especially in its early stages, primarily as an expression of various elite communities, grouped around either religious or regional interests. Moreover, these writers trace the efforts of these communities to displace British power in India merely to a dislike of foreign rule, a dislike relegated to the status of "emotion." Spear's explanation of the origin of the nationalist movement in *A History of India: Volume Two* (1965) runs as follows:

In looking for the roots of Indian nationalism we can begin with an emotion and a tradition. The emotion was dislike of the foreigner which in India for many ages has gone along with a tolerance of his presence. The tradition was that of Hinduism deeply rooted and the basis of what has been called the fundamental unity of India. The Arab philosopher Albiruni noted in the eleventh century that the Hindus believed "that there was no country like theirs, no king like theirs, no religion like theirs, no science like theirs." The foreigner was impure in a stronger sense than the barbarian to the Greek or the Gentile to the Jew. Foreign rule was thus impure, whether it was Muslim, Turkish, or Christian. (Spear 158–59)

In Spear's estimation, nationalism in India developed not because of an increasingly intolerable colonial condition, which, as many Indian and British historians point out, kept every Indian in a state of subjugation, but because foreign rule was "impure" according to the beliefs of the predominantly Hindu population. Spear's construction of this seemingly natural aversion on the part of the Hindus to foreign rule of any kind erases Britain's responsibility for inciting rebellion against its particular brand of imperialism. For if Hindus despise any rule that is not indigenous, it is hardly the fault of the British and their colonialism that a national movement rose up to oust them.

Both Spear and Heimsath also repeatedly depict the Hindu and Muslim people of India as fundamentally divided along clear-cut religious lines. In the above passage, for example, Hindus are made to seem the native inhabitants of India while Muslims are lumped in with the British as conquerors. That many of India's Muslims are descendants of Hindus or that the two religious groups might share certain cultural values or nationalist aspirations are rarely presented as relevant issues. Moreover, by constructing Hinduism as a coherent faith, to be counterpoised against an equally coherent Indian Islam, Spear and Heimsath demonstrate their indebtedness to one of the most influential and long-lasting of all Orientalism's inventions—namely, that there was, before the British arrived, a religion such as Hinduism, practiced by people who identified themselves as Hindus. Romila Thapar, in her powerful critique of current Hindu fundamentalism in India entitled "Imagined Religious Communities? Ancient History and the Modern Search for a Hindu Identity," gives us an alternative view of what is now commonly held to be the single, inclusive religion called Hinduism with a similarly communal history. The reality of pre-British and pre-Islamic Hindu India, according to Thapar, "lay in looking at it as a cluster of distinctive sects and cults, observing common civilizational symbols but with belief and ritual ranging from atheism to animism and a variety of religious organizations identifying themselves by location, language and caste. Even the sense of religious identity seems to have related more closely to sect than to a dominant Hindu community" (228–29). The attempt to conceive of these often diverse forms as something cohesive, as Hinduism, arose out of an impulse in Orientalists, inherited later by nationalists, to understand the indigenous religious traditions of India in terms of Christianity, which, in spite of its factions, was a coherent faith, with a central figure and a fundamental text. My point here is not to lambaste Spear and Heimsath for seeing India as religiously segregated, since the argument that Indians in the nineteenth century did at times affiliate along somewhat monolithic lines can certainly be substantiated with evidence from that period (as can the argument that they increasingly joined together along nationalist lines). Instead, what I mean to show is that these two western historians have created their histories of Indian nationalism not from so-called "objective reality," but from traceable traditions of historiography, traditions whose origins can be located in such a politically interested discourse as Orientalism. It is the political investments and agendas behind their versions of India's history that I want to expose rather than their correctness or lack or correctness about the "facts." Finally, let me add that, as a result of Orientalism's legacy to Indian nationalism, something that can be loosely understood as a 'Hindu identity' has been established in India today, though it is not without its outspoken and numerous detractors, who see it either as fallacious or as detrimental to the status of a democratic nation. But whether or not a sharply drawn line between Indian Islam and Hindu India can be said to have existed during the historical periods that Heimsath and Spear examine—the late nineteenth century and earlier—surely needs to be questioned in light of Thapar's recent insights into the constructedness of Hinduism and its discursive links to an imperialist era.

Spear and Heimsath further argue that the divisiveness of the Indian people stalled the emergence of nationalism, nationalism, that is, "in the commonly accepted Western sense" (Spear 158), meaning a desire for self-government based on shared aims and a common culture. The country lacked those "conditions obviously conducive to the development of a sense of national unity" (Heimsath 134). Being of western origin, nationalism, we are meant to assume, is a concept foreign to Indian minds. When it is transplanted into Indian soil, something therefore goes awry.

What did emerge in the second half of the nineteenth century, according to Heimsath, were the first stirrings of nationalist feelings, stirrings which originated independently of one another, in Bengal, in the Maratha area surrounding Poona, in central India, stirrings which were often articulated as regional patriotism or as social reform or as Hindu revivalism. Thus, in spite of the founding of the Indian National Congress in 1885, Indian nationalism in the nineteenth century — seen through the eyes of an American professor writing in the 1960s — consisted of many nationalisms, each of which was grounded in a different assumption about the nature of the nation and the aims of the nation-builders. For some nationalists, the ideal of nationhood was rooted in indigenous religions and institutions, in, for example, the worship of the Hindu god Ganapathi and the celebration of the Maratha warrior Shivaji; for others, particularly for Indians who received an English education either in England or in India, European social and political conceptions of nationhood were privileged over those of the East. India's nationalisms were, therefore, often at odds in Heimsath's portrait of the movement, and the heated debates that were waged in the English-language and vernacular newspapers over such concerns as widow remarriage, age of consent, and the efficacy of social reform in general attested to the passionate convictions among these competing groups.

Nationalism, in the unified sense that Heimsath defines and constructs it, was struggling to come into existence in India in the last two decades of the nineteenth century, and its many voices were an indication of the fervor and the growing power of that struggle. He writes,

> Nationalists were religious and social reformers, political agitators, poets, saints, and statesmen; they were British-born as well as Indian-born. Some had programs for change, others merely criticized conditions around them, and still others were content to express devotion to an India which existed only in religious and mythological symbols. The absence of an observable nation and a sense of common nationality

among the people in general was not an impediment to the development of nationalism among that educated and often well-travelled group. A nation could not be discovered; it had to be created. (135–36)

Although Heimsath acknowledges that nationalism is never spontaneous but is rather the result of "consciously propagated ideas" (135), his emphasis on the friction and dissension within the nationalist movement leads his reader to wonder how Indians managed to unite long enough to depose the British. Indeed, his book ends with an analysis of nationalism in the first decade of the twentieth century, when its momentum was brought almost to a halt by a disagreement between the two major Congress factions, the moderates and the extremists, *and* when the British were still forty years away from relinquishing political power.

While western and particularly conservative writers of modern Indian history tend to concentrate on the diversity and the dissent present in nationalist agitation for self-government, Indian historians focus on the solidarity that the Congress leaders were able to achieve in spite of or, some would argue, because of India's immense heterogeneity. In the introduction to *India's Struggle for Independence* (1989), Bipan Chandra, a well-known writer of nationalist histories, outlines the historical assumptions from which the five co-authors have proceeded. One of these assumptions is that the Indian National Congress was not a political party, as some western writers have assumed,[2] but a movement; although "all political trends from the Right to the Left were incorporated in it," these "currents" were unified by a "common aim," namely to overthrow British hegemony. Unlike Heimsath, who sees some fundamental debility in the nationalists' various and often discordant stances, Bipan Chandra believes the Congress was able to contain these voices without silencing them and without curtailing their power: "While intense debate on all basic issues was allowed, the diversity and tension did not weaken the cohesion and striking power of the movement; on the contrary, this diversity and atmosphere of freedom and debate became a major source of its strength" (14). In his determination to show that there was very little dissonance, however, Chandra glosses over such potentially unharmonious events as the founding of Aligarh College in 1875 by Sir Syed Ahmed Khan, who, as Spear is quick to point out, saw himself and his college for Muslim men as standing in opposition to the Indian National Congress (Spear 226). Various statements made by Syed Ahmed at this time attest to his belief that the British and not the Congress could best safeguard the interests of the Muslim community in India and, consequently, that Muslims should rally behind the government and remain politically passive. While Bipan Chandra briefly mentions what he calls Syed Ahmed's "communalism" (414), he does so about three hundred pages *after* his discussion of early nationalism. The effect of this is to suggest to the reader that the refusal of some Muslims to participate in the Congress was not, in fact, part of the political landscape of the late nineteenth century but was of relevance only to later developments, such as the Muslim agitation for a separate state.

There is no question that the issue of Muslim participation in early nationalism is truly problematic, which goes some of the way toward explaining why Spear and Bipan Chandra erase the Muslim community in their histories of this era. It is certainly easier to avoid the problem entirely than to concede that Muslims occupied a precarious middle ground, which could be made to work for either imperialism or nationalism or for neither. The Muslim voice at this point in history was, I think, a powerfully subversive one, for it potentially threatened both the interests of the imperialists and the nationalists of the time as well as the constructions of Indian history by later neo-imperialist and neo-nationalist historians, such as Spear and Bipan Chandra. Spear's assertion that Indian nationalism was the product of an inherent Hindu aversion to foreign rule does not stand up in the face of a speaking, protesting Muslim community. Nor could Bipan Chandra confidently posit his image of nationalist "cohesion" if he were to acknowledge the reality of Muslim dissent. The historical validity of both Spear's and Bipan Chandra's recreations of early nationalism is dependent upon the absence of the Muslim people from the nineteenth-century political arena in India. That we can use this commonality in their work to critique their apparently oppositional constructions of Indian history points, I think, to a fundamental affinity in their political commitments. Both Spear's neo-imperialist history and Bipan Chandra's neo-nationalist one rely on the Orientalist assumption that Hinduism constituted the bedrock of India.

Ram Gopal in his 1967 history, *How India Struggled for Freedom*, confronts this matter of Muslim dissent. He notes that in the early nationalist movement, the Muslim community was itself split, with some men following Syed Ahmed and others joining the Congress. In spite of Syed Ahmed's enjoiners to Muslims to remain loyal to the British government, Muslim participation in Congress was increasing year after year. At the 1888 meeting of the Congress, Gopal reports, the Muslims numbered 221 to the Hindu majority of 965 (82). Moreover, Gopal is careful not to undercut the importance and the power of Syed Ahmed's political position, while at the same time making it clear that certain imperialist institutions, such as the Indian government and some British newspapers in England and in India, found it advantageous to support Syed Ahmed in his dual role as the rehabilitator of the socially depressed Indian Muslim community and the loyal advocate of British rule.

Gopal also draws attention to the constructed nature of Indian nationalism when he uses quotations from *The Times* of London to demonstrate how some Englishmen chose to interpret this Muslim dissension. The 1886 Congress session received the following treatment in *The Times:*

> The Mohammedan community appear to hold aloof from this kind of thing on the ground that they prefer not to hamper the Government at a time when it is doing its best for the natives of India. This incidentally shows what the real aims and results of the "National Indian Congress" are considered to be by the natives of India themselves. . . ." (quoted in Gopal 81)

It was, as Gopal points out, entirely within the interests of the British government and the British people to maintain rule in India, since imperialism was not only a very profitable enterprise but also provided careers for numerous young British men and women. And in order to ensure the continuance of that rule, the British press must have felt that it had to defuse the threat of nationalism by undermining its actual or potential power to mobilize the masses of Indian people. *The Times* is repeating what was a common belief at the time when it suggests that the Congress was in reality the work of only a small group of Indians and did not engage the sympathies of the "real" people, who in the above quotation are conflated with that part of the Muslim community which did not attend the 1886 Congress. Lord Dufferin, the Viceroy from 1884–1888, said much the same thing at his farewell dinner when he characterized the Congress as a "microscopic minority" (quoted in Gopal 69).

Although they wrote their histories in different decades and with different notions of historiography, Gopal and Bipan Chandra both construct an early Indian nationalist movement that is essentially cohesive. Bipan Chandra does so by maintaining that the many religious and special interest groups within the movement managed to rally behind the secular aspirations of the Congress. And Gopal suggests that the most debilitating dissent in the movement, caused by a partial Muslim boycott of the Congress, was the result of the machinations of the British government. These writers seem to be implicitly calling into question the frequent claim made by many western historians that at no time during the British Empire was India one country: instead, it was an almost haphazard collection of peoples and religions, none of which had any particular attachment to any other.[3] While not openly disputing this imperialist assertion, Bipan Chandra and Gopal choose to lay emphasis on the leaders of the freedom struggle, who, they insist, had a vision of India's unity which eventually brought about its actual unification in the twentieth century. Bipan Chandra writes,

> National leaders from Dadabhai Naoroji, Surendranath Banerjea and Tilak to Gandhiji and Nehru accepted that India was not yet a fully structured nation but a nation-in-the-making and that one of the major objectives and functions of the movement was to promote the growing unity of the Indian people through a common struggle against colonialism. . . . This process of the nation-in-the-making was never *counterposed* to the diverse regional, linguistic and ethnic identities in India. On the contrary, the emergence of a national identity and the flowering of other narrower identities were seen as processes deriving strength from each other. (23)

By stressing the role of the nationalist leaders and the transformative power and secular aims of the movement, Gopal and Bipan Chandra effectively sidestep the western historians' representations of a disunified India. In their histories Indian nationalist leaders emerge as farseeing and dedicated individuals who consistently place the nationalist cause over their own concerns and allegiances.

The problem at the heart of this construction is that these leaders are often emptied of their personality, and their political choices are made to seem only the consequence of their nationalism and not at all a product of their personal commitments and lives. For instance, Gopal states that Bal Gangadhar Tilak, an early extremist leader, approached politics from a secular standpoint: "he made no distinction between Hindus and Muslims and was prepared to go to any extent to accommodate Muslim demands" (98). And yet Gopal does not address the issue that western historians find so important in Tilak's politics, namely the inherent communalism in his agenda, a communalism that is evident, they insist, in his focus on Ganapathi, a Hindu deity, and on Shivaji, a Hindu hero of the Maratha wars. Tilak and a few other early nationalist leaders were involved in the Hindu revivalism that swept India in the 1890s and 1910s. This revivalism lent a new religious dimension—specifically Hindu—to the nationalist movement. About this, Heimsath goes so far as to comment, "Indian nationalism had in fact become by the first decade of this century Hindu nationalism among the Hindu leaders of the movement" (312). These leaders, and he cites Tilak and Aurobindo Ghosh, identified the nation with Hinduism. While Heimsath delineates Tilak's communalism in great detail and the growing Hindu revivalism Tilak propagated at the turn of the century and Spear suggests that Hinduism and nationalism went hand in hand in India, neither Gopal nor Bipan Chandra nor even Nehru examine in any depth the possible effect of powerful Hindu leaders on a fledgling nationalist movement.

When it was not ignoring the Indian political scene altogether, which was the most frequent reaction among British writers before 1900, Anglo-Indian literature of the late nineteenth and the first decade of the twentieth century employs images and ideas similar to those found in the work of Spear and Heimsath. These writers often dismiss the nationalist movement with the argument, provided by Lord Dufferin, that its appeal was limited to an inconsequential segment of the population, namely the newly created westernized class, and they offer as an alternative a continued maintenance of the status quo. As Indian agitation for political reform began to attract more and more attention, however, especially in the first years of the 1900s, a few British writers responded by focusing on a single faction of nationalism, usually a violent one that had ties to Hinduism, in order to undermine that particular faction and, by extension, all the others as well.

Rudyard Kipling and Sara Jeannette Duncan seem, at least in this regard, to be telling representatives of the Anglo-Indian writing community,

for they each either ignore Indian nationalism or portray it as a violent
and therefore inviable movement. Of the many short stories Kipling wrote
about India, only two address the issues implicit in the nationalist position, despite the fact that his writing career did not properly begin until
after the founding of the Congress in 1885. Kipling's concern is to establish an Empire, or an ideal of empire, based on a masculine work ethic.
Consequently, when he finds fault with the nationalist cause, as he does in
"The Enlightenments of Pagett, M.P.," it is often because he claims that it
does not do any work. Kipling depicts Indian nationalism as a movement
that attracts lazy and confused Indians, who are the unhappy products of
a western education. Such is the character of Wali Dad in "On the City
Wall." His representation of nationalism, therefore, stands in stark contrast to his almost religious vision of Empire that permeates story after
story. Furthermore, his emphasis is on a peasant India, an India which
retains its strong attachment to an ancient feudalism and an agrarian economy. Nationalism, with its commitment to democratic processes, seems
out of place in such a setting.

Duncan, on the other hand, credits nationalism with more scope, and
she delineates it as an expression of a modern, urban India. In her 1909
novel *The Burnt Offering,* she explores the turn-of-the-century Bengali resistance that erupted into violence and resulted in the assassination of a
number of British officials. Despite her obvious interest in the continuance
of British rule in India, she still admits to the validity of some of the nationalists' complaints, and she still attempts to examine and sympathetically
to portray the intense emotional investment behind the violence. However, Duncan centers her novel on a conception of law and order that takes
precedence over every other allegiance which her characters might have,
and the result is that, at the close of the story, nobody wins, not those Indians who sought nationalism, not those who supported the British right
to rule, not even the British themselves. What triumphs is only law and
order. Although Duncan is much more willing than most Anglo-Indian
writers to tackle Indian nationalism in her work, she ultimately strives to
negate it.

Kipling is as problematic a writer as they come. His work has engendered more debate on more levels—the political, the aesthetic, the ethical—than almost any other writer in or outside the Victorian and mod-

ernist canons. His position in those canons is also precarious; he is either defensively admitted at least to the margins, as T. S. Eliot seems to allow in his famous essay on Kipling, or he is roundly excommunicated. Excommunication is clearly what Lionel Trilling was trying to accomplish in 1943 when he published an essay entitled simply "Kipling." In it, he castigates Kipling for his poetry, his politics, and, surprisingly, his personality: "although he makes much to-do about manliness, he is not manly. . . . His imperialism is reprehensible not because it *is* imperialism but because it is a puny and mindless imperialism. In short, Kipling is unloved and unlovable not by reason of his beliefs but by reason of the temperament that gave them literary expression" (126). Eliot L. Gilbert in his 1970 study is determined to save Kipling from judges such as Trilling. But in doing so, he ignores 'the bad Kipling,' the political one with whom all liberal critics contend, and concentrates instead on 'the good Kipling,' who, he maintains, was able artistically "to synthesize apparently disparate elements into a satisfying aesthetic experience" (10). What these extremes in opinion manage to convey is the real difficulty that previous generations of literary scholars had in addressing Kipling on a political level. I would guess that one of the reasons for this difficulty is that he functions as the repository of so much western guilt about imperialism.

Still, in spite of the primarily negative reception of his work in the twentieth century, Kipling's name, his poetry, and his fiction never entirely disappear from the pages of literary scholarship. Eliot found that he could not dismiss him, Hemingway confessed to being influenced by him (Plimpton 227), and even a strident anti-imperialist such as George Orwell enshrines a Kipling he obviously despises by declaring that "tawdry and shallow though it is, Kipling's is the only literary picture that we possess of nineteenth-century Anglo-India" (50). There were other pictures of this period and of these people—for instance, Duncan's, Maud Diver's, and Flora Annie Steel's. Seemingly against the intent of his essay, which appears designed to consign Kipling to oblivion, Orwell's effacement of these alternative Anglo-Indias keeps Kipling alive at least as a historically relevant author. The republication by Penguin Classics of nearly all of Kipling's major fiction and the renewed interest in Kipling among postcolonialist scholars suggests that his work is further from oblivion than it has ever been.

I will not venture to examine Kipling's aesthetic staying power in the face of great odds, as Eliot did, since I do not have an adequate answer. But I will admit to believing that the "quest for value," as Catherine Belsey calls it, is erroneous (22). Barbara Herrnstein Smith in her important article "Contingencies of Value" uncovers certain matters that have been elided by conventional discussions of literary texts and questions discussions fueled by some belief in innate literary merit. She argues that such a belief led many literary scholars, particularly of the modernist era, to assume that, since merit or value was or was not inherent in a text, critical evaluation was unnecessary. Evaluation was therefore effectively banished from literary study and along with it went the potential for any analysis of those contingent forces that contributed to its production. She writes, "One of the major effects of prohibiting or inhibiting explicit evaluation is to forestall the exhibition and obviate the possible acknowledgment of divergent systems of value and thus to ratify, by default, established evaluative authority" (11). Although Kipling's writing has been evaluated to the point of tediousness, the largely unspoken taboo against applying evaluative judgments to works of literature prevented his critics from examining the nature of the evaluative process itself, which alternately denounced and praised him. But Kipling's liminal status in the Victorian and modernist canons calls this process into question. For if value is indeed inherent, as so many earlier scholars assumed, then the contents of any canon should not require debate.

In the thirties and forties the "established evaluative authority"—and I am referring here to canonizers like Eliot, Orwell, and Trilling rather than to publishers or general readers who also participate in canon building— was predominantly liberal and decidedly anti-imperialist in tone. Kipling's avid imperialism no longer fit England or even America's image of itself and consequently had to be expunged from the roll of literary texts that scholars, such as the ones mentioned above, studied. Eliot was clearly reluctant to let Kipling go entirely and so agreed to write the introduction to the 1941 Faber and Faber edition of Kipling's poetry. But Trilling, Orwell, and indeed most other influential modernist critics appeared determined to erase his work and his name from the ranks of the canonized or even semi-canonized English literary text. In this study, I would like to "revitalise the present"—to use Belsey's words (22)—and I believe I can do this best not by sweeping Kipling and the implications of his imperialist discourse under the rug. What interests me about Kipling is the extent to which his fiction can be made to engage contemporary controversies and concerns. In *Tropics of Discourse* White observes that historians writing now should investigate the past, "not as an end in itself, but as a way of providing perspectives on the present that contribute to the solution of problems peculiar to our own time" (41). The same can be said of the literary critic, especially one who interprets literature within the context of history. In this study, I choose to address the issue of Kipling's imperialism because its basis is discursive. Other white men and women contributed to British imperialism in more tangible ways, serving in the Indian Civil Service, for example, but Kipling chose to write about it, to construct imperialism through discourse. The neo-imperialism of various western countries, to which India has been subjected in the decades since its political independence, also has its discursive aspect.

Finally, I must confess that what prompts me to tackle Kipling's imperialism in this study is a guilty love for his India. Among contemporary literary scholars writing in the wake of imperialism, finding pleasure in Kipling's fiction is no more acceptable than it was in the modernist age. Now, although we are expected to know Kipling, we are hardly encouraged to enjoy him. But I appreciate his love for India and his exuberant renditions of the nineteenth-century Indians and Indian landscapes, particularly in such works as the novel *Kim* and the short story "On the City Wall." His approach to India is at times so passionate that I find myself wanting to share it. But there is a danger in identifying too intensely with Kipling's emotional attachment to the country. His love for India and his detailed delineations of Indian customs, people, and places often function as smokescreens, disguising not only the structures of power that underlie his work but his use of knowledge about India to perpetuate those structures. We must not forget that, as a white, middle-class, male writer, Kipling himself benefited from British imperialism.

The problems of knowledge and power—those catchwords of postmodern literary theory—are, then, very much in evidence in Kipling's fiction. In "The Enlightenments of Pagett, M.P." and "On the City Wall" these issues are particularly relevant because the protagonist and the narrator are confronted with a threat to the established power they represent.

Both stories deal with some form of Indian nationalism. In each, Kipling inscribes a different strategy for rendering powerless the nationalists' challenge to imperialist authority. Although in "The Enlightenments of Pagett, M.P." the protagonist does manage to nullify the nationalist discourse by containing it within an imperialist framework, in "On the City Wall" the narrator is not so successful. In the end he becomes implicated in the knowledge he endeavors to subvert.

"The Enlightenments of Pagett, M.P." is something of an anomaly among Kipling's fiction about India. It is one of the few stories he wrote that consistently undermines the image of the glamorous East, an image that he was largely responsible for creating. The story seems to be predominantly concerned with demystifying India. From the beginning, it establishes Orde, a British official of the Indian Civil Service, as the 'demystifier.' Orde possesses this ability to delve beneath the glossy rhetoric of both liberalism and nationalism and see the true India, because he is an Anglo-Indian who has lived there for twenty years: this apparently makes him an expert. His visitor, Pagett, on the other hand, is newly arrived, and although he thinks he knows India because he is a British M.P. with liberal leanings who has done some research into the Indian political situation, it is the purpose of the story to show him that he is wrong.

The intrusion of the visiting M.P. into the world of British India is a convention in Anglo-Indian literature. Duncan uses it in both her first and last Indian novels, *The Simple Adventures of a Memsahib* and *The Burnt Offering*. This convention points to a certain defensiveness on the part of the Anglo-Indians, which was not altogether unwarranted, since they were often subject to the criticism of the public at home and the M.P. functioned as the representative of that condemning voice. Defensiveness of this kind led some Anglo-Indian writers, such as Kipling and Duncan, to assume the role of an apologist.[4] This is fundamentally what "The Enlightenments of Pagett, M.P." is about: it is a defense not only of British imperialism in India but specifically of the Anglo-Indian expression of colonial power.

Orde's defense of Anglo-India is sparked by Pagett's interest in the Indian National Congress. Leaving his constituency in England, Pagett has traveled to India to learn "what popular feeling in India is really like, y'know, now that it has wakened into political life." He is operating under the assumption that the "National Congress . . . must have caused great excitement among the masses" (98). "The Enlightenments of Pagett, M.P." was written in 1890, five years after the founding of the Congress. The picture Bipan Chandra paints of this very early period of Indian nationalism emphasizes its anger, its restlessness, and its developing vision. Even in these initial stages, he insists, the Congress was attempting to alter the political composition of India, although the changes the nationalist leaders wanted to implement seem minor in comparison to the later independence movement. According to Bipan Chandra, one of the most important demands the leaders made was for the expansion and reform of the legislative councils, which they felt were unrepresentative of Indian opinion (115). Not only were there few Indians on the councils, but these few tended to be wealthy businessmen who were in favor of British rule because of their financial stake in it (114). Moreover, the councils were not elected bodies; their members were appointed by the government. The early nationalists called for the admission of a considerable proportion of elected members. Given that the British government in India was an imperialist rather than a democratic institution, this was, he argues, an extremely subversive demand (72).

In contrast to Bipan Chandra's detailed illustration, in Kipling's story we get a vague sketch of the Congress as a "parcel of Babus, pleaders, and schoolboys" (103) who are miserably uninformed about the state of their own country. Pagett never meets an admitted Congress member in the course of the story, and the closest he gets to its propaganda is a circular, which announces that the movement is *"for the remission of tax, the advancement of Hindustan, and the strengthening of the British Government"* (110). But Pagett does not actually see this circular; Orde communicates its contents to him. Almost everything we learn about the movement comes to us through Orde himself, or through Orde's manipulation of both the Indian and white people who stop in at his bungalow.

Orde's viewpoint, then, is at the center of this story. He serves as the mediator of knowledge about the Congress, about India, and as a representative of imperialism. The conflict implicit in this double role seems to escape him entirely. When Pagett suggests that as an Anglo-Indian official, Orde is hardly a fair judge of the nationalist movement, he replies that he too grew up in England, reading the same books and thinking the same thoughts as his visitor. Just because he and a few hundred other Englishmen are now living in another country is no reason to assume that they are any less open-minded. "No," he says, "I think you will get no fairer or more dispassionate view of the Congress business than such men as I can give you" (99). For Orde, even other Englishmen have only a partial understanding of the Indian people and political situation. A manager of a local bank, Reginald Burke, gallops up to the house on his polo pony and delivers a short speech which is mildly critical of the Indian government's economic policy. Once he leaves, Orde asserts that Burke's evaluation of things is biased toward his own business community. A commercial interest like Burke's might, according to Orde, "hamper a Government intent in the first place on the larger interests of humanity" (123). The story suggests that men like Orde of the Indian Civil Service (ICS) are best able to determine the "larger interests" of India's humanity.

In *The Discovery of India,* Nehru examines these rulers of India, the white men of the ICS. He states that, particularly in the nineteenth century and even after "the East India Company handed over its estate of India to the British crown" (202) in 1858, ICS men played the part of feudal landlords. As landlords, they felt they thoroughly understood their subordinates' needs and identified these needs with their own: "They ran India, they were India, and anything that was harmful to their interests must of necessity be injurious to India" (Nehru 203). The Indian National Congress was unquestionably harmful to the interests of the ICS because it prescribed that Indians be permitted to participate in the government of their own country by occupying higher positions in the ICS and the even higher seats on the legislative councils. Until the 1919 reforms, Indian civil servants were largely confined to lower-ranking jobs. Furthermore, the nationalist leaders held democracy as an ideal and encouraged the growth of a more democratic society in India. Not surprisingly, Anglo-Indians of the ICS were resistant to the change demanded by the Congress because this change threatened the feudal system that was the basic source of their power.

Nehru's description of the nineteenth-century British civil servant in India is congruent with Kipling's character Orde for a number of reasons: Nehru's historical recreation of the past is undoubtedly dependent on his own present, his perception of the ICS officials he encountered throughout his years living in colonial India, *as well as* on such depictions in literature.

Anglo-Indian fiction is particularly noted for its tendency to mythologize what imperialists believed was the British mission in India, and the ICS official was a common and central figure in the fiction that contributed to this myth. By Nehru's time, the British civil servant had acquired a heroic stature, at least in the eyes of Anglo-Indians. Nehru's demythification of the ICS, his attempt to show that these men were not simply responding to the needs of the so-called peasants when they adopted the role of landlord but had an interest of their own in preserving feudal power, is relevant to this analysis of Kipling's most famous ICS character because it is fundamentally a reaction if not to Kipling then certainly to the nineteenth-century Anglo-Indian myth that he was instrumental in creating. It is through demythification that we come to recognize that something is a construct.

Orde's feudal vision of India, as Nehru's analysis has led us to suspect, is evident in his description of the general population. He tells Pagett,

> You are in another land, another century, down on the bed-rock of society, where the family merely, and not the community, is all-important. The average Oriental cannot be brought to look beyond his clan. His life, too, is more complete and self-sufficing and less sordid and low-thoughted than you might imagine. It is bovine and slow in some respects, but it is never empty. . . . Why should such folk look up from their immemorially appointed round of duty and interests to meddle with the unknown and fuss with voting-papers?" (110)

The Indian people depicted in the story—the Sikh woodcarver, the Muslim landowner, and the Jat farmer—fulfill Orde's description in every detail: they are tradition-bound, clannish, and extraordinarily distrustful of one another. Without him and the British government, we are supposed to believe, they would all probably kill one another. Orde's depiction of Indian diversity is regressive, for it is rooted in a simple and very British construction of the Indian past, and it does not allow for the possibility of unity in the future. Nowhere in the story do we see Orde acknowledge what Bipan Chandra insists the early nationalist leaders knew, that India was a "nation-in-the-making" (23) and that in order for that nation to emerge, its people had to be convinced of the importance of ties other than those of the family or the clan. On the contrary, Orde chooses to see Indians as eternally unchanging, indeed incapable of change.

Of all the Indian characters in the story, Rasul Ali Khan, the Muslim landowner, demonstrates the kind of archaic behavior that Orde believes is the essence of India. After meeting him, Pagett announces, "What an old fossil it is!" (108). Nevertheless, Rasul Ali Khan earns Orde's respect in a way the other Indians do not. Orde calls the Muslim community "the most masterful and powerful minority in the country." "They have controlled the land," he proclaims (108), undoubtedly referring to the Mughal period of Indian history when Muslims held the highest positions in the government. Under the election system promoted by the Congress, Orde predicts that the Muslim population will become extinct presumably because their minority status will make it difficult for them to secure any seats in the legislative councils. Orde sees the British people in India as protectors of the Muslims and of the other minorities who would be suppressed by a Hindu majority, if the government were to give in to Congress demands for a more democratic society. In light of Ram Gopal's examination of the Hindu-Muslim dissonance, encouraged by the nineteenth-century government, readers can conclude that Orde's line of argument coincides with those divisive tactics used by imperialists during the period of early nationalism. As part of the same imperialist discourse, Kipling's story advances the notion that Muslims and Hindus have no cultural, political, or financial interests in common.

It is often the case in Anglo-Indian literature—and this is certainly true in Kipling's work—that Muslims are valorized because they belong to a so-called "martial race," which once ruled a huge part of the country, while Hindus, and particularly Bengalis, are criticized or even ridiculed. Anglo-Indian fiction rarely depicts Indian characters as individuals with personal ambitions and desires that might contradict the basic precepts of whatever community or race to which they belong. Instead, they are types, who represent entire traditions. We are to understand Rasul Ali Khan not only as a "courtly" Muslim landholder of the late nineteenth century (107) but as an embodiment of all the past glory of the Muslim people in India. Similarly, Dina Nath, who belongs to the "new literary caste" (119) for which Orde has so much contempt, is a sort of 'stand-in' for that Hindu caste as a whole. Orde's repudiation of him is meant as a repudiation of all westernized Indians and all Indians who espouse the cause of nationalism, since in this story Kipling does not differentiate between one group and the other.

It is not clear if Dina Nath is actually a member of the Congress, and, in Kipling's totalizing view, it does not matter. Dina Nath is associated with the Congress both because he has been educated in English and because he purports to be devoted to such English institutions as Milton and the parliamentary system. Although he tells Pagett that the Congress is *"the* greatest movement of modern times" (115), he is barely able to name and completely unable to defend its major demands. Readers are expected to dismiss Dina Nath's beliefs and ideals and, by extension, those of the Congress as well, once Orde reveals the final truth that closes all further discussion of the Indian youth: "He is a sort of English schoolboy, but married three years, and the father of two weaklings, and knows less than most English schoolboys" (117). Dina Nath's weakness, evident in the "weaklings" he has fathered, is implicitly contrasted with the "masterful and powerful minority" that Rasul Ali Khan represents. Weakness is therefore associated with sedition and nationalism, while loyalty to British rule confers strength and virility. These associations are made possible by the polarity between the Muslim and the Hindu, which Orde's imperialist discourse goes to such lengths to establish.

The tendency on the part of Kipling and other Anglo-Indian writers of the nineteenth century to see Indians in terms of some minor collectivity but never as a nation—or even a potential nation—is one of the key elements in the imperialist construction of Indian nationalism. It is what lies behind Lord Dufferin's famous denunciation of Congress as a "microscopic minority," which, significantly enough, Orde quotes in "The Enlightenments of Pagett, M.P." Indeed, Kipling's entire story seems dedicated to the task of proving that this metaphor is accurate—that Indian nationalism *is* the work of a very small group of misfits, infinitesimally small in relation to India's millions, hence the British do not have to bother worrying about it. Every character manages in some way to testify to the truth of Lord Dufferin's statement, from Mr. Edwards, the English tradesman, at the beginning, who says that his Indian workers never speak about the Congress, to Bishen Singh, the Sikh woodcarver, who professes a complete lack of knowledge on the subject, and finally to the American doctor at the end, Eva McCreery Lathrop, who passionately insists that "what's the matter with this country is not in the least political, but an all-round entanglement of physical, social, and moral evils and corruptions" (125). Lord Dufferin's metaphor and Kipling's reproduction of it are Anglo-Indian attempts to incorporate a new and possibly threatening movement into an already well-established ideal of British colonialism.

In his discussion of the noble savage theme in eighteenth-century European thought, White examines the function of metaphor in the discourse of human societies which are in the process of assimilating unfamiliar objects or ideas. He states that "when we have to identify things that resist conventional systems of classification, they are not only functionally useful but necessary for the well-being of social groups. Metaphors are crucially necessary when a culture or social group encounters phenomena that either elude or run afoul of normal expectations or quotidian experiences" (*Tropics* 184). Indian nationalism was just such a phenomenon facing the Anglo-Indian culture of the late nineteenth century. By this period Anglo-Indian society had become firmly ensconced in India, and it justified its presence by means of an elaborate ideology of service, based on the assumption that since Indians were unable to govern themselves — because of the eternal conflicts between the many Indian communities and because of their own innate inability to do so — Englishmen and women would sacrifice their well-being and sometimes their lives to do it for them. At the end of "The Enlightenments of Pagett, M.P.," Orde calls up this ideology to silence Pagett's criticism of the ICS. He dramatically declares, "our death-rate's five times higher than yours — I speak now for the brutal bureaucrat — and we work on the refuse of worked-out cities and exhausted civilisations, among the bones of the dead" (128). The Indian National Congress does not fit comfortably into Orde's ideology of service in India because it implicitly challenges the imperialist "sacrifice" behind that service. Orde is clearly against allowing Indians any form of self-government whatsoever, not even the concessions that the Congress was demanding. And his argument is grounded in the proposition that the "facts" of India cannot accommodate nationalism: "if, in short, India were a Utopia of the debating-room, and not a real land, this kind of talk might be worth listening to; but it is all based on false analogy and ignorance of the facts" (117), he explains to Pagett. Whether or not Orde is actually right or wrong about the "facts" is beside the point. The nationalists might well have been at that time a "microscopic minority," although many Indian historians state that this was not so. But that they would continue to be a "microscopic minority" is, it seems to me, the purpose of the metaphor. In his efforts to support the colonial power of Britain in India, Kipling offers his readers—many of whom would be Anglo-Indians—a metaphor of Indian nationalism that familiarizes it, makes it seem less dangerous to the status quo, and that effectively disregards any relevance the nationalist movement might have to the future political situation in India.

The strategy he uses in "The Enlightenments of Pagett, M.P." to defuse the threat of nationalism is predominantly containment. Although the Indian National Congress seems at first to represent a power that resists imperialist authority, by the end Orde has circumscribed it within an overall framework of colonialism. Nationalism becomes only one of many competing groups that exist in India under the control of the British government, and this group does not even have to be taken as seriously as the Muslims or any of the other "warlike races" (105). Orde manages to accomplish this marginalization of the nationalist movement because he is able to generate knowledge about India from a position of strength—and not simply generate it but pass it on to other powerful people in authority, such as Pagett, M.P. Orde is, therefore, a supreme Orientalist in Said's definition of the word, since, for him, knowledge of an Oriental people is a means of colonial management. Said writes, "knowledge of subject races or Orientals is what makes their management easy and profitable; knowledge gives power . . ." (Orientalism 36). It is because Orde knows the ins and outs of Indian society, the customs, allegiances, and weaknesses of all its many communities, including the "new literary caste" associated with the Congress, that he ultimately succeeds in dismissing nationalism as the work of a "microscopic minority." Moreover, Kipling allows no authority other than Orde's to stand in opposition to the imperialist vision that dominates the text.

But if knowledge gives power in some of Kipling's stories, in others it exposes an Englishman to forces that not only question his right to that power but also entangle him in actions and ways of thinking that subvert that power. "On the City Wall," written in 1888, is one of Kipling's most complex pieces of fiction. It offers no feasible solution to the problems of knowledge and power in an imperialist society and instead mystifies the issues of nationalism and imperialism by implicating them in a web of sexual relationships and religious convictions. Said's assertion in *Oriental-*

ism that the colonial management of Oriental peoples is achieved through a knowledge of "their race, character, culture, history, traditions, society, and possibilities" (38), an assertion that works so well in "The Enlightenments of Pagett, M.P.," seems only half true in "On the City Wall." The male, English narrator in this story, though he strives to maintain a tone of knowing worldliness, is unable to contain the power of nationalism within an Orientalist, dominating discourse because he is attracted to this nationalism and to the people who represent it. Rather than using his knowledge of the East to control the nationalist threat, which is Orde's method, he runs the risk of being subsumed by this same knowledge.

On the surface the story appears to move toward demystification of the myth of the glamorous East; this accounts for the narrator's sarcastic voice, especially in the first few pages. Like Orde, the narrator is critical of the Pagett types, those visitors who "come from England, spend a few weeks in India, walk round this great Sphinx of the Plains, and write books about its ways and its works, denouncing or praising it as their own ignorance prompts" (305). Similar to "The Enlightenments of Pagett, M.P.," there is a polarity between those who know—such as the narrator—and those visitors who think they know, but who are, in fact, ignorant. From the beginning, the narrator establishes himself as the truth-teller in this tale. Moreover, just as Orde serves as a sort of corrective to Pagett, so too in "On the City Wall" does the daily toil of the ICS hero, described in the narrator's panegyric, counteract the misinformation provided by the misguided visiting politician:

> Year by year England sends out fresh drafts for the first fighting-line, which is officially called the Indian Civil Service. These die, or kill themselves by overwork, or are worried to death, or broken in health and hope in order that the land may be protected from death and sickness, famine and war, and may eventually become capable of standing alone. It will never stand alone, but the idea is a pretty one. . . . (305)

Here is the conventional justification of British rule in India: Indians need to be governed by the British ICS because they are incapable of governing themselves and, furthermore, the British man proves his fitness for rule by his willingness to sacrifice himself for the cause of India. However, what is also conveyed in these lines is a certain pointlessness to British imperialism. If indeed its official purpose is to ensure that India does "eventually become capable of standing alone," a goal unattainable according to the narrator, then British imperialism is fundamentally meaningless, even absurd. This note of intense pessimism is one of the first indications in the story that we are not in Orde's predictable and controllable world.

The narrator's delineation of work as a component of imperialism is another common theme in Kipling's fiction. In "The Enlightenments of Pagett, M.P." the subject is raised by one white man after another and finally culminates in Orde's statement, "after all, the burden of the actual, daily unromantic toil falls on the shoulders of the men out here" (128). "On the City Wall" espouses a similar belief system when it sets up a dichotomy between those men who do "the work of pushing and coaxing and scolding and petting the country into good living" (305), namely the white, middle- and upper-class ICS officers, and the Indian others such as the western-educated Wali Dad and the prostitute Lalun, neither of whom appear to do any work at all. It is significant that the work of the Empire is consistently depicted in Kipling as the property of British men rather than of British people. Moreover, his work ethic is masculine both in its inclusion of men only and in its tendency to emphasize the type of work that British men of the nineteenth century would have engaged in, jobs associated with the government administration, the military, and with the British Secret Service. Although the Raj did, in fact, include women and women's work outside the home—white women in India occupied positions in the religious, teaching, service, and medical professions—Kipling chooses to focus almost exclusively on the "toil" of the white man. The few women whose work he recognizes as valuable, such as the American doctor who visits Orde's bungalow, are exceptions in his stories. Kipling's fiction also completely elides the domestic work of white women. Their roles as mothers and keepers of the home are undercut by the presence of Indian servants, who are shown doing all of the chores that women in nineteenth-century England would normally have done, such as cooking, cleaning, and managing the children. Most of Kipling's white, female characters are idle and consequently prone to the immoral behavior readers witness in a Mrs. Hauksbee or a Mrs. Reiver, both of whom spend their time hatching sexual plots and enticing British men. While it is apparent from the various texts written by English men and women who went to India during Victoria's reign that the middle-class Anglo-Indian world abounded with servants, the making of a home was a job women seem to have taken very seriously, though it often involved, for example, overseeing the daily shopping instead of doing it oneself. Furthermore, Kipling conflates the middle and upper classes with the lower class when he assumes that all women were without domestic work. The wife of a British soldier, a missionary, or a clerk was hardly in a financial position to hire a battery of servants to do the housework.

Significant points of contact would seem to exist between this story and "The Enlightenments of Pagett, M.P.": both depict an opposition between those who know and those who don't; the narrator's ironic tone suggests that the tale will demystify some of the myths about the East; the ICS officer has been heralded as the hero of the British Raj; and work, specifically men's work, is held up to the reader as the great British sacrifice for the cause of India. But the stories do not lead to the same place. What was relatively simple in "The Enlightenments of Pagett, M.P."—the acquisition and transmission of knowledge—is a complex and mysterious process in "On the City Wall." And India, which was made to seem so knowable and therefore so manageable in the first story, is entirely unknowable in the second.

The mystification of India in "On the City Wall" is in part the result of its feminization. Not only does the narrator refer to the country as "this great Sphinx of the Plains," suggesting that India is a lady with a secret, but the story itself is predominantly concerned with the activities of another secretive Indian lady, Lalun the prostitute. India and Lalun are extensions of one another. They are identical in their secretiveness and in their possession of immense knowledge. Indeed, Lalun's knowledge has no boundaries. According to Wali Dad, her most ardent admirer, "Lalun *is* Lalun, and when you have said that, you have only come to the Beginnings of Knowledge" (307). Even the English narrator, in spite of his ironic voice and his own pretence to knowledge, is compelled to speak in impossible extremes when describing what Lalun knows:

She knew all the songs that have ever been sung. . . . She knew how to make up tobacco for the pipe so that it smelt like the Gates of Paradise and wafted you gently through them. She could embroider strange things in gold and silver, and dance softly with the moonlight when it came in at the window. Also she knew the hearts of men, and the heart of the City, and whose wives were faithful and whose untrue, and more of the secrets of the Government Offices than are good to be set down in this place. (309–310)

That the narrator is attracted to this knowledge is evident in his attraction to Lalun; she is what she knows, and she both *is* and *knows* things that are unfathomable, unobtainable to the English narrator, and dangerous.

The way she passes on her secret knowledge contributes to the larger picture of Lalun as a mysterious woman, for she communicates through songs, puns, poetry, and equivocations. At one important moment in the story, she sings before an audience consisting of Wali Dad, the narrator, and Khem Singh, an old Sikh warrior who is not actually in the room with the other three but is listening from the ramparts of the fort in which he is imprisoned. Her song recounts the story of a seventeenth-century Indian guerilla fighter who mounted numerous successful campaigns against the Mughal Empire. It is clearly a call to arms:

> With them there fought who rides so free
>   With sword and turban red,
> The warrior-youth who earns his fee
>   At peril of his head. (310–311)

Furthermore, it is meant only for the ears of Wali Dad and Khem Singh in the fort; this becomes obvious when the Sikh responds to Lalun's music by calling back the last line and singing his own song, which, significantly, the narrator is not able to understand. Nor do Lalun and Wali Dad bother to translate it for him. When Khem Singh later escapes from the fort and, through Lalun's clever manipulation of the narrator, is taken to a group of people who are organizing a rebellion against the British government, we realize that Lalun's song and the Sikh's answer contain some secret message about the planned escape. But because Lalun speaks in code, neither the reader nor the narrator is allowed access to this information. Contrasting this means of transmitting knowledge with Orde's relatively simple lecture to Pagett on the loves and hates of the various Indian peoples shows that the India Kipling constructs in "On the City Wall" is so much more intricate than the one that Orde masters in "The Enlightenments of Pagett, M.P." Lalun's India is inaccessible to the western mind and, therefore, cannot be contained by an Orientalist discourse.

But although her knowledge is fundamentally uninhabitable by the narrator, Lalun manages to implicate him in it. She is able to do this because of his desire for her. When he interrupts Lalun as she is pulling Khem Singh up through her window, she elicits his help by lying about the Sikh's identity. Then she embraces the narrator to keep him from seeing the exchange of money between her maid and Khem Singh, which is occurring behind his back, and finally she gets him to transport the Sikh across the city, saying, "He is a friend of mine, and thou art—more than a friend—therefore I ask this" (325). Not until the end of the story does he realize that he has been Lalun's pawn in a scheme of sedition. What is significant about Lalun's actions is not merely that she manipulates the English narrator into participating in an act of rebellion against the British government, but that she is able to manipulate him at all. The narrator's susceptibility to Lalun, his desire for her, makes him vulnerable in a way that Orde never is. In spite of the fact that it is the narrator and not Lalun who is a member of the ruling race in India, Lalun holds the power in the story. Although the rebellion falls through and the threat that Khem Singh represents is eradicated when he returns to his prison in the fort, the last line still shows the English narrator contemplating his part in the rebellion and Lalun's power over him. The boastful and worldly tone that he adopts at the beginning of the story, with its note of superiority about the white heroes of the British Raj, is overturned at the end when the narrator realizes that he has been subject to another's will: "But I was thinking how I had become Lalun's Vizier after all" (329). This strange reversal of the power positions in the story attests to a certain ambivalence on Kipling's part about the nature of Indian sedition.

It is not nationalism in general that Kipling appears to abhor, but only nationalism of the type that Dina Nath advocates and Orde dismisses in "The Enlightenments of Pagett, M.P."—a nationalism that sees change occurring as a result of constitutional reform. Kipling believes that this nationalism is the sole prerogative of the westernized classes of India, who have absorbed English ideals of government but not its fierce work ethic. As I pointed out earlier, one of Orde's justifications of British rule in India is his assertion that the "daily unromantic toil" involved in the protection and management of the Indian people is carried out by English men. Indian nationalists are generally depicted as incapable of this work. However, Kipling seems willing to give another kind of Indian nationalism at least some measure of credibility, some claim to power. This other nationalism, represented by Lalun, Wali Dad, and Khem Singh in "On the City Wall," is not satisfied with making legislative changes—as Wali Dad makes clear when he scoffs at the thought of himself as a "member of a Legislative Council" (311). It is instead grounded in a belief in the necessity of violent rebellion. Khem Singh's long life is condensed to a few violent episodes in Wali Dad's description to the narrator:

> "He fought you in '46, when he was a warrior-youth; refought you in '57, and he tried to fight you in '71, but you had learned the trick of blowing men from guns too well. Now he is old; but he would still fight if he could." (311)

Khem Singh is accorded some dignity in this portrait of his life and in other accounts offered by Lalun and the young Subaltern who is his jailer at the fort. Wali Dad, too, is shown at his best when he defiantly argues with the narrator and refuses to fulfill the role that his English education has given him. His resistance to his own westernization parallels Kipling's criticism of the "new literary caste" in "The Enlightenments of Pagett, M.P." Moreover, the reader is permitted to sympathize with Wali Dad, a member of that caste, precisely because he has repudiated that style of living and that style of nationalism.

Not simply violent nationalism but violence of any kind receives a certain approval in "On the City Wall." When the British troops from the fort are turned out into the city streets in order to quell a riot between Muslims and Hindus, the brutality that results is portrayed as an almost gleeful activity for the English soldiers as well as for the Indian rioters. After Wali Dad plunges somewhat joyfully into the fight, the narrator makes his way to the fort, where he observes, "Once outside the City wall, the tumult sank to a dull roar, very impressive under the stars and reflecting great credit on the fifty thousand able-bodied men who were making it." And about the native and British soldiers waiting to enter the city, he quips, "I am sorry to say that they were all pleased, unholily pleased, at the chance of what they called 'a little fun' " (323). Finally, at the height of the riot, Kipling presents us with an image of British imperialism in India that is surely one of the most chilling and, simultaneously, the most ridiculous in all of Anglo-Indian literature:

> Parties of five or six British soldiers, joining arms, swept down the side-gullies, their rifles on their backs, stamping, with shouting and song, upon the toes of Hindu and Mussulman. . . . They were routed out of holes and corners, from behind well-pillars and byres, and bidden to go to their houses. If they had no houses to go to, so much the worse for their toes. (327)

By making violence seem absurd and even fun, Kipling avoids its serious implications for both British imperialism and Indian nationalism.

Yet it is because he sidesteps these questions that Kipling is able to relay two important suggestions at the end of "On the City Wall": first, that British imperialism in India is not such a bad thing at all since it keeps the peace in such a way that no one, at least no one of importance, is really hurt by it; and second, that the only legitimate expression of Indian nationalism is a violent one. Anything else is depicted as emasculating for its adherents. However, this last idea creates a catch-22. Although violent nationalism is the only form of nationalism that Kipling and his narrator will affirm, this nationalism is no longer possible in India because Indian men have already been emasculated by the imposition of western education and western ideals on traditional Indian society. Khem Singh lends credence to this notion of the deterioration of Indian masculinity when he returns to the fort after recognizing that Indian men are no longer able or willing to fight off the English. And Wali Dad is the perfect example of the consequences of this kind of westernization in India. His English education has demoralized him to such an extent that he is unable to act in any kind of thoughtful or productive way. The only action he does take—rushing blindly into the riot—leaves him "sobbing hysterically" and "frothing at the mouth" (327), hardly what Kipling would demarcate as masculine behavior. Ultimately only Lalun is capable of effective action, but her Indian womanhood, powerful as it is within her own sphere, limits her. She is confined to her house on the city wall; her actions cannot extend into the city itself. Hence the violent Indian nationalism that Kipling creates in "On the City Wall," attractive as it is to the male English narrator, is destined to be a lost cause. For in Kipling's construction, the times are no longer conducive to organized violence directed against the British Government, as they once were in Khem Singh's angry youth. Consequently, the only violence that can occur is disorganized, meaningless, and finally absurd.

Kipling's representation of Indian nationalism in the last decade of the nineteenth century has two faces. On one side is nationalism that seeks to bring about change through constitutional methods and gradual political reform. This nationalism Kipling's tales consistently dismiss as weak, dishonorable, and inauthentic, because it is considered the domain of a small class of western-educated Indians who endeavor merely to copy western ideals and practices. On the other side is violent nationalism, which Kipling seems to respect but which has become impossible in India as a result of the emasculating effects of westernization. Although this type of nationalism is not explicitly identified as such, it is nationalism insofar as it is depicted as a cause that unites Indians of different communities (Lalun is Hindu, Wali Dad is Muslim, and Khem Singh is Sikh) in an effort to overthrow British rule in the land. One nationalism is seen as the recent product of British policies of westernization; the other is said to have its roots in a glorious past, when Indians and Englishmen met in battle and made history. While "The Enlightenments of Pagett, M.P." can be summarized as a denunciation of the former nationalism, "On the City Wall" is a sort of requiem to the latter.

Where Kipling's two nationalisms meet, however, is in their impetus. The Indian characters in both stories have set themselves in opposition to the government because they share some dissatisfaction with the way the country is being run by the British. But exactly what this dissatisfaction might be is not spelled out in either story. In "The Enlightenments of Pagett, M.P." the English tradesman Edwards clearly states that Indians have nothing to complain about. He tells Pagett,

> They haven't got any grievance—nothing to hit with, don't you see, sir; and then there's not much to hit against, because the Government is more like a kind of general Providence, directing an old-established state of things, then that at Home, where there's something new thrown down for us to fight about every three months. (103)

In "On the City Wall" Wali Dad is the only character who openly expresses his disapproval of the government, but his opinions are undermined by Kipling's portrait of him as a languid, unhappy, and irresponsible youth. His specific criticisms are never examined, and instead readers get a general picture of him as a perpetual whiner: "Wali Dad was always mourning over something or other—the country of which he despaired, or the creed in which he had lost faith, or the life of the English which he could by no means understand" (309). Kipling's nationalisms, then, have no foundations, or at best are founded on vague and insubstantial feelings of discontent on the part of certain Indians. This nebulousness at the heart of each story connects Kipling to the later imperialist discourse about Indian nationalism, of which the work of the British historian Spear is an example. As I mentioned earlier, Spear attributes nationalism in India to an emotion that he identifies as "dislike of the foreigner," an emotion, moreover, which he believes has no precise origins but which has always existed in India. Within these conceptual parameters, nationalism emerges as a simple reaction to foreign rule.

The disturbing thing about this vision of Indian nationalism is that it allows its adherents to evade any responsibility for civil unrest in India. If Indians have always had a vague dislike of foreign rule, as Kipling and Spear suggest, then it is not the British government in particular that is at fault, since any foreign government would be equally disliked. Kipling's separate constructions of Indian nationalism—whether of the violent or the constitutional variety—are safe constructions, palatable to the nineteenth-century British taste. They do not require an Anglo-Indian reader of his fiction to examine his or her possible participation or the participation of the British government in the oppression of Indians. Moreover, they are comforting constructions, which serve to familiarize and defuse a movement that threatens the Anglo-Indian status quo in India. Having said this, however, I should also acknowledge the different degree to which these two stories are successful in offering safety and comfort to Anglo-Indian readers. "The Enlightenments of Pagett, M.P." is, I think, relatively straightforward in its surface intentions and in its overall effect. Because the usual narrative devices—plot, characterization, denouement—are all employed to debunk Indian nationalism, the story effectively quells any internal dissonance which might lead the reader to question the predominant imperialist viewpoint, centered in the character of Orde. But the more complex narrative technique in "On the City Wall" allows in many voices and many silences, silences which are pregnant with repressed meaning. We are acutely aware throughout that neither we, the readers, nor the narrator himself are permitted to hear the whole story about Lalun's and Wali Dad's Indian nationalism. What we do not know and *that* we do not know are disquieting in the story. On one level, "On the City Wall" comforts its readers when it depicts Wali Dad's failure and the defeat of Khem Singh's violent aspirations. On another, deeper level, the story snatches that comfort away.

2

A Memsahib and Her

Not-So-Simple Adventures

In *Apprentice to Power*, Sir Malcolm Darling, writing in the first decade of the twentieth century, describes the typical Anglo-Indian attitude to the rising nationalist movement in India.[1] While at a dinner party with other ICS officers, Darling hears the Indian National Congress and its declared aim of self-government dismissed as "bunkum" by someone called "Sir Charles." Later, in a letter home, he writes, "Bunkum it may be . . . I think much of it is, but when you see a spark near gunpowder, it is better to take the thing seriously. That is the English fault—a defect of the imagination . . . (128). In his autobiography, Darling sees himself as one of the few Anglo-Indians who is able to understand and appreciate the desire of educated Indians for political power in their own country. The book encourages readers to regard him as an anomaly—an Englishman who *did not* suffer from this "defect of the imagination." However, while Darling often quotes from letters and a diary written between the years 1904 to 1908, the narrative itself was actually composed some sixty years later, after he and every other British civil servant had left India for good. Darling wrote his autobiography not only with the benefit of hindsight but also with the additional advantage of knowing that his 1960s readers, conscious of the success in 1947 of Indian nationalism (not to mention numerous other nationalist movements around the world), would be less inclined to disagree with some of his statements about Indians and their aspirations to power. The politics of the western nations in the sixties had moved a long way away from where they were in the first decade of the century. Imperialism was in the dumps.

Sara Jeannette Duncan, who wrote all of her novels about India between 1893 and 1909, addressed a different readership. It was a readership that was pro-imperialist more often than not, since imperialism, as it was expressed in the various texts that contributed to British culture at this time, was becoming increasingly noisy, militant and self-congratulatory.[2] It was also a readership steeped in notions about India garnered from such sources as Kipling's more romantic fiction and the adventure tales of Maud Diver and Flora Annie Steel. Duncan's novels of social realism, of the domestic world of white women in British India, stand as an exception to this rule in Anglo-Indian literature of the late Victorian and early Edwardian period. Her novels generally challenge the stereotypes that had become entrenched in the British imagination, stereotypes about English heroes and heroines bringing civilization and cultural enlightenment to the darker races of India. In her depictions of English life in India, an insightful woman protagonist is usually surrounded by people who, though they may proclaim loudly their superiority over the indigenous population, are nevertheless ordinary and dull: "illustrations of the great British average," she calls them in one of her books (*Simple Adventures* 129).

Although occasionally Duncan sympathizes with the British people in India, acknowledging their feelings of exile and their sense of displacement, generally she is her society's critic, a writer who makes fun of its foibles and pretensions. And when we consider that her readership largely consisted of either Anglo-Indians or other English readers whose imperialism was strident, we must give her credit for taking the stance she did. At the time she was writing, the books that sold well celebrated the glories of the British empire. Duncan almost never does this, at least not until her last novel about India, *The Burnt Offering*. Paradoxically, this is her most courageous piece of fiction, because it examines in detail the Indian nationalist movement at the turn of the century. It is often extremely critical of the Indian and the English characters who propagate nationalism— Duncan was, after all, an imperialist herself—but the novel raises questions about the implications of the British presence in India, and these are questions that few western novelists before or after her had raised.[3] The typical Anglo-Indian "defect of the imagination," which Darling encountered again and again during his first three and a half years in India and which he interpreted as an unwillingness on the part of the British to confront the issue of nationalism, is absent in Duncan's *The Burnt Offering*.

This novel is about nationalism and imperialism's relationship to it, and it is about the people, Indian and English, who are forced to negotiate this relationship in their personal lives.

The predominant metaphor that informs the novel is marriage. Duncan suggests that the colonial relationship between India and Britain can be understood as a marital one. However, our comprehension of this metaphor is complicated by the actual marriages and potential marriages that make up the plot of the novel. In the end, we are left wondering how much credence we should give to the ideals expressed in the surface text and how much we should allow the subtext to subvert it, for the subtext implies that another kind of relationship to India is possible, a relationship that does not necessarily involve the British. The novel finally stands as a testament to the internal conflict that Duncan herself must have felt as an imperialist and a woman, who was also distrustful of patriarchal dictates, in a country struggling to throw off the oppression of a paternalist system.

The central marriage in the novel—central because it indicates how all the other marriages are to be evaluated—is between Britain and India. Duncan is not the first Anglo-Indian writer to use this metaphor in an attempt to explain the relationship between the two countries. Kipling occasionally employs it in his journalism.[4] For Kipling, however, the marriage metaphor and his congruent construction of India as a seductive woman, evident in numerous short stories, serve to justify the hierarchy that he repeatedly establishes between Britain and India. As the ruling country, England obviously retains the dominant masculine position in Kipling's work, while India is cast into the feminine role, with its implicit suggestions of inferiority and subjugation.[5] Duncan's use of the metaphor in *The Burnt Offering* is somewhat different than Kipling's, although, like him, she offers it to her reader as a justification of British rule in India.

Duncan's metaphor of marriage is articulated by a particularly powerful figure in the novel, an Indian teacher or *guru* whose opinions readers are encouraged to respect. Yadava is the spiritual advisor to two of the major characters, Kristodas, an Indian judge, and his daughter, Janaki. Kristodas is moderate in his political opinions, a supporter of the British; Janaki has nationalist leanings. It is for Janaki's benefit—to dissuade her from pursuing further the nationalist cause—that Yadava comes up with the metaphor. He says it simply, aligning himself very clearly with the forces that stand against nationalism:

> England is the husband of India. We talk of the Mother as if we had but one parent. . . . But we are the children of England also. Can we deny it? . . . There are those . . . who would make their mother a widow. I am not of them. (165)

In contrast to Kipling's fiction, there is little sense here that the feminine, namely India, is devalued or made subordinate because of her femininity. Yadava seems to regard the relationship and India's place within it as a liberating one. The English, he insists, colonize India only to protect the land and keep the peace so that Indians, or more specifically the upper caste Brahmins, can "sit and rule and tell their tale of God" (166). Undoubtedly, this is Raj rhetoric, rendered more credible, perhaps, because it issues from the mouth of an Indian.

In much of Kipling's fiction, India is either depicted *as a woman* or is represented *by a woman* who needs to be controlled by the British because she is dangerous and immoral when left to her own devices. Figures such as Lalun the prostitute in "On the City Wall," the desirable but seditious Indian woman, are plentiful in Kipling's work. Clearly we are not dealing with an analogous formulation in Duncan's *The Burnt Offering*. First, there are no seductive Indian females. The predominant Indian woman in the text is Janaki, and her character is drawn with the same exploratory and tentative strokes that Duncan uses on all of her protagonists. And second, when India is feminized, as in the passage quoted above, the perspective from which readers are permitted to observe her is not an androcentric one. We are *not* looking at India through the eyes of a male English narrator, as we do in "On the City Wall; instead, we see her from a female vantage point, female because it is the perspective of the wife in the marriage metaphor. In Duncan's novel, the metaphor is produced by an Indian, Yadava, for the benefit of other Indians, Kristodas and Janaki. The effect of this is to allow the reader to regard Indians as capable of self-creation and self-identification. Contrasted with the tendency in Kipling's fiction to objectify India, to treat the country as a female who is subject to the male gaze, we can appreciate, I think, the great distance between these two Anglo-Indian constructions of India as wife. One, Kipling's, depicts India, and by extension Indians, as passive recipients of the husband's (Britain's) ministrations and attentions; the other, Duncan's, constitutes India and Indians as acting rather than being acted upon. It seems important not to forget, however, that the imperialism implicit in Duncan's metaphor—in the notion, for example, that India would be "widowed" were British rule to end—constantly undermines it as a potentially empowering image.

If the relationship between Britain and India is a marriage, then in *The Burnt Offering* it is a marriage in which the husband does not love his wife. Yadava himself admits this. Prior to his discourse on marriage, he states,

> But it is my grief that they as a people seem to have little affection for us as a people. For some of us yes—for our peasants and our princes. . . . But men like themselves—no. You would embrace them—they nod uncomfortably and move away. For myself I would rather be worse governed and better loved. (164–65)

A common complaint among Indians writing about the Raj has been that the Anglo-Indians were concerned solely with the lowest or the uppermost classes, the peasants or the princes. The rising middle class in India, mostly composed of Indians educated in English, was dismissed as an unimportant minority which could be overlooked because it was not the 'real India.' For all his liberal leanings, Malcolm Darling partially promotes this kind of attitude. Throughout Darling's autobiography, the peasants are represented as possessing authentic Indianness. He frequently waxes eloquent about this segment of the population and is particularly impressed by a group of villagers he meets in the hills, an encounter which prompts him to rhapsodize on "the *true* Baluch—the Baluch in his native fastnesses untouched by the sophistication of modern life" (99, my emphasis). Although Darling expresses an interest in the educated, middle-class Indians under British rule, he does not appear to know what to do with them. Moreover, his obvious bias toward Indian peasants and princes in his book— numerous paragraphs are spent describing and analyzing them while the middle class receives little of his attention—leaves the reader feeling that he is comfortable with the places assigned by Anglo-Indian tradition to the lower- and upper-status groups in India and decidedly uncomfortable with the issue of the westernized Indian. For him, the 'real' Indian is one who is free of the taint of the modern world. According to this definition, an English-speaking Indian can only appear to be lacking something.[6]

Rashna B. Singh, in her 1988 work on British fiction about India, argues that one of the contradictions of imperialism was that it promoted western education for Indians and then "scorned" those who tried to put it to use:

> Educated Indians were a challenge and a threat to the continuance of British rule. Often they questioned the claim that the British were ruling in the best interests of India. . . . For as long as the British could go on believing that those who posed an intellectual or political threat to them were not "real," they could continue to believe, placidly, in the beneficence of their Empire. (94)

That an Anglo-Indian novelist writing at the "climax of the British Empire" (Brantlinger 227–28) should allow one of her Indian characters to point out this blind spot on the part of the British suggests that Duncan was not as willing as some "to believe, placidly, in the beneficence of their Empire." Nor is she willing to attack it openly, particularly in this novel, which tries, more than the others, to justify British rule. Her method throughout the novel is covert. Readers merely receive hints that there is something wrong with the British governance of India, hints that are often difficult to get at because of her overt imperialist agenda.

Yadava, then, is referring to this British inability to assimilate the Indian middle class into their picture of the 'real' India when he speaks of the discomfort that Englishmen in India exhibit in their relations with men who are "like themselves," that is, of the same class. The novel supports him in this statement. One of the text's most prominent themes is that the English and the middle-class Indians do not understand, sympathize, or love one another. Events occur again and again which demonstrate the social incompatibility of the two groups. A gathering of both cultures at the Victoria Club, for instance, rapidly disintegrates into "little groups [formed] on strictly racial lines" (95) when a telegram arrives announcing the arrest of a popular nationalist. And a "Ladies' League" party is portrayed as a sadly ridiculous effort because neither coterie of women in attendance, Bengali or English, can speak the other's language. For Duncan, the Indians and the British of Calcutta are "two tides that did not mingle" (120), and the novel seems to ascribe the blame for this primarily to the British who adamantly refuse to step out of their roles as rulers of India and treat the people they govern as equals. Considering this situation of lovelessness, the idea that the two races are participating in a marriage degenerates into absurdity. A marriage without love, indeed with almost no meeting ground whatsoever, is hardly a marriage in any culture's definition of the term. Although we are encouraged on the surface to accept as accurate Yadava's metaphor of marriage, other more subtextual intimations undermine its supposed accuracy.

Ultimately, Duncan's marriage metaphor differs from Kipling's because she does not lend it her wholehearted support, as Kipling does. He does not question in his fiction the necessity and the structure of marriage, dictating that wives occupy a secondary and passive role. Duncan does. Furthermore, Kipling's metaphor assumes that the relationship is based on love and desire, at least from the British point of view.[7] Duncan's novel asserts, however, that such affection should but does not exist between the two polities in India, the rulers and the ruled. Hence, there is a difficulty at the heart of her marriage metaphor, which is not explained away in the course of the narrative. The problem emerges even further when we take into account the other marriages that the novel examines.

The first marriage introduced is Michael and Lucy Foley's, and it is actually the only marriage in the novel that is in any way successful. The others flounder before they even reach the altar. The Foleys' marriage, therefore, serves as a standard in the text. The narrator pays such close attention to its quotidian details, such as the couple's ritual of early tea on the terrace and the planning of dinner parties, that readers assume that other Anglo-Indian marriages in Calcutta are conducted with similar rituals and similar conversations. Lucy and Michael Foley are, we think, a typical British couple living in imperial India at the turn of the century. The narrator expects us to like them both for their averageness and especially to like Lucy, for she is portrayed as gracious, charming, and efficient, indeed the feminine heart of Anglo-India. However, as a standard, this marriage is founded on some questionable principles: Michael is dominant and Lucy is clearly and problematically subordinate. When the two are sitting on their terrace, discussing the arrival in India of the socialist M.P. Vulcan Mills and his daughter Joan, Michael absentmindedly kicks his slipper at the crows that cluster around them. Just as absentmindedly, the narrator tells us, "Mrs. Foley . . . trailed across in her dressing-gown, picked up the slipper and replaced it on her husband's foot" (14). Lucy's action receives no further comment from the narrator at all, and perhaps readers might disregard it if it did not recall a similar incident in chapter 1.

Bepin Behari Dey, a Bengali, is invited to share a first-class train compartment with the Mills, after having been denied entry into another carriage by two Englishmen. Responding to the Mills' indignation over the obvious racism directed at an Indian in his own country, Dey remembers his father, who suffered worse treatment at the hands of two English officers at an earlier time in India's history:

> They were very angry finding my father in the carriage, and told him to get out. He refused to get out, so when the train started they ordered him to pull off their boots. He refused this also, but they stood over him and compelled him to do it, and being an old man he dared not resist. (9)

This action of stooping at the feet of an Englishman becomes an emblem in the novel of the oppression of Indians. When Lucy does the same thing less than six pages later, we cannot help but be struck by the connections between the two incidents and cannot help but wonder whether Duncan wishes, consciously or unconsciously, to imply that Lucy's marriage to Michael Foley perpetuates a similar oppression. Duncan's characterization of Lucy seems to suggest this is the case.

Lucy is probably the least enigmatic of all the novel's characters. Open-hearted and sympathetic, she is also prone to the prejudices of her community. She is appalled at the thought that Joan Mills, her old friend from school, should cultivate a friendship with Bepin Behari Dey, who is a young, attractive Bengali man. Because she is steeped in Anglo-Indian notions of propriety, notions which not only determine the relationship between the sexes but between the races as well, she advises Joan, "The fact is, dear . . . if you must go about with a Babu it really ought to be an old Babu" (121). Although she finds Joan's "extraordinariness" (14) compelling, she has no desire to emulate her because Joan threatens the Anglo-Indian world that both Lucy and her husband work hard to sustain. Within the context of Duncan's other novels—in which it is the extraordinary woman who invariably receives her most detailed approbation because of the excessive difficulty inherent in being extraordinary in Anglo-Indian society—Lucy is, for the most part, a pleasant but ordinary woman with ordinary values and attitudes.

If Lucy is ordinary and, therefore, a typical Anglo-Indian woman, her tendency to situate herself as a vehicle for her husband's voice is particularly disturbing, for it suggests that what Duncan is pointing to is a certain self-negation among the married women of British India. For Anglo-Indian women, marriage appears to mean the suppression of one's own ideas and feelings about the world in favor of those of one's husband. Lucy does this repeatedly throughout the novel. She echoes Michael's beliefs, never claiming them herself but instead always acknowledging their source. Since Michael is, more often than not, a spokesman for the British Raj, Lucy adopts this role as well. At one point in the novel, after learning that the Viceroy's band plays only western music, Joan asserts, "Whatever our instruments produce in India, it isn't music." Lucy almost erases herself in her reply: "I'm not clever enough to argue about it, but I think Michael would say that we're not here altogether for that purpose" (122). The Raj rhetoric that frequently comes out of Lucy's mouth lacks authenticity because she is continually quoting or paraphrasing Michael's statements. The novel points to the fact that for many of the British women in India, this rhetoric is inappropriate because it does not articulate the domestic reality of their lives. Women like Lucy are not permitted to participate in the predominantly masculine work of British India. But the rhetoric whose purpose is to justify this work is, nevertheless, used by both white men and women, the result being that women's work for the Raj is elided, since they are expected to align themselves with the work that their men do. Readers are given no indication that Lucy harbors alternative ideas about imperialist rhetoric, but her disinclination to claim this rhetoric as her own implies that she does not identify with it to the same degree as Michael or his friend John Game. Lucy's use of Raj rhetoric affirms her subservient position in her marriage and in the Empire. It is as if, in lending her voice to the discourse of imperialism, a discourse which dictates her subservience, she is acquiescing to that position.

The current debate among historians about the role and reality of the memsahib of the British Raj is exemplified in the character of Lucy; for it is women like Lucy, unremarkable and generally conventional women, who have been memorialized as a result of that debate. From Pat Barr's *The Memsahibs: The Women of Victorian India* (1976) to Marian Fowler's *Below the Peacock Fan* (1987) to a later addition to the conversation, Margaret MacMillan's *Women of the Raj* (1988), the typical women of Anglo-Indian society have been remembered with praise, sympathy, and only a little censure. These three authors all wrote their books on the memsahibs in reaction to the sexist supposition, put forth in many texts about British India written by men, that the cause of the dissent between English and Indian men was Englishwomen. E. M. Forster is the most famous proponent of this theory in his novel, *A Passage to India,* but there were numerous other male writers who shared his views and propagated them in the fiction and nonfiction of Anglo-India. MacMillan addresses the reputation of the memsahibs with this statement: "The memsahibs have often been blamed for the gap that opened up between the rulers and the ruled in the nineteenth century. But it was a gap that was produced by circumstance as much as choice—and the men also wanted it" (10). A paragraph later she adds, "The men themselves rarely questioned the justice of British rule. How much less likely that their wives should presume to do so" (11). The memsahibs were as much the victims of the social situation in nineteenth-century India as they were its perpetrators. Victorian society demanded the conformity of its women even more than its men and did not tolerate female rebellion. The cost of any unconventional behavior was usually "the full disapproval of their peers" (200), but sometimes those women who rebelled faced total abandonment by their countrymen in India. The example MacMillan gives is of an Irishwoman identified only as "Florence" who married an Indian maharaja and was never again invited to mix with British society (215).

Stressing the extreme social restraints imposed on white women in India, MacMillan, Fowler, and Barr all valorize ordinary Anglo-Indian women who, to use Barr's words, "loyally and stoically accepted their share of the white people's burden and lightened the weight of it with their quiet humour, their grace, and often their youth" (1). When I use the word 'ordinary' here, I don't just mean 'middle class'; I mean the opposite of 'extraordinary.' Fowler's book is entirely about the most politically powerful white women of the Raj, the vicereines, but she emphasizes the burden of convention that so circumscribed their lives. The four vicereines whose stay in India she chooses to elaborate are Emily Eden, Charlotte Canning, Edith Lytton, and Mary Curzon. Though she calls them "remarkable women" (3) in her introduction, they are repeatedly applauded for being gracious hostesses and dutiful wives or sisters to husbands or brothers who often neglected them or were sexually unfaithful to them—in short, they are remarkable for upholding the conventions of British society in India often to the detriment of their own welfare. This accomplishment was also singularly unremarkable because every memsahib did it.

By deciding to focus on the ordinary memsahib of the Raj, MacMillan, Barr, and Fowler relegate the truly 'extraordinary' woman, the woman who defied her society in one way or another, to the margins of their texts. In the 1820s and 30s Fanny Parkes left behind her customs collector husband again and again in order to travel around India and meet its people, and although she is mentioned in all three books, her life, her ideas, and her writings are hardly examined at all and certainly not with the detail that these three authors devote to the more conventional memsahibs.[8] MacMillan, Barr, and Fowler, then, are doing much the same thing in their books that Duncan does, at least on the surface, in *The Burnt Offering:* they are paying tribute to the moderate and respectable women of the Raj instead of those women who did not conform to its strictures. This is a particularly unusual construction for Duncan, since in her first Indian novel, *The Simple Adventures of a Memsahib,* it is the ordinary memsahib, represented by the unoriginal Helen Browne, who is the object of her fierce satiric wit. Prior to *The Burnt Offering,* the female protagonists on whom she lavishes her most careful attentions are invariably extraordinary; they are deep-feeling and deep-thinking women who are out of step with their society because of these sensibilities.

I think we have to recognize here that seventy or eighty years separate Duncan's novels about India from these three contemporary reinterpretations of the memsahibs. The events and attitudes that prompted Duncan to construct her ordinary memsahibs (and I am referring primarily to Lucy Foley and Helen Browne) are not the same as the events and attitudes that produced the numerous histories in praise of the Victorian and Edwardian women of Anglo-India and which have been published during the last twenty years or so. Duncan created Helen Browne, with her "character of stunning normality," as Thomas E. Tausky has aptly described her in the introduction to *Simple Adventures,* in response to the *femme fatale* figures who Kipling popularized in his earliest collection of short stories, *Plain Tales from the Hills,* which was published in 1890, three years before Duncan's *The Simple Adventures of a Memsahib.* Mrs. Hauksbee and

Mrs. Reiver are notorious female types who repeatedly turn up in Kipling's Indian fiction. Wicked, adulterous, and disdainful to lesser female beings, those with less sexual power over men, they are depicted as dominating the summer society at Simla. In *Simple Adventures,* Duncan suggests that Kipling's construction of the Anglo-Indian woman had a definite effect on the expectations of British people visiting India. At one point in the story, a traveling M.P. looks for the Kipling type everywhere in British India and is disappointed to find that Helen Browne does not fit the mold (195). The rather mundane character of Helen Browne functions as a sort of corrective to Kipling's larger-than-life rendition of Anglo-Indian womanhood. But *The Simple Adventures of a Memsahib* is much more complex than such a statement suggests, since the narrator's satiric tone, which she maintains until the end, subverts as well as inscribes Helen's ordinariness.

Obviously a different rationale exists behind the creation of Lucy Foley in *The Burnt Offering.* The glorification of her character is a reaction to what Duncan and many other Anglo-Indian novelists of the Edwardian period perceived as a threat—namely, the growing Indian nationalist movement and the support it received from liberal politicians and certain private citizens in England. Lucy's pleasant but ordinary personality, her routine and unconventional ways, serve as the novel's stabilizing force. In the midst of extreme conflict between the races in *The Burnt Offering,* Lucy is an anchor of easy, unoffensive normality. The range of character types that Duncan's memsahibs represent is much broader in the novel immediately preceding *The Burnt Offering.* In *Set in Authority,* published in 1906, there are a variety of Anglo-Indian women: from the intelligent and passionate Dr. Ruth Pearce, who is the protagonist, to Mrs. Biscuit, about whom the narrator comments that she had come to India in eager anticipation of "the many interesting situations from which she should extricate herself within a hair's breath of compromise" (36), to the ambitious Mrs. Lenox and the "keen little chota-mem" Mrs. Lamb (35), whose pluck and good nature the narrator clearly admires. In *Set in Authority,* Anglo-India is not confronted with an external threat which would require a character such as Lucy in *The Burnt Offering* to function as a safe, conservative presence; therefore, Duncan is free to create a diversity of memsahibs, some ordinary, some extraordinary, while others exist in between these extremes. The narrator's sympathy with these women, moreover, varies according to the situation. We do not find Duncan in the untenable position she creates for herself in her delineation of Lucy in *The Burnt Offering*, the position of having to offer unmitigated support to a character she would normally treat ironically.

Understanding the process behind the construction of Duncan's ordinary memsahibs, scholars have to wonder why would Fowler, Barr, and MacMillan, writing seven or eight decades after Duncan's work was published, demonstrate a similar tendency to enshrine the same type of Anglo-Indian woman in their histories. Perhaps it has something to do with the fact that women writers of the Raj are not the ones who are remembered and canonized. In her book on Anglo-Indian literature, *Delusions and Discoveries: Studies on India in the British Imagination 1880–1930*, Benita Parry claims that British India produced only one masterpiece, Forster's *A Passage to India* (8). Rashna B. Singh adds Kipling's and George Orwell's fiction to her list of "major" Anglo-Indian writers in *The Imperishable Empire* (17). Since the academy traditionally cherishes and studies only the work of male writers who wrote about British India, it is hardly surprising that their version of Anglo-Indian womanhood, which many memsahibs have insisted was exaggerated and distorted, is the one that has survived the British Raj. We can, therefore, see the three women's histories, Barr's, Fowler's, and MacMillan's, all of which substantially draw upon the writing produced by Anglo-Indian women, as attempts to recover a women's history of British India and to recover the character of the memsahib as she was perceived, created, and defended by the memsahibs themselves.

In spite of the clear commitment in these four texts—the three histories and the novel—to champion the cause of the ordinary memsahib, there are other less overt and more oppositional voices. MacMillan and Barr make some effort to document the lives of those Anglo-Indian women who belonged to the lower economic classes. We are occasionally told about a soldier's wife or a governess: women who did not attend viceregal balls, did not send their children home to England to be educated, and did not move to Simla during the hot season. But neither of these histories go much beyond a passing acknowledgment that these women existed, and, as a result, readers are left only with a vague picture of the degradation inherent in being white and poor in British India.[9] In Fowler's book, the narrative voice seems to grow increasingly tired of the superficial lives it is recreating. Among the final words of the book is the following quite contemptuous description of a portrait of Mary Curzon wearing her famous peacock dress: "There she stands, transfixed, transported in her finest hour. For the peacock, symbol of royalty for the Mughals, object of worship for the Hindus, that was the final indignity: to find itself seamed and darted between frothing lace at one extreme, and fake white roses at the other" (308). Fowler's history moves, therefore, from an unequivocal expression of sympathy for the highest female members of the ruling class of British India to an implied sympathy for the ruled, symbolized by the peacock feathers sewn into Lady Curzon's gown.

In Duncan's *The Burnt Offering,* the oppositional voice that strains against the narrator's apparent commitment to defending and justifying the ways of Lucy, the average memsahib, belongs to Joan Mills. She is the most extraordinary woman in the novel, the least conventional and typical of all the other female characters, and she is also the novel's pariah. Her judgments about Anglo-Indian lifestyle and politics are often very perceptive, despite the narrator's repeated attempts to call her motives into question. For example, she is able to reveal the assumptions of racial superiority that lie at the base of John Game's theories about governing India. During one of their many arguments—this one about the entrance requirements for the ICS, a subject in which John has a vested interest since he is an ICS officer—she manages to manipulate John into admitting his prejudice. Having learned that Ganendra Thakore's son, an Indian, had brilliantly passed the written exams but failed the riding test and was therefore not admitted to the prestigious ICS, Vulcan Mills suggests that perhaps such qualifications are ridiculous. John's reply, that riding is an indispensable skill for a civil servant, prompts the following exchange between Joan and himself:

> "Are many Englishmen ploughed for riding?" she asked quietly.
> "I should think not. Most Englishmen are naturally able to ride."
> "As all Englishmen are naturally able to govern."
> "Precisely." (55)

John's race consciousness and confidence here betrays a simplicity that Joan is easily able to expose. We, therefore, begin to question John's beliefs because Joan questions them. John's conviction that he and other

Englishmen are naturally able to rule is one of the linchpins of the imperialist belief system. In this story, readers cannot help but wonder about the validity of Raj rhetoric in general, coming as it does from such naive and easily outwitted men.

The marital structure in which the woman generally submits to the man and to his conception of the world would also not be so plainly problematic in the novel, if it were not undermined by Joan's vehement criticism. Joan is its outspoken critic. She receives two marriage proposals in the course of the story, one from Bepin Behari Dey and one from John Game. In refusing John's proposal, Joan makes a clear argument against the kind of marriage that Lucy has accepted. Joan and John have been adversaries from the beginning. Joan's entire reason for coming to India was to join the nascent nationalist movement in Bengal. John, on the other hand, is an established officer of the Raj. He believes the rhetoric and subscribes to the myths that the Anglo-Indians have propagated to explain their presence in India. The two of them engage in one disagreement after another about the contemporary political situation, but John still manages to fall in love with Joan. When he asks her to marry him, the terms of his proposal, and the words in which he couches those terms, suggest that he views marriage with Joan as a way finally to win the argument:

> And after, we will settle everything. I will explain everything—you will understand everything. You will find a new focus for the affairs of this perplexing country—after all, we are doing our best. You will soon feel that it is your race and your husband who is, who are, doing their best. (229)

What John is offering Joan is a place in Anglo-Indian society and the kind of marriage that this society encourages, a marriage like Lucy and Michael Foley's, in which the wife becomes merely the voice of her husband's and her culture's creed. But the cost of such a marriage is that Joan must forfeit her right to entertain any alternative ideas about Indian politics. Joan certainly interprets John's proposal in this manner. She turns him down, saying, "You seem to think that by marrying me . . . you would obtain some sort of influence over me, and even over my father—that you would be able to dictate our private beliefs and public actions. That may be a natural official expectation, but . . . it is a very great mistake" (230).[10]

Joan is not only refusing to marry John Game, but she is also refusing membership in his society. Shocking the conservative Michael Foley early in the novel, Lucy states that Joan has been "a great leader of the women's movement" in England (15). The novel suggests that a woman who has a history of fighting for women's suffrage would hardly make a suitable Anglo-Indian wife. And her unsuitability has everything to do with her unwillingness to embark on a marriage that will suppress and circumscribe her personal convictions.

Joan's acceptance of Bepin as a marriage partner is, in part, her reaction to the restraints and prejudices of Anglo-Indian society. The Indian culture into which she plans to marry has its own very pronounced restrictions and prejudices, especially those pertaining to women, but Joan chooses to overlook these. She conceives of her upcoming marriage to Bepin as something she must do not because she loves him but because it presents an opportunity to sacrifice herself in the cause of Indian nationalism. Explaining her choice to her father, she insists that the circumstances of British imperialism have made interracial marriage a "duty": "How else can one so completely devote one's self to these unhappy brow-beaten people. . . . How can one do *anything* short of identifying one's self with them?" (197). The ardent and overblown language that Joan uses here suggests that she is immature in her notions of marriage, but her fierce need to identify with the Indians because of their subjugation points to an area that the novel does not explore on the surface, but which still emerges through the subtext—namely the connection between white women living within a patriarchal system that undervalues them and their personal lives and Indians who experience a parallel oppression under British imperialism.[11] The novel has already implied that such a connection exists through its portrayal of Joan as both an advocate of Indian nationalism and a suffragette, and further when it showed Lucy in chapter 2 repeating the same action—stooping at the feet of an Englishman—that Bepin had said his father was forced to do years before. By chapter 14, when Ganendra Thakore, the popular Indian nationalist, first raises the idea of a possible marriage between Joan and Bepin, the connection becomes even more apparent.

Ganendra initially proposes the marriage because he believes that Joan will be a steadying influence on Bepin and will dissuade the young Bengali from adopting a violent form of nationalism. In trying to win Vulcan Mills to the idea, he exclaims,

> Let him take all I can give him, and carry on the cause. And with your daughter to guide him, restrain him, and inspire him, to what point might he not carry that cause? My friend, let us make this political marriage. (136)

Ganendra has perceived that Joan and Bepin meet on some very important political grounds: the two are equally ardent nationalists. But while the novel supports him in this last assumption, it proves wrong his belief that Joan will act as a sort of safety valve for Bepin, keeping him from pursuing a more violent expression of his nationalism. At one point, Bepin takes Joan to the secret *asram* (religious retreat), where young nationalists are trained and where explosives and rifles are hidden, in order to ascertain the extent of her dedication to the cause. When she begins to understand that Bepin's nationalism incorporates violence, Joan gives her wholehearted assent. They are brought together not only by the machinations of Ganendra but also by their shared devotion to India and their willingness to approach the strategy for its liberation in a similar manner. They have more in common than even Ganendra realizes.

The proposed marriage between Bepin and Joan has a highly symbolic purpose in this novel in which marriage as a political and personal institution comes under such scrutiny. Its symbolism echoes back to Yadava's notion of an English/India marriage in which England is the "husband of India" (165). But something is altered when that model is overturned by the actions of the characters in the novel. What the plot eventually puts before us is not a British husband and an Indian wife but a British wife and an Indian husband. Yadava's metaphor, when translated into the actual lives of English and Indian people, is reversed. I contend that the proposed marriage of Bepin and Joan recasts both our perception of the gender roles implicit in the original marriage metaphor and our perception of the entire political relationship. These recastings bring into the text the possibility of a new alliance between India and England.

The novel presents a paradigm of marriage in which the feminine role is doubly encoded. Joan Mills is the potential female partner to an Indian man, in contrast to Yadava's depiction of India as the wife of Britain.

However, Joan's anger and rebellion against two traditionally masculine power structures, patriarchy and imperialism, does not jibe with Yadava's description of the feminine India's willing acceptance of English imperialism. The novel posits, then, two types of wives, one nationalist, the other imperialist; moreover, their nationality is variable—the feminine is not always Indian nor, by the same token, is the masculine always English. The potential marriage of Bepin and Joan undermines, therefore, the metaphorical marriage of India and England and vice versa because each is a reversal of the other, at least in terms of the gender roles. Consequently, what breaks down is the idea, introduced by Yadava and supported by imperialists such as John Game, that there can be any sort of fixed relationship between the two countries or between the people of the two countries. By not standardizing these relationships into a single unequivocal pattern, the novel lets in the possibility that a change can and might occur. The relationship between Bepin and Joan represents a potential future for India and England, a future in which the former struggles toward self-government with the support of the latter.

However, although this may be suggested at a subtextual level, the surface of the text works to bring about the re-establishment of British imperialism. Joan and Bepin do not end up marrying because ICS officers such as John Game and Michael Foley manage to stop the ceremony by arresting Bepin for theft. Later, he kills himself after an unsuccessful attempt to assassinate the Viceroy. Joan stays on in India with his family, hoping to continue the nationalist struggle, but later is asked to leave by his female relatives, who are concerned that her presence in their home will attract further attention from the white authorities. At the end of the novel, Bepin and Joan seem permanently disgraced. Their relationship and the nationalism they held on to so fervently are trivialized. The narrator's last words on Bepin offer an impression of him as merely a foolish and misguided man:

> It looked as if the old gods had checkmated Bepin in a move too high for him; they are known to prefer to keep the game in their own hands. His name went into the shadows with him. He became, with cruel quickness, the mere accident that finally turned a people of philosophers from the methods of madness. (315)

This last phrase, "methods of madness," remains unexplicated by the narrator. Should readers assume that what is being condemned here is merely violence as a "method" of nationalism, or has the entire nationalist movement been dismissed as "madness" of sorts? The last few chapters of the novel seem to point to this second interpretation, since various events occur in rapid succession which undermine the nationalist movement, and these events are designed to make us assume that the destiny of India lies with a power greater than that wielded by any of the human characters. As the above passage suggests, the "old gods" are at work and they appear determined to prove the beneficence of British imperialism in India. This effect is accomplished through the valorization of the English characters and the death, disgrace, or withdrawal of the Indian ones.

For example, it is not Bepin, the novel finally asserts, but John Game who seems the real martyr. His death, in the same incident that prompted Bepin to commit suicide, is depicted as a cause for great mourning by English and Indian alike. No longer an enemy to the nationalists, John, after his death, comes to be regarded as a friend to India, and the narrator encourages readers to envision him in this way. The close of the novel reaffirms the old imperialist relationship between Englishmen and Indians and between England and India. The two countries move back into the positions Yadava originally assigned them: England is the husband and India the wife. This is reiterated when Janaki, who has secretly loved John throughout the novel, retreats from the world and adopts a widowhood she had renounced: "The Rani Janaki has returned to her widowhood, but I do not know—I do not know for whom she prays" (320). The narrator leads us to believe that her mourning is for John, an English husband for an Indian wife, a husband made even more sovereign and powerful because of his status as a martyr in the cause of her country.[12]

Still, in spite of the firm closure that Duncan tries to impose on the plot, we must not underestimate the dissenting voice that the novel allows to be heard. This voice is stridently anti-imperialist, and it is the voice of many characters in the text, Ganendra, Bepin, Joan, Vulcan, even Janaki. Ganendra's passionate defense of nationalism at his trial is one of the high points of the novel. Charged with inciting sedition, he refuses to regard his actions on behalf of India as seditious. His speech in court calls into question any definitions of treason imposed by a foreign ruler: "I am accused of exciting to hatred and disaffection; but I submit that these harsh words do not truly describe the new emotion which is beginning to thrill the hearts of my countrymen" (245). Ganendra represents the strength of nationalism in the novel. Although he is punished with ten years' exile and he finally dies, saddened by Bepin's failure, his courtroom words remain powerful. Nationalism has a voice in *The Burnt Offering,* and not even Duncan's efforts in the end to justify imperialism can silence that voice.

The novel raises a truly radical alternative to the imperialist marriage of England and India, and this relationship vies with the marriage metaphor for predominance throughout the text. I am referring here to the mother/child paradigm that the nationalists use, in which India is constituted as a maternal figure and the Indians see themselves as her children. Early in the novel, Bepin explains to Joan the relationship that Ganendra and potentially all Indians have with their native country:

> "He lives only for God, and for the Mother."
>
> "For the Mother?"
>
> "For India."
>
> "Oh, yes—the motherland. I understand," she said.
>
> "To us she is the Mother," Bepin told her. "It is the language of the heart. If it were not for her I think Sri Ganendra would be altogether a holy man—recluse. But our Mother calls him." (31)

The call of the Mother is heard by many disparate characters. Even Janaki, who has previously identified herself as a moderate, finally admits to Yadava that she has been giving money to the nationalists because, she explains, "I have wished to help—to free the Mother" (297). This familial relationship with India, then, is not confined solely to Indian men (although Ganendra often speaks of the Mother's children as if they were men alone); it is a feeling and an aspiration in which Indian women can share as well. The only people who do not and cannot take the metaphor to heart are the English. They are left out of it entirely, or to put it more accurately, they fit into the picture only as something to be ejected. When the Viceroy appropriates the metaphor at the end of the novel, shouting "*Bande Mataram*" or "Hail to the Motherland" after having announced certain civil reforms that will enable more Indians to enter the upper reaches of the ICS, it loses some of its emotional significance. For India is not the motherland to Englishmen, and the Viceroy is, therefore, not speaking "the language of the heart" which, as Bepin suggests above, has produced the notion of India as mother in the first place.

Among Duncan's novels about India, *The Burnt Offering* is the one most firmly embedded in its historical moment. The chanting of *Bande Mataram,* the attempted assassination of a high official (although it was the Lieutenant-Governor of Bengal who was almost killed by Indian revolutionary terrorists in 1907), the trial and conviction of a major Indian political leader, the introduction of much-needed reforms—these details, taken together, situate the time of the novel in the six-year period between 1903–1909. Considering the numerous references and allusions that Duncan makes to contemporary events and ideas, we can regard *The Burnt Offering* as its author's attempt to provide Anglo-Indians and the English reading public with the conceptual tools to assimilate the powerful nationalist tensions in India at that time. To some degree, the novel works much like Kipling's short story, "The Enlightenments of Pagett, M.P." It strives to contain Indian nationalism within a discourse of British imperialism. But, as I have tried to suggest, *The Burnt Offering* lets in too many alternative voices and visions to be entirely successful in this endeavor.

I use the plural here—"voices and visions"—instead of the singular because the novel does not present us with a unified Indian nationalism. Not only is it split into various streams, the extremist faction, which Ganendra embodies, and the revolutionary terrorism that Bepin practices in the end, it is divided along gender lines as well. The Indian women in the novel do not participate in the nationalist movement in the same way that men do. Because of the feminine roles Indian society assigns them, they are not permitted into its limelight. Consequently, their nationalism goes on in the private sphere of the home. This becomes evident in Chapter 11 during the Ladies' League party. Janaki tells Joan, "Every Bengali woman in this room is in her way a politician. But, naturally, they will not speak of that" (113). They do not speak perhaps, but they do sing. When asked by her English hostess to sing in Bengali, Mrs. Das, a well-known composer and singer, chooses a patriotic song, one that unites the Indian women and excludes the English:

Suddenly from her immobile little person, where it sat, the song began to issue, rather a cry than a song, harsh and plaintive. Two or three of her sister-guests exchanged half-frightened glances; the rest looked with covert smiles at the floor, the lips of one or two moved in unison. . . . When it was over, something like a sigh lifted the bosoms that had understood, but it was lost in the complacent applause of the Anglo-Indian ladies. (114)

Janaki understands the political statement implicit in the song itself and in Mrs. Das's decision to sing it in front of the English women in the room. It is, of course, an act of solidarity. As a nationalist, however, Janaki's personal allegiances interfere with her patriotism. When she learns that there will be an attempt on the Viceroy's life during a parade which both her father and John Game plan to attend, she betrays her nationalist affiliations in order to save their lives.

In *The Burnt Offering* readers see the politicization of Indian women in the cause of nationalism. Such a construction is by no means common, even in Anglo-Indian literature written later in the century, when the subject of nationalism becomes more prevalent. Invariably, and particularly in novels written by Anglo-Indian men, Indian nationalism is depicted as a predominantly masculine movement. That Duncan, writing as early as 1909, should include Indian women among her nationalist characters puts her in the forefront not only of novelists but of historians writing about Indian nationalism. In her 1985 article entitled "*Swadeshi* Movement and Women's Awakening in Bengal, 1903–1910," Bharati Ray observes that although this period has received much attention in Indian historiography, "one significant aspect has been left almost totally unexplored, namely, the women in the movement" (73). Because Duncan is one of the earliest novelists, English or Indian, to write about the entrance of Indian women into the nationalist arena, her construction of the event, as it is delineated through the character of Janaki, merits some comparison with a few of the major points in Ray's reconstruction, written some seventy-six years later and from the vantage point of a post-independence Indian woman.

It is hardly surprising that Duncan attributes Janaki's nationalism to her stay in England, during which she "fell into the family of a Radical don of Oxford, where for five years she was treated with indignant pity and taught to think politically. Mrs. Sidney Gray placed in her hand the latest flag of applied democracy . . ." (41). The notion that Indian nationalism was a product of western culture and ideals is frequently found in English histories. Spear, referring to the late nineteenth century in British India, writes, "No one could be in contact with Englishmen at that time for long or read Shakespeare . . . without catching the infection of nationalism" (166). Ray, on the other hand, maintains that Indian women heard the call of nationalism not from English people or from English literature but from Indian men: "the menfolk of Bengal, who had acquired some experience of political deliberations since the mid-nineteenth century, built up the protest movement and . . . it was they who invited the women to partici-pate in the struggle" (75). The difference between these two perceptions of the same event is clearly a political one. By suggesting that the origins of Indian nationalism lie with the English themselves, which is a common supposition in Anglo-Indian fiction and nonfiction, imperialist writers, such as Duncan, avoid confronting the possibility that it was the British oppression of Indians which gave rise to nationalism in India. But Ray is writing within a long tradition of Indian historiography about modern Indian history, a tradition which searches for the origins of nationalism in Indian culture. Although she mentions in her article the influence of west-ern political practices on the early nationalists, her perspective remains primarily that of an Indian looking at the developments of an Indian in-stitution and the effects of that institution on an Indian population. The British figure in her argument only as a colonial structure against which the nationalists reacted.

The most significant difference between Duncan's and Ray's separate constructions of the politicization of Bengali women in the first decade of the twentieth century, however, lies in the feminine roles that these writers ascribe to these women. According to Ray, middle-class Bengali women began to establish themselves as a powerful force in Indian politics during the *Swadeshi* movement, which consisted of a massive boycott of British goods to protest Lord Curzon's decision to partition Bengal in 1905. While Indian women had in the past generally been denied the right to partici-pate in politics, Ray asserts that the partition was viewed by the men as a "national crisis" (75) and the massive co-operation of the women was thought to be essential to the success of the cause. Bengali women were able to enter the public arena without entirely discarding their traditional images and roles because nationalism, by the time the *Swadeshi* movement got underway, had adopted a spiritual form. Ray states, "The motherland had become the Mother Goddess, *Bandemataram* the new mantra (hymn) and the politico-economic agitation a *mahayajna* (holypuja) [*sic*]. . . . The conversion of politics into religion made [women's] participation in it easy and natural" (77). The potential radicalism inherent in the emergence of hitherto secluded women into public affairs was tempered, Ray suggests, by both the religiosity of the *Swadeshi* movement and by the fact that it appealed to women as mothers and sisters rather than as wives and lovers. She cites as the reason for this the tendency in Bengali families to privilege the mother-son and brother-sister relationships over other familial and marital ties. "In most Hindu families," she writes, "a wife was not yet permitted to speak to her husband during the day" (78).

Despite Duncan's use of the India as mother metaphor, *The Burnt Offering* is principally concerned with Bengali women in their roles as wives and lovers. The major conflict in Janaki's life, for instance, is generated by a romantic liaison gone awry. Moreover, near the close of the novel, as John Game recollects his long-time service in the ICS, Janaki and India itself are conflated into an image of the ideal wife or lover:

> He felt a fresh tenderness for her; perhaps she stood to him for India as he thought of her—the India of his old dreams, the bride of his country, the enchantress of his race. India then could be kind to those who served and loved her. (303)

From the beginning of the novel, readers are encouraged to see Janaki as the potential partner of an English man, and in the end she is finally idealized into that role. Since her allegiances are inevitably split between the English man she loves and the country whose freedom she longs for, the extent of Janaki's politicization is seriously limited. Within the context of Duncan's novel, the role of the wife or lover emerges as a means of controlling an Indian woman character and restraining her nationalist aspirations.

Assessing Duncan's achievement in *The Burnt Offering* means acknowledging that she dared to write sympathetically and in detail about Indian nationalism at a time when almost no other British writer would tackle the subject. The historical period that informs the novel was one that British and Indian historians alike represent as a tumultuous period in India. But most Anglo-Indian writers, by the turn of the century, were engaged in writing romantic adventure stories rather than realist narratives, and, consequently, the reality of the early Indian nationalist movement went almost undepicted in western literature. Kipling's *Kim,* for example, was published in 1901, and the novel is remarkable for its refusal to address in any way the issue of nationalism in India. The India that exists in *Kim* is one that is virtually free of internal political dissension. The only threats to British rule come from outside the country, from the Russians. I have earlier called *The Burnt Offering* Duncan's most courageous work of fiction. Its courage lies not only in its choice of subject matter but in the degree to which Duncan was willing to affirm the pull of nationalism for many elite Indians who were growing increasingly dissatisfied and disenchanted with the ideology of British imperialism.

The novel takes risks in another area as well. It dares to delineate a relationship between an Indian man and a white woman, something few other pieces of fiction at or before that time had done. Interracial marriages or love affairs are touchy topics in Anglo-Indian literature generally, and if the subject is broached at all, the relationship invariably involves a white man and an Indian woman. Furthermore, it usually ends in disaster, with the Indian woman dying or killing herself.[13] While Duncan remains true to convention when she dooms the relationship between Bepin and Joan, her fundamental assumption is revolutionary. The possibility of sexual attraction and emotional compatibility between white men and Indian women is conceived of as "natural" in Anglo-Indian literature. That the same might be true in reverse is not even entertained. Duncan, then, disputes the gender and racial stereotypes that the English perpetuated in their fiction about India. More than this, her portrait of Joan's and Bepin's friendship suggests that there might be a meeting ground other than sexual attraction for English and Indian people living in India.

In my interpretation of *The Burnt Offering,* I have concentrated on those aspects that seem extraordinary to me given the other texts produced during the same historical period, and I have chosen to do this because I think that Sara Jeannette Duncan is a vastly underrated and under-read author. In Allen J. Greenberger's *The British Image of India: A Study in the Literature of Imperialism, 1880–1960,* Duncan is not even mentioned. Nor does Benita Parry bother to take her into account in her much-quoted *Delusions and Discoveries.* The omission is an unfortunate one because

Duncan's fiction calls into question many of the generalizations that both of these texts tend to make.[14] Neglecting Duncan's work means neglecting the alternative constructions she offers, alternatives to Kipling, Forster, Leonard Woolf, George Orwell, and to the women romance writers of her own day who chose India as a subject or a setting. Duncan allows readers to see Anglo-Indian society in ways that the other writers do not—with a critical eye, because she does not subscribe to all the myths of British imperialism or of patriarchy, but also with an eye focused on the small details, focused on the particular more than on the universal, on the everyday more than on the timeless. She also frequently introduces characters whose ideas challenge the prevailing imperialist ideology of her fiction. Duncan's novels invite multiple and sometimes contradictory interpretations. This openness is her work's greatest strength.

3

Liberal Imperialism as a Passage to India

For Kipling and Duncan, writing their Indian fiction before 1910, imperialism was a creed standing in no need of justification; for its justification was to some extent a given, or at least presented as if it were a given. Certain fundamental assumptions of imperialism, such as the right of one people to rule over another and to reap the benefits implicit in that sovereignty, are never addressed and consequently never defended. Even their fiction about Indian aspirations for self-government does not so much attempt to vindicate the British presence in India as it strives simply to discredit nationalism—its followers, its leaders, and its ultimate goals—and consequently does not bother to offer an all-out defense of the Empire. If, on occasion, their work points to the existence of doubts about the administration of India or, as in Duncan's case, about the advisability of subjugating a progressively angrier people, inevitably these are swept away by a fundamental belief in the efficacy of imperialism, which dominates and controls the direction of their texts. Around 1910, however, and especially after World War I, the literature of Anglo-India becomes a site for the open contestation of political power. The result is that while Anglo-Indian fiction of the late nineteenth and very early twentieth centuries usually takes for granted the idea that imperialism is basically a good thing, by the 1910s this 'fact' becomes a disputed issue, to be struggled with on the surface of the text. What prompted this shift in literary practice, this new foregrounding of tension (as opposed to the kind of tension-under-erasure that Kipling and Duncan propagate)? It might be linked to any number of historical occurrences, depending on the school of historiography to which one subscribes.

The ten years that began around 1909 were marked by the decline of the Swadeshi movement, the rise of revolutionary terrorism, and constitutional reforms. Ending in 1919 with the first nationalist *satyagraha,* the massacre at Jallianwalla Bagh, and more constitutional reforms, the decade contained many events which Indian and British historians have traditionally identified as hugely transformative moments in the history of India and the Empire, moments which could be seen as contiguous to or somehow allied with the changes occurring in the tone and political content of Anglo-Indian literature. I have chosen to focus on Mohandas K. Gandhi's 1915 appearance on the Indian political scene and the British government's declaration in 1917 of its commitment to self-government in India because these incidents allow me to tap into two elaborate and cherished myths about Indian independence, the details of which have been painstakingly fashioned by historians on both sides of the political fence.[1] These myths are particularly useful in reading Forster's *A Passage to India,* because they were conceived during the eleven-year period in which Forster wrote his novel, from 1913 and 1924, and they inform almost all subsequent interpretations of this text.

On August 20, 1917 during his tenure as Secretary of State for India in the British parliament, Edwin Montagu made a statement which some liberal historians, especially those with imperialist leanings, look back on with pride. That day saw the government in London announcing for the first time its pledge to work toward a radical alteration in the political make-up of the Indian administrative system:

> The policy of His Majesty's Government . . . is that of the increasing association of Indians in every branch of the administration and the gradual development of self-governing institutions with a view to the progressive realisation of responsible government in India as an integral part of the British Empire. (quoted in Schuster 74)

What is new about this statement is not its promise to increase Indian participation in the administration of the country, since this was the substance of the 1909 reforms. Its novelty lies in its guarantee of eventual self-government.

Mridula Mukherjee, one of the six co-authors of *India's Struggle for Independence,* sees this declaration as the British government's reaction to the Home Rule movement. Under the leadership of Tilak, the early nationalist whose participation in Hindu revivalism has been the source of so much debate among historians, and the English Theosophist Annie Besant, the campaign for home rule began in 1915 to build up agitation around the demand for Indian independence. Having set up Home Rule Leagues boasting thousands of members, Besant and Tilak moved through India spreading the word about nationalism. When Besant was arrested in June 1917, angry citizens all over India rose up in protest, which, Mukherjee suggests, forced the government to adopt a more "conciliatory posture," and the end result was the August pledge.

While she acknowledges that this new policy represented a leap ahead for the nationalist movement, because "after this the demand for Home Rule or self-government could no longer be treated as seditious," Mukherjee also notes that a deliberate delay was inscribed in the pledge itself through an accompanying clause, which stated that "the British government and the Government of India, on whom the responsibility lies for the welfare and advancement of the Indian people, must be judges of the time and measure of each advance" (quoted in Chirol 149). It was the prerogative of the government alone to decide on the nature and timing of the progression toward home rule. The British parliament could, therefore, retain its hold over India indefinitely, since the clause "gave it enough leeway to prevent any real transfer of power to Indian hands for a long enough time" (168). Mukherjee, then, interprets the government's 1917 pledge as a seriously circumscribed advance for the nationalists but an advance nevertheless.

Liberal imperialist historians have produced a different reading. For them, the pledge was proof of a liberal course working in Indian history, a course which had been present almost at the beginning of Empire and which shaped one enlightened policy after another throughout the nineteenth century. George Schuster, in his 1941 book entitled *India and Democracy,* articulates this liberal myth of imperialism:

Yet when the Indian story is reviewed over the whole period of the British connection, whether it be followed in the record of acts in India or of comment and debate in England, it is possible to trace a steady and consistent purpose inspired by a spirit which in the main has not varied. The purpose has been the establishment of self-government in India, the spirit has been one of liberalism. (xiii)

This is, of course, a relatively easy assertion to make in 1941, over twenty years after the August 1917 pledge, and just two years after the *latest* British promise of self-government in 1939, which yet again delayed the event until the close of World War II. To maintain that home rule has been the British hope for India all along at a time when it is obvious that no other outcome is likely can be construed as an attempt to appropriate responsibility for India's imminent political independence.

Moreover, Schuster's suggestion that English liberalism, with its commitment to Indian self-government, was at the heart of imperialism all along is in accordance with the hidden agenda of his book, which is to convince his readers of the need for India to maintain its political connections with Britain, even after independence. His premise is that India should not strive for complete freedom from England but should remain a member of the British Commonwealth. Speaking to an imaginary Indian reader in the epilogue of his book, Schuster argues his point by stating that India does not have the strength or unity "to stand alone in the world" (439), and, therefore, "Her best chance of obtaining freedom and security to develop her own destiny on her own lines lies in remaining a member of the British group" (440). It is only by constructing British imperialism as a fundamentally benevolent institution with the same hopes and ideals and goals as Indian nationalism that Schuster is able to justify his argument. A conservative approach, which constitutes the British presence as a necessity since, according to this view, Indians are incapable of ruling themselves, would simply alienate the Indian nationalist leaders, who by 1941 had clearly assumed positions of power among the Indian people and would therefore take over the reins of government when the British departed.

Schuster's support for his theory is provided by the co-author of the book, Guy Wint. Wint retraces Indian history, selecting various events and finding in them evidence of a liberal tradition in the practice of British imperialism. He concentrates specifically on the numerous constitutional reforms instigated in India—from 1853, when the first legislative council was established to what he calls the "great Act of 1935," which, he insists, "reached the goal of full parliamentary government in the provinces" (72). Within this explanatory system, the British declaration of 1917 emerges as the first explicit statement of a political program that had actually been operating in India for over one hundred years. "The British deliberately fostered the growth of political organs which were bound to end by super-seding their own administration. Nor did they fail to recognise this," Wint confidently asserts (73).

He admits, however, that not all British officials in India have been sympathetic to this program. Some have been determined to maintain British power over Indians out of a mistaken belief in the Englishman's right to rule. But he dismisses these particular men as having "developed frankly Oriental conceptions of the relation of the ruler and subject" (74), and here readers are meant to equate the qualities of despotism and incompetence with Oriental rule, having in the preceding chapter been briefed on the practices of the traditional Indian monarch (14–17).

Wint's reworking of Indian history reaches a crescendo in his affirmation of "the British parliament, the British public, and British ideas" (74), an influence on India which, he insists, "was anything but 'imperialist'." Finally he invokes a conventional fiction about the Empire—that the English acquired India absentmindedly and continue to hold the country inattentively: "the builders of the largest empire in history . . . have seemed over long periods to be almost unconscious of what they had achieved, or to be anxious deliberately to ignore it" (75). That this statement contradicts his earlier insistence on the carefully thought out program of liberalism, which had been in effect in India for almost a century, seems to escape his notice. Wint wants to have it both ways. On the one hand, he wants to preserve the liberal imperialist ideal, which holds that policy in India had always been shaped with a view toward the eventual transfer of power from the English to the Indians. On the other, he also wants to envision the Empire as a phenomenon that the British encountered almost by chance, and so he calls up the conservative imperialist fiction of English absentmindedness. The former notion points to deliberate designs and to the planned and purposeful suppression of the Indian people in the interests of empire building and free trade; the latter removes some of the English guilt over the conquest of India because it relegates the responsibility for the creation of the Empire to forces, like Providence, beyond individual or even national control. By such myths, and the inevitable blind spots that they encouraged, was the British Empire sustained and vindicated.[2]

Perhaps in response to the liberal appropriation of India's independence, perhaps simply as a means of affirming itself and its autonomous power, Indian nationalism produced its own myths, one of which grew up around the figure of Gandhi. The return of Gandhi to India, after twenty years in South Africa, is usually interpreted by nationalist historians as the signal of a basic and irreversible change in political conditions on the subcontinent. Nehru in *The Discovery of India* represents the event as a profound psychological experience for the entire Indian people. World War I, he states, left Indians feeling humiliated and betrayed by the British government, which had promised constitutional reform and the Indianization of the civil service in return for recruitment, and delivered instead martial law in the Punjab. Nationalism too was at a "low ebb"; a disagreement between the two prominent factions, the moderates and the extremists (271), had produced a debilitating split that almost paralyzed the Congress. But when Gandhi came "like a powerful current of fresh air . . . like a beam of light . . . like a whirlwind," he altered the state of the nation forever because he transformed the people. They were suffering, Nehru writes, from a "pervasive, oppressing, strangling fear" under British rule (274), and Gandhi brought them release and truth:

> As fear is close companion to falsehood, so truth follows fearlessness. The Indian people did not become much more truthful than they were, nor did they change their essential nature overnight; nevertheless a sea change was visible as the need for falsehood and furtive behavior lessened. It was a psychological change, almost as if some expert in psychoanalytical method had probed deep into the patient's past, found out the origins of his complexes, exposed them to his view, and thus rid him of that burden. (275)

Nehru was one of the first politicians—but many followed his lead—to identify Gandhi as *the* pivotal figure in nationalist history. Gandhi's status as such rests on the assumption that he, more than any other leader, was responsible for bringing the so-called "masses" into the Indian movement for independence. The significance of this act in the historiography of modern India is apparent in the fact that it is the mobilization of the people that nationalist and imperialist historians alike regard as the distinguishing feature of twentieth-century nationalism in India.

The nineteenth-century nationalists, we are told by Heimsath, Nehru, Bipan Chandra, and Spear, were certainly effective on some level, but they were unable to engage the populace in their struggle. Although the Swadeshi movement in the first decade of this century is often cited as the moment at which large numbers of people first entered the Indian political arena, historians also tend to add that these numbers were predominantly from the middle class and further that their participation was elicited primarily in response to the partition of Bengal. It was not until Gandhi appeared on the scene that the "masses" were mobilized for the express purpose of ousting the British and achieving *swaraj* or independence. In Indian and western historiography, then, Gandhi is clearly constructed as the father of the modern Indian nationalism, which is, more so than the earlier variety, credited with the overthrow of imperialism.

What is particularly interesting about the discourse historians have built up around Gandhi is not so much that it mystifies the man—through the use of such words as "magic" when describing his political strategies (Spear 202), the ascription of nebulous powers to him (Nehru 281), and the tendency to add the respectful suffix "-ji" to his, and no other leader's, name whenever it is mentioned (Bipan Chandra)—but that it simplifies the people over whom he was supposed to have had such a profound influence. In order to constitute Gandhi as their savior and teacher, the "masses" of India are made to seem homogeneous, acquiescent, uneducated in political action, and somewhat helpless. This is certainly what Nehru means when he speaks of India's "people." He repeatedly makes a distinction in his writing between "the small westernized group at the top and the masses" (281), at one point going so far as to describe these two categories as "the small thinking minority and the unthinking masses" (59). It is because the Indian people are depicted only as a clump, rather than as a collective comprised of separate constituents and constituencies, that Nehru can make a declaration like "Gandhi knew India, and especially the Indian masses" (363). Otherwise such an achievement would seem impossible and the statement ridiculous.

Spear sets up a similar binary opposition in *A History of India: Volume Two*. For him, Indian people can be reduced to the "masses" and the

"classes," the "classes" being the university-educated Indians who, he asserts, were responsible for organizing the nationalist movement and the
"masses" being everyone else in India who was not British. Using this
paradigm, he represents Gandhi's effect on the nationalist movement in
the following manner: "He could persuade the masses to follow the classes
because they believed him to be a good Hindu, a great soul; he could persuade the classes to accept his Hindu and, as many of them thought, his
primitivist habits because it won them the masses" (200). The idea that
the Indian nationalist movement consisted of two such immense camps
influenced by one powerful man has a number of ramifications. First, it
reinforces the imperialist image of the Indian people as a mob, unrespon-
sive to everything save a spiritual appeal and, second, it smooths over any
dissenting voices that might exist within either group. Thus, the Indian
Communist Party, which frequently disagreed with Congress politics to
the extent that it often refused to support Gandhi's organized protests,
is left out of the picture entirely, as are those peasant or working-class
groups who, for various reasons, chose occasionally to exceed Gandhi's
authority or not to align themselves with him at all.[3] (Spear also makes it
appear as if all the people in question are Hindu, which, of course, elides
the Muslims, Christians, Jews, and Parsees, who would not be particularly concerned whether or not Gandhi was "a good Hindu.") That Spear
should see the matter in this light seems hardly surprising considering his
tendency to rely on imperialist notions of India. But that he should participate with Nehru in the polarization of the Indian people into two distinct
groups, one of which thinks and reasons while the other does not, suggests that he has been influenced by a nationalist construction of society.
For although imperialists often use the divide-and-conquer method in the
writing of their government policies as well as in their history, they are
much more inclined to fragment the Indian people into many factions
rather than just two. By doing so, imperialist writers seek to establish that
Indians comprise a fundamentally fractured society and further to make
it evident that any achievement of unity in India is a singularly British
achievement. For example, Kipling's short story "The Enlightenments of
Pagett, M.P." insists on the existence of many races in India, all of which
are at each other's throats, and none of which have anything in common
beyond their shared status as subjects of Britain. It was nationalism, and

especially Nehru's variety of it, that sought, in its quest for Indian unity, to minimize the differences among the people of India. Spear's ability to draw on both the discourses of imperialism and nationalism in his history of modern India—to contain them both within his argument without the one theoretically undermining the other—points to the basic connectedness of these two systems.

Until this moment in this study, I have been representing imperialism and nationalism in India as oppositional political ideals and systems. This is a conventional way of understanding the politics of modern India; it is usually the explanatory paradigm that Anglo-Indian and Indian national-ist fiction writers choose to depict the situation. At this point, however, it becomes important that we recognize the ground on which imperialism and nationalism meet, a ground, I might add, much larger than most histo-rians acknowledge. The extent, the meaning, and the political implications of this ground have been the subject of much debate in contemporary scholarship on Indian history and postcolonial literary criticism. I turn to this scholarship now in order to situate traditional historiography about India, which I have already outlined in this and the preceding chapters, in relation to it.

Although imperialist, nationalist, and Marxist interpretations have tended to dominate historiography about the colonial period in India, re-cently a new trend has produced alternative readings of the same era. This trend, which participates in the current structuralist and post-structuralist critique of the sovereign subject, is responsible for two different but con-nected historiographies, one of which calls itself Subaltern Studies and the other I will delineate as "post-Orientalist," following Gyan Prakash's lead in his excellent article "Writing Post-Orientalist Histories of the Third World: Perspectives from Indian Historiography." Both of these approaches to historical writing challenge and rewrite imperialist and nationalist constructions of the colonial period in Indian history, and they do so on the basis that neither of these systems of thought tells the whole story. Invariably something is left out or even concealed when, as Prakash notes, "issues are posed as India versus Britain" (401).

Partha Chatterjee in *Nationalist Thought and the Colonial World* argues that the complicity between Indian nationalism and British imperialism has been erased by this model of polarity. While it is true, he says, that nationalism challenged the imperialist notion of India—insofar as it conceived of India and Indians as active and sovereign where imperialism saw only passivity, otherness, and dependency—it also accepted the intrinsic premises on which that notion was built. Nationalism committed itself to the same essentialist ideology that imperialism had used in order to objectify India. Like imperialism, nationalist thought idealized reason; it idealized history and progress. Moreover, it adopted imperialism's belief that the East and West were distinct entities geographically, culturally, and spiritually. In doing so it affirmed the post-Enlightenment typology which constructed a transcendent subject and a non-transcendent object of knowledge: "There is, consequently, an inherent contradictoriness in nationalist thinking, because it reasons within a framework of knowledge whose representational structure corresponds to the very structure of power nationalist thought seeks to repudiate" (Chatterjee 38). India remained for the nationalists something to elucidate, to chart and explain, the only difference being that while Indology had previously been an exclusively European discipline, when it was in the hands of the imperialists alone, now it was a discourse that Indians could produce as well.

Chatterjee and other post-Orientalist historiographers like Lata Mani and Gauri Viswanathan tend to concentrate on existing texts of history, both those that have been published, such as Nehru's and Gandhi's writings, and those that remain in archives in India and Britain. They deconstruct the colonial discourses of nationalism and imperialism and expose what has been placed under erasure by these discourses. The Subaltern Studies historians, on the other hand, though they too participate in this kind of scholarship (Chatterjee is one of the founding subalternists), are more concerned with recovering a lost history. For them, what has been elided by traditional "colonialist and neo-colonialist" and "nationalist and neo-nationalist" historiography (Guha I: 1) is the struggle of the subaltern.[4] Ranajit Guha, the editor of the series of books, delineates the subaltern as a shifting category of subordination in South Asian society. Because it is shifting rather than static, the subaltern has various manifestations. It can be expressed, he states in his preface to the first volume, in terms of "class, caste, age, gender and office or in any other way" (I: vii). Defined as "not subaltern" are those groups which are usually subsumed under the classification of "elite," specifically the dominant foreign groups, such as

British officials of the colonial state and other foreign planters, industrial-
ists, and merchants, as well as the dominant indigenous groups, including
those classes and interests which sought either to maintain the colonial
status quo or simply to displace it with yet another system perpetuating
the subordination of the subaltern. Among these elites, Guha places the
mainstream nationalist leaders.

The historiography that these leaders either wrote, as in Nehru's case,
or of which they were the subject tends to emphasize their participation,
their contribution, and their organization of nationalist politics. But Guha
insists that such writing masks the nationalists' complicity in the colonial state and structure. In their hands or under their direction, Indian
nationalism emerges as a

> phenomenal expression of the goodness of the native elite with the an-
> tagonistic aspect of their relation to the colonial regime made, against
> all evidence, to look larger than its collaborationist aspect, their role
> as promoters of the cause of the people than that as exploiters and op-
> pressors, their altruism and self-abnegation than their scramble for the
> modicum of power and privilege granted by the rulers in order to make
> sure of their support for the Raj. The history of Indian nationalism is
> thus written up as a sort of spiritual biography of the Indian elite. (I: 2)

A history that recounts only the story of the Indian bourgeoisie, however,
cannot ultimately explain nationalism in India, Guha insists, because it
excludes what he calls *"the politics of the people"* (I: 4), and by "people"
Guha is referring to the subaltern groups. (The terms 'people' and 'subaltern' *and* 'nation' are all synonymous in his writing.) The gaps left by
this type of historiography are apparent when it is used to explain the
numerous instances of popular revolt "in defiance or absence of elite control" (I: 3), and here Guha cites as examples the anti-Rowlatt riots of
1919 and the 1942 Quit India movement, both of which resulted in violent
clashes between the Indian people and the police and Gandhi's subsequent cancellation of these *satyagrahas*. Since nationalist historiography
cannot adequately elucidate such occurrences, Guha argues that it cannot be employed to interpret the contribution made by the subaltern to
the nationalist movement. Guha goes so far as to assert that these gaps in
nationalist and neo-nationalist historiography, gaps which are indicative

of subaltern insurgency, actually point to what he calls "an important historical truth," namely, "the *failure of the Indian bourgeoisie to speak for the nation*" (I: 5).

To rectify the historiographical situation, Guha and the other subalternists offer alternative histories of nationalism in India, histories which reveal the workings of subaltern resistance as well as the efforts on the part of nationalist leaders and writers to suppress its emancipatory potential. Gyan Pandey's essay in Volume I of the Subaltern Studies series, entitled "Peasant Revolt and Indian Nationalism: The Peasant Movement in Awadh, 1919–1922," is just such an attempt to engage this other look at modern Indian history. Rather than focus on the events to which historians typically turn when considering these dates—Gandhi's anti-Rowlatt *satyagraha* of 1919, the massacre at Jallianwalla Bagh, and the pan-India Noncooperation Movement of 1920–22—Pandey chooses to see the Indian nationalism of this three-year period in terms of the increased politicization of the Awadh peasant. He recognizes the difficulty inherent in his efforts: "The peasants' view of the struggle will probably never be recovered; and whatever we say about it at this stage must be very tentative. Yet it seems important to try and piece together some part of it, from the isolated statements of peasants found in the documents and from the only other evidence we have—the message contained in their actions" (I: 150). He goes on to demonstrate that the "Peasants' Perspective" (I: 166), far from being irretrievable, is, in fact, implicit even in the elitist documents which are available to us.

The interpretation that Pandey offers of specific events in the Awadh region and of larger movements like Gandhi's Non-cooperation is significantly different from most nationalist and imperialist views of this period in particular and of the peasant in general. The peasant is constructed as an active participant in his own local politics and in national politics. He is shown operating independently of the elite Congress and even at times in defiance of this organization. Pandey describes in detail the establishment, demise, and reformation of the Kisan Sabhas or peasant associations, which were formed by peasants for the purposes of addressing issues pertinent especially to them. He also delineates the attempts of the nationalist leaders such as Gandhi and Jawaharlal Nehru to appropriate these associations in the interests of the Non-cooperation Movement and its tactics of non-violence. Although Pandey recognizes the influence of Gandhi on the peasant political consciousness, he cautions against exaggerating the role of any urban politician in rural politics. Gandhi's achievements, he says, certainly served as inspiration to the peasants in Awadh, but "the timing of the peasants' revolt and the violence of their actions" (I: 177) suggest that they had gone beyond Gandhi's or the Congress's control.

Pandey asserts that the Awadh peasants in their struggles against their landlords, offered Congress a much more radical conception of *swaraj* than it was prepared to accept. By the end of their movement, it was clear that the peasants sought not only to overthrow colonialism in India but also to be free of oppression coming from indigenous landlords. Gandhi and the Congress leaders, however, were determined to strive for an all-India unity, a unity which would include landlords and peasants both. In their efforts to win the landlords to their cause, the elite nationalists instructed the peasants to sacrifice their personal battle against their land-lords and to fall in line with the larger anti-imperialist movement, which would relegate them to the position of followers and Gandhi devotees. Pandey's reading of this moment stands in stark contrast to that of the typical nationalist historian. Instead of constituting the educated intel-ligentsia as the "thinkers" and the advocates of change, Pandey depicts the peasants and the social transformation implicit in their struggle as far more revolutionary in character:

> the Congress' insistence in 1921–22 on a united front of landlords as well as peasants and others, was a statement in favour of the *status quo* and against any radical change in the social set-up when the British finally handed over the reins of power. The advice to peasants to give up organizing 'meetings' and 'disturbances' and to leave politics to the professionals, was a statement against mass participatory democracy and in favour of the idea of "trusteeship"—the landlords and princes acting as trustees in the economic sphere, Gandhi and company in the political. (I: 187–88)

Gandhi's Non-cooperation Movement, which is often interpreted as a suc-cess in spite of its failure to reach its stated goal of *swaraj* (see M. Mukh-erjee in Bipan Chandra 195), is clearly enormously insufficient in Pandey's portrait of it from the peasants' perspective; and not merely insufficient, it also represents a betrayal of the peasant by the 1920–22 Congress leaders.

The work of the subaltern historians does offer a real alternative to traditional historiography about India in its attempts to give voice to those actors in history who have previously been silenced. Where it falls short, however, is in its tendency to draw the peasant as exclusively male. With the exception of one essay by Julie Stephens in Volume VI, which examines the western feminist construction of the Indian woman, and Gayatri Chakravorty Spivak's articles in Volumes IV and V, Subaltern Studies is almost entirely a historiography of men. Women appear in these texts as incidental to the events of history, as objects of exchange between men, as a feature of the domestic rural world of the peasant, along with his cattle, but rarely do they emerge as contributors to the struggle. There is, of course, much evidence to suggest that Indian women played a large and revolutionary role in nationalist events (see Sarkar and Ray); that they are given such a small part in the Subaltern Studies histories attests to a "bankruptcy" on the part of the subalternists akin to that which Guha discerns in nationalist and neo-nationalist historiography (3). Furthermore, woman as a symbolic entity in these texts is an extremely disquieting figure. Spivak notes that "the continuity of community or history, for subaltern and historian alike, is produced on . . . the dissimulation of her discontinuity, on the repeated emptying of her meaning as instrument" (IV: 362). The subaltern woman is effaced in these texts, and, as Spivak suggests, her effacement on both the historical and symbolic levels is intimately tied up with the discursive traditions that have mediated the work of the subaltern historians and in which they are participating. In other words, they are the male heirs to a fiercely androcentric tradition in Indian and British historiography.

The importance of the Subaltern Studies group's efforts at recovering a subaltern history and constructing a subaltern narrative that is capable of disrupting nationalist historiography cannot be underestimated. While not wishing to undermine the fundamental significance of the group's project, I would like nevertheless to question the notion of the subaltern as he is constructed by the subalternists. Guha, Pandey, and the other historians have shown him to be a shaper of history. Still, he is not the writer of his own subjectivity but the object of somebody else's scrutiny. Furthermore, he has no access to the truth that he is made to represent. His position as the object of the historians' gaze is as problematic a construction in the Subaltern Studies texts as it is in imperialist and nationalist histories. In the history of colonial India, the peasant is always a site of power, a battleground on which historians of various schools wage a war of possession. In the late nineteenth century, the Viceroy Lord Dufferin dismissed nationalism because it did not speak to or for the peasant; he assumed that imperialism did. With the arrival of Gandhi in India, the nationalists laid their claim to the peasant's ear and the imperialist writers backed off this terrain. In the 1980s and 90s, the subaltern historians assert their right to the same territory, with the argument that imperialists and nationalists have been appropriating the subaltern all along. The theories change, but the ground remains the same. This connection to imperialist and nationalist historiography is something I would like to see the subalternists explore.

And surely all of us who have some interest in the history of subaltern peoples must start asking ourselves what else besides an abstract belief in justice is behind the desire to investigate or simply pay attention to subaltern practices. The reading that follows of Forster's *A Passage to India* is very much indebted to some of the insights provided by the subaltern historians, but it is also a product of my own tendency to distrust middle-class perspectives of reality, a tendency that arises out of my experience as an academic whose background has not been identifiably middle class. I choose to look for the subaltern in two middle class, male-authored texts—Forster's and, in a later chapter, Anand's *Untouchable*—because the places where the oppressed are created are vortexes of unintentional meaning, which have the potential to disturb the assumptions on which these works rest. The assumptions of novels by middle-class authors and the assumptions of the middle-class academy are often congruent, and, in spite of the decades of Marxism's presence in universities and in scholarship, these assumptions have not been adequately examined or undermined. For me, then, analyzing the construction of the subaltern in literature and history is one of the ways I use to point out the inability of middle-class texts to speak for us all.

Forster's *A Passage to India,* a powerfully influential middle-class text, has been accorded special supremacy by literary critics all over the world. Viewed as the pinnacle of Anglo-Indian literature, this English novel is frequently presumed to be the one that best delivers the truth about the

British Raj and about India. As a result of this mostly uncontested canonization, scholars have for years treated this novel as a social and historical document. It is often discussed as if it were an exact depiction of the mood which characterized the Anglo-Indian/Indian relationship in the early 1920s, and Forster is consequently heralded as one of Britain's foremost interpreters of modern India. John Beer in his forward to G. K. Das's *E. M. Forster's India* declares that Forster's attitudes, conveyed through both his novel and his journalism about India, "helped to prepare the ground for the final cession of English power as it took place, by revealing to many politicians in England the shaky kinds of foundation on which that power had been built, and the need for a graceful retreat" (xiv). Not only literary critics but historians as well have been known to credit Forster with achieving such an accurate representation of India that his novel can be taken as coincident with history. His influence on the British interpretation of politics in India is enacted in the already-mentioned 1942 history of Indian nationalism, *India Today,* by Duffett, Hicks, and Parkin. At one point in their text these three authors use Forster's novel as evidence for their statement that "most British officials were unable to have any feelings of real friendship for their educated Indian associates" (71).

What this respect for Forster as a historical writer has encouraged is a penchant among critics for reading *A Passage to India* as a novel which is so closely allied with the history of twentieth-century Indian nationalism that the major events, figures, and opinions of the day can be discerned in its pages. Hence in spite of the fact that Gandhi is never mentioned, Frances B. Singh is able to see in the novel some of the fundamental principles of Gandhian ideology. Forster and Gandhi are depicted as thinking the same thoughts and believing in the same politics, the only difference being that Forster chose fiction as his medium. I would be the last one to suggest that fiction is not amenable to a historical reading. Indeed I have no doubt that there are traces of early Gandhism in Forster's book. My point in picking out Singh's article from the mountain of scholarship available on Forster is not to disparage it but simply to use it as an example. It is one of the latest in a long line of literary analyses that taps into a particular tradition that has been built up around Forster's novel in the years since it was published in 1924.

This tradition constructs Forster in opposition to Kipling, as an Anglo-

Indian writer who, for the first time, offered the British public a critique of imperialism and a passage out of its totalizing narratives. Benita Parry articulates its basic tenet: "Against the grain of a discourse where 'knowing' India was a way of ruling India, Forster's India is a geographical space abundantly occupied by histories and cultures distinct from the Western narrative of the world and the meanings this endorses" (Parry, "The Politics of . . ." 29). Forster is seen as doing much the same thing as the Indian nationalists; that is, he is reputed to have created an alternative history of India, which posits the autonomy of the Indian, thereby putting the West in its place. Although many, but not all, of these critics recognize the limitations of his vision—namely, his inability to break entirely with an imperialist perspective—they are unwilling, nevertheless, to dislodge Forster any further from this vaguely nationalist, anti-imperialist space.

Earlier in this chapter, I discussed the way in which nationalism's complicity with imperialism has become the subject of much recent historiographical scholarship. This desire to re-evaluate conventional assumptions about the era of imperialism in India has swept certain literary circles as well. In consequence Forster's investment in the structures and symbolic order of the political system he devalued has been re-examined in light of the new postcolonial literary criticism. Sara Suleri's "The Geography of *A Passage to India*" provides a fascinating and original interpretation of the novel and, additionally, an implicit critique of a critical tradition that has refused to consider this angle of the Forsterian myth.

Suleri delineates *A Passage to India* as the initiator of a western narrative mode that converts the historic site of India into a "vast introspective question mark." Forster, she argues, has produced the quintessential modernist novel, a novel that turns endlessly in on itself, transforming its subject, India, into an extension of the "writing mind of the West" (169). Contrary to the scholarly tradition that regards Kipling as the father of all subsequent representations of India—and Forster therefore as a disrupter of the imperialist discourse in Anglo-Indian literature—Suleri sees Forster as the founder of the western and colonialist image of India:

a text like *Kim* in fact reinforces the reality of India by seeing it so clearly as the other that the imperial West must know and dominate. *A Passage to India*, on the other hand, represents India as a metaphor of something other than itself, as a certain metaphysical posture that translates into an image of profound unreality. It thus becomes that archetypal novel of modernity that co-opts the space reserved for India in the Western literary imagination, so that all subsequent novels on the Indian theme appear secretly obsessed with the desire to describe exactly what transpired in the Marabar Caves. (170)

The Orientalist code, within which Kipling worked, divided the world into two sections, the East and the West, and the aim of the West was to apprehend the essence of the East in order to understand and hence to rule it. According to Suleri, however, Forster's approach to India "is perhaps even more fraught with violence" than the Orientalist one because *A Passage to India* refuses to 'other' the East. It implies instead that India, far from being an other, is merely a passageway back to the West. The picture of India as illusory, amorphous, and unattainable, the image for which the novel is famous, leads ultimately to the western mind itself, and as a result India becomes an expression of the ineffability of that mind. Later narratives about India, she observes, pick up on Forster's model, and India comes to be represented within the English literary tradition as a hollow or a cave, with which western protagonists must grapple but which inevitably defeats them. Thus, the modern response of the West to the difference of India is to excavate any autonomous meaning it might have.

Suleri goes on to suggest that the failure of the liberal humanist imagination to apprehend the otherness of India is actually translated in the novel into a failure on the part of India itself. The novel, she says, charts "the desire to convert unreadability into unreality" (171). Again and again the English protagonists in *A Passage to India* are confronted with the unreadability of India, but rather than acknowledging this as a western or perhaps specifically English deficiency, the novel grafts it on to the country and its people, especially on to the Hindus, as the following much-quoted passage demonstrates:

> The fissures in the Indian soil are infinite: Hinduism, so solid from a distance, is riven into sects and clans, which radiate and join, and change their names according to the aspect from which they are approached. Study it for years with the best teachers, and when you raise your head nothing they have told you quite fits. (289)

The English inability to interpret the otherness of India is not differentiated from the novel's depiction of India's essential unreality. The "bou-oum" in the cave (159) consequently becomes an Indian rather than an English problem. The final step in the novel toward annihilating the unreal otherness of India involves the transformation of that unreality into a positive quality and the identification of it with the ineffability of the western literary imagination, the narrator's mind and even, I suspect, Forster's. What readers are left with in the end is the narrator's frustration with a land and a people that he cannot interpret, and the novel finally becomes the record of his attempt, as a result of that frustration, to colonize the intellectual territory of India. Considering that the novel holds the potential for this type of reading, Suleri admits that it is "a matter of some perplexity" (174) to her that so many of Forster's readers persist in seeing *A Passage to India* as a text sympathetic to the nationalist movement and cynical about British imperialism. I would add that the desire of some western academics to characterize Forster as an advocate of Indian nationalism, sometimes to the exclusion of any other possible meaning for his novel, is perhaps indicative of a certain willful unawareness of the ideological effects and manipulations of imperialism. Such determination runs the risk of reinscribing imperialist narratives, complete with the requisite blind spots.

This co-optation of the geography of India, which Suleri has uncovered in her article, corresponds on some levels to the liberal myth of imperialism. Once the British government had pledged itself, in August 1917, to the promotion of self-governing institutions in India, a space was left wide open for the appropriation of nationalism by imperialist mythmakers. Of course, it was *liberal* historians who moved into that space and began to interpret that pledge as simply an overt acknowledgment of what had been all along imperialism's covert movement toward Indian independence, a movement which Schuster and Wint insist dates back to government policies of the nineteenth century. Both Forster's internalization of India's mystery and the rewriting of history by Schuster and Wint in order to locate traces of a British origin for Indian nationalist aspirations are acts of colonialism, attempts on the part of the dominant discourse to colonize an area belonging to the subordinate culture. That all three of these authors are committed to some form of liberalism—Forster to liberal humanism and Schuster and Wint to its political expression—attests to the colonizing impulse of the liberal ethic when it is transplanted into imperialist ground.

English liberalism has a long history in India. Some historians date its emergence as far back as the first years of Britain's encounter with India. Others have found its source in the social reform movement of the early nineteenth century. The difficulty inherent in identifying the moment of liberalism's birth in India lies in distinguishing it from a conservative or Orientalist position, which most historians consider the original politics of British imperialism. These two streams appear to approach the task of governing Indians from different perspectives, with different philosophical goals and tools. However, as Lata Mani has demonstrated in her article on the discourse of *sati* (the voluntary or involuntary immolation of a Hindu wife on her husband's funeral pyre), in actual practice liberalism and conservatism often displayed the same purposes and achieved the same ends. In keeping with the theoretical bent of Mani's article, it could also be argued that their places of intersection are more important in many respects than their dissimilarities. Suffice it to say that when historians do try to differentiate the liberal from the conservative or Orientalist variety, what they tend to focus on is its insistence on introducing change into Indian cultural, educational, and legal institutions. Liberalism is therefore often associated with an evangelical posture toward India; implicit in this attitude is, of course, a certain contempt for Indian society and, conversely, an abiding trust in the superiority of western and especially British civilization.

Exactly how an ethic that promoted such principles as freedom from the constraints of government, equality between men and women, and tolerance of difference was made conducive to an imperialist agenda is, I think, one of the most interesting twists of the nineteenth century. The writings of John Stuart Mill chart the process of this metamorphosis. Undoubtedly the most influential liberal of his time, Mill was also—at least in terms of India—one of the most powerful. His position in the East India Company, where he worked for thirty-five years of his life, first as a clerk and later as Examiner, allowed him to formulate policies which, once ratified by the English parliament, were implemented by ICS officers in India. We have in Mill, then, an example of a liberal imperialist whose political ideas and beliefs had a direct effect on the governance of the Indian subcontinent.

In his "Considerations on Representative Government," Mill states that the highest form of government is a democracy in which "the whole people participate" (412). However, not all people are "fit" for such government. The English and the Americans—who provide, he declares, "the foundation of the best hopes for the general improvement of mankind" (409)—and even the Australians and Canadians possess the moral qualities necessary for the construction and maintenance of a representative government. Indians unquestionably do not. Mill gives various reasons to explain his evaluation of the Indian people as morally unfit for democracy, none of which goes much beyond an unsubstantiated condemnation, but he is not fundamentally concerned with pointing out their flaws. What he is intent on establishing is that a hierarchy of societies exists in the world, a hierarchy presided over by England and the United States. Located somewhere near the bottom of this hierarchy are "backward," "savage," or "barbaric" communities, and, for Mill, India falls into this latter category. As his use of the above words suggests, his political theory is based on a belief in social progress and evolution. A certain society requires a certain form of government depending on the evolutionary stage it has reached.

The best government for a country such as India, Mill insists, is a benevolent despotism. However, if the despot is of the same race or community as the people over whom he rules, he is not exempt from their faults and hence cannot properly lead them to self-government, the ideal toward which all despots should strive. Foreigners "belonging to a superior people or a more advanced state of society" do not possess the defects of the subject population (418). Consequently, they are supremely suited to introduce the idea of representative government to the people of the morally inferior society. Mill is therefore convinced that the subjugation of India as a result of Britain's imperialist project was a fortunate occurrence for the Indian people: "subjection to a foreign government of this description, notwithstanding its inevitable evils, is often of the greatest advantage to a people, carrying them rapidly through several stages of progress, and clearing away obstacles to improvement which might have lasted indefinitely if the subject population had been left unassisted to its native tendencies and chances" (419). Mill is concerned with ruling the Indian people not for the sake of the rule itself but for the purposes of promoting their 'progress,' a key word in the liberal vocabulary. In their enthusiasm to reform the Indians, English liberals, like Mill himself, often put aside their famous tolerance and their beliefs in liberty, individuality, and equality, which had characterized their politics in most other spheres. Only by constructing India's civilization as inferior and its people as "backward" could such a displacement be justified.

Since the fundamental goal of liberalism in India has been the reformation of Indian society, a reformation conducted along western lines, one of its attendant effects is the smoothing out of the differences between the two cultures. Liberalism seeks to transplant British methods of education and politics and, additionally, British values onto Indian soil. In order to do this, difference must be suppressed and homogeneity encouraged. A liberal ideology emphasizes those things that Indians already have in common with the British; these are often communicated in rhetoric that speaks of Indians' access to universal truths and inalienable rights. This process of homogenization deals with the distinctness of India either by dismissing it as negligible or even immoral, ignoring it entirely, or by subsuming it into a British hegemony. An example of this might be the numerous texts that have been and still are being written, which compare Christianity with such Indian religions as Islam, Hinduism, and Buddhism. Invariably these texts flatten out the differences of Indian religiosity. Krishna, Buddha, and Mohammed are understood in terms of Christ, and those qualities and teachings that are incompatible with a Christian reading are marginalized, omitted from the discussion altogether, or treated with patronizing contempt.

Examining Schuster's and Wint's book in light of this discursive tradition of liberal imperialism, it becomes more and more apparent that their appropriation of an Indian difference is a product of liberal imperialism. When confronted with nationalism, a difference which was not part of the imperialist agenda and which was too large to ignore or marginalize, Schuster and Wint co-opt the Indian movement to British imperialism. Indian nationalism is, as a result, constructed as the inevitable outcome of the social and constitutional reformation initiated by British liberalism in India. Those aspects of nationalism that cannot be fully incorporated into this picture are underplayed, undermined, or simply left out. Hence, Gandhi's critique of modern civilization, with its emphasis on the materialism and the consumerism of the West, and his commitment to a Hindu style of ascetic life are treated with condescension in *India and Democ-*

racy. Repeatedly, Schuster and Wint dismiss Gandhi as politically and religiously archaic—"his is a personality which might conceivably have existed in the European middle ages" (113)—and his disapproval of western consumer values is attributed to the fact that he lives in an undeveloped culture that has not yet come to terms with industrialization: "Thus far he manifests in India a line of thought which occurred in England when our own society was at a somewhat similar stage of economic evolution as that which India has reached to-day . . ." (107). By comparing Indian society and an Indian political figure with earlier periods and personalities in British history, Schuster and Wint minimize the differences between the two cultures and, consequently, are able to colonize Indian nationalism and nationalists in the name of Britain. Such colonization, moreover, is clearly an attempt to eradicate the threat that nationalism presents to the liberal program of imperialism.

In Forster's novel, something far more complex is occurring, although it too can be understood as resulting from the liberal discursive tradition. Like Schuster's and Wint's history, *A Passage to India* appropriates the difference of India. It does so because it constructs Indian, but specifically Hindu, spirituality as a danger to the western mind. The process begins with the novel's recognition of the unreadability of Hindu India—hence the repeated assertion by various characters that India is a "muddle." Then that unreadability is converted into an unreality, which is nihilistic and therefore destructive of a western sensibility. Mrs. Moore's fate is a case in point. Her confrontation with the "bou-oum" in the caves robs her of her tolerance and generosity and seems ultimately to be the cause of her death at sea. That it is only Hindu India that represents a menace is evident in the novel's treatment of Islam. Since Islam is not depicted as a metaphysically dangerous religion in the novel, it is discounted in the end. Fielding concludes the text's examination of Islam with a statement that undermines it completely: " 'There is no God but God' doesn't carry us far through the complexities of matter and spirit; it is only a game with words, really a religious pun, not a religious truth" (272). Hinduism, on the other hand, is a persistent threat and cannot be dismissed with Islam. On the contrary, it comes to be associated with an emptiness which the western traveler must negotiate in his or her own spiritual life, and in the process it ceases to be the 'other.'

This appropriation of Hinduism in the interests of the western literary imagination is clearly well within the liberal tradition of imperialism. We might even read into the novel a certain reformist tone, especially in such passages as the one that describes Fielding's voyage home: "The buildings of Venice, like the mountains of Crete and the fields of Egypt, stood in the right place, whereas in poor India everything was placed wrong" (277–78). That India is somehow "wrong" and Europe is "right" is one of the basic assumptions of the liberal imperialist ethic in India. This assumption prompted liberal policies such as the abolition of *sati* in 1829, the gradual introduction of English education into Indian schools throughout the nineteenth century, and the Hindu Widows' Remarriage Act of 1856, all of which sought to correct a perceived flaw in Indian society. Moreover, when the narrator declares, "The Mediterranean is the human norm" (278), he is adopting yet another liberal stance, insofar as he is speaking in universals and, more important, measuring those universals from the perspective of Europe.

But *A Passage to India* goes even further than the typical liberal appropriation of difference, which we have already encountered, for example, in the history of British imperialism-cum-Indian nationalism as told by Schuster and Wint. The novel problematizes gender and sexual orientation, thereby making classically "liberal"—albeit misogynistic and homophobic—interpretations of the narrative exponentially more complicated. The representation of womanhood and the concomitant homoeroticism in *A Passage to India* are intricately bound up with Forster's version of liberal imperialism. Like India itself, womanhood does not constitute a difference in the novel because the space it usually occupies in the masculine literary imagination is co-opted in the interests of masculine relationships, specifically the relationship between the male characters and the relationship between the narrator and the male personification of India, exemplified in the figure of the punkah wallah. That the novel is engaged in this kind of homoeroticism, which effectively erodes any influence the feminine principle or the female characters might have, is the argument I will take up for the remainder of this chapter. Nevertheless, what I hope finally to demonstrate is that the punkah wallah and Forster's other beautiful images of Indian subaltern maleness indicate a way out of the liberal imperialist reformative discourse that dominates the text.

Let me say from the outset that my reading of *A Passage to India* is a troubled one. Like most other fans of this book, I am convinced that *A Passage to India* is extraordinarily complex. It offers us contradictory images and feelings about India, and it does so by means of a writing style that is supremely fluid and graceful. It seems a shame to interrupt our reading in order to question some of the novel's presuppositions. But I nevertheless think we should stop and question them. As I've stated above, *A Passage to India* has been privileged over virtually all other British fiction about India. It has been repeatedly proclaimed a masterpiece, a declaration which invariably discourages the kind of critique I am offering here. For the reputation of this novel gets in the way of seeing the process of its construction—the historical, social and political allegiances which contributed to its making. Western readers have placed a great deal of trust in Forster's vision of India because it is thrilling and provocative and because it tries to be a generous vision. It does not always succeed. My reading focuses on those moments in the text when Forster's generosity fails him, when *A Passage to India* is unable to encounter the other without somehow undermining it or him or her. These failures are important; they point us toward the novel's sad suspicion that the liberal ethic did not live up to its ideals in India.

A Passage to India is hard on women. It portrays them unfavorably—as shrewish harpies, silly gigglers, confused spinsters, and cranky old ladies; it accords them only one outlet, marriage, for meaning and value within a patriarchal system, and then it persistently undermines that outlet; and it valorizes the cross-national alliance of men at their expense. When Elaine Showalter writes, "I think we must accept the fact that Forster often saw women as part of the enemy camp" (7), I can hardly help but agree with her. Yet the novel is not so much a record of Forster's animosity toward women in general, as Showalter's use of the word "enemy" suggests; it is a record of his indifference. Women don't really count in the patriarchal economy of *A Passage to India*. Certainly Forster lavishes much careful expository detail on Adela's sexual angst and Mrs. Moore's dark night of the soul, but these female characters and issues by and large lie outside the orbit of the novel's course.

A Passage to India is a novel principally about men, about their attempts to reach across continents, across cultures, across race in order to understand and even to love one another. It announces this intention in its title, which is a reference to Walt Whitman's poem of the same name. Whitman's "Passage to India" celebrates, with feverish intensity, the history of man's explorations to the New and the Old World. Christopher Columbus is its muse ("Ah Genoese thy dream! thy dream" [l. 65]), and Vasco da Gama, Alexander the Great, Tamerlane, the Mughal Emperor Aurungzebe, Marco Polo, and Batouta the Moor are its heroes. Notably, each of these characters from history was a conqueror or a merchant, and all of them were engaged in the task of colonization, either for the purposes of political power or for trade. As much as anything Kipling ever wrote, Whitman's "Passage to India" is a poem that glorifies imperialists and their mission to the world:

> Passage to India!
> Lo, soul, seest thou not God's purpose from the first?
> The earth to be spann'd, connected by network,
> The races, neighbors, to marry and be given in marriage,
> The oceans to be cross'd, the distant brought near,
> The lands to be welded together.
> A worship new I sing,
> You captains, voyagers, explorers, yours,
> You engineers, you architects, machinists, yours,
> You, not for trade or transportation only,
> But in God's name, and for thy sake O soul. (ll. 30–40)

Whitman's vision addresses itself almost exclusively to men. It praises male professions (or what would have been male professions in 1871 when "Passage to India" was first published) and depicts the journey implicit in its title as a predominantly male endeavour. Women are hardly present in the poem. The "marriage of continents" (l. 118), which he holds up as an ideal, must therefore be read as a union between men and between masculine knowledges, powers, and discoveries.

Forster's novel is much less blind to the feminine presence, but it nevertheless shares Whitman's vision. The narrator makes this clear when he describes Fielding's approach to life: "The world, he believed, is a globe of men who are trying to reach one another and can best do so by the help of goodwill plus culture and intelligence . . ." (80). One can make too much of the connections between Fielding and Forster or between Fielding and the general attitude of the novel itself. However, events in the novel repeatedly lend support to Fielding's belief. At one point in the story, Aziz and an unidentified Englishman develop a brief affection for one another while playing a game of polo. When it is over, the narrator tells us, "Nationality was returning, but before it could exert its poison, they parted, saluting each other. 'If only they were all like that,' each thought" (76). The famous moment at the end of the novel when Aziz and Fielding attempt to embrace and are prevented from doing so by the hundred voices of the Indian landscape, which announce "No, not yet . . . No, not there" (316), relies for its emotional efficacy on the notion that a loving relationship between the two men *should* be possible and *would* be, if the time were right. Both of these events, and numerous others in the novel, assume that it is the friendship of men that will bring about the union of the nations.

Women are not included in this union because they tend to function in the novel not as active participants in the creation of these friendships but instead as obstacles to them or, conversely, as conduits, which enable the friendship to come about or continue. Wives in particular serve this latter purpose. Aziz's relationship with Fielding achieves a depth and permanence by means of his dead wife. A photograph of her, which he allows Fielding to see, becomes a token of Aziz's trust and affection for the Englishman. When Fielding responds with gratitude to the gesture, Aziz tells him that had his wife been alive, he would have been permitted to see her in spite of the purdah (seclusion of women). He adds, "All men are my brothers, and as soon as one behaves as such he may see my wife," to which Fielding answers, "And when the whole world behaves as such, there will be no more purdah" (128). Beyond being a vague memory which Aziz calls up when he is feeling poetic, his wife has no autonomous existence in the story. Her primary function is to serve as a vehicle for the affection of her husband and his friend. Furthermore, the act of viewing her photograph is linked to the utopian possibilities that the friendship of Aziz and Fielding represents. When Whitman's and Forster's vision is realized and all men recognize their brotherhood, purdah will end because men will no longer feel the need for it. There is, of course, an erasure here of the wife's will. Were she alive, she would apparently have no say either about meeting Fielding or about the practice of purdah in her household.

Despite the importance of the purdah custom to the workings of this paradigm in which females are tokens, such nullification of women is not confined solely to Indian culture. Englishmen also have wives to exhibit. Fielding returns Aziz's compliment toward the end of the novel when he uses his wife, or, more accurately, information about his wife as a means of demonstrating his feelings for the other man. One of the narrator's comments establishes that this is indeed his motive in revealing Stella's spiritual restlessness to Aziz: "And, anxious to make what he could of this last afternoon, he forced himself to speak intimately about his wife, the person most dear to him" (313). In *A Passage to India*, wives, or at least "good" wives, seem to exist to further the friendship between husbands and the ties between nations. Speaking about the discourse of *sati*, to which Indian men of the upper caste and English ICS officers contributed but from which the testament of the widows who practiced it is entirely left out, Spivak observes that, "Between patriarchal subject-formation and imperialist object-constitution, it is the dubious place of the free will of the sexed subject as female that is successfully effaced" ("Rani" 144). Spivak's widows and Forster's wives are caught between these two mutually supportive systems and effectively silenced.

The female characters in the novel who refuse to be silenced earn the resentment of their men and the narrator's disapproval as well. These are the Anglo-Indian wives, and they are the characters we are least encouraged to like. Forster's condemnation of Anglo-Indian women has a discursive history that goes back before *A Passage to India* was published. In a 1922 article for the journal *The Nation & the Athenaeum,* Forster lambastes all Anglo-Indians for the social ineptitude toward Indians for which they have become renowned. But he saves his most scathing reproof for Anglo-Indian women:

> If the Englishman might have helped the Indian socially, how much more might the Englishwoman have helped! But she has done nothing, or worse than nothing. She deserves, as a class, all that the satirists have said about her, for she has instigated the follies of her male when she might have calmed them and set him on the sane course. (615)

In Forster's eyes the Anglo-Indian woman is more responsible than her male counterpart for the appalling racial situation in India, and, therefore, all the social blunders of the British Empire are laid at her feet. The attitude toward these women in the novel is much more calm, much less vociferous, but nevertheless hostile. Throughout the novel, they are blamed for standing in the way of their men. We are told on one occasion that the men would have made a greater effort to socialize with the Indian guests at the Turton's 'bridge' party but were "prevented from doing so by their womenfolk whom they had to attend, provide with tea, advise about dogs, etc." (66) Moreover, at a particularly crucial time for the Anglo-Indian society in the novel—when the women feel threatened because of Adela's experience (or imagined experience) of attempted rape and the men have assumed roles as their protectors—the novel relays the Collector's inmost thought, and it is, not surprisingly, a misogynistic one: "After all, it's our women who make everything more difficult out here" (217). Anglo-Indian women are the novel's scapegoats; they bear the brunt of Forster's anger about English conduct in India. The Anglo-Indian men, on the other hand, are criticized but are usually accorded some sympathy because of the difficult jobs they are required to do.

The text's resentment toward these women may also be a part of their refusal to accommodate its utopian ideal. For whatever reasons, they will not do what is expected of them, that is, be a passageway for the easy flow of friendship between English and Indian men. On the contrary, the women force their men to choose sides. Fielding recognizes this early in the novel: "He had discovered that it is possible to keep in with Indians and Englishmen, but that he who would also keep in with Englishwomen must drop the Indians. The two wouldn't combine" (80). Fielding initially chooses Aziz and his Indian friends, but when he marries an Englishwoman, his continued relationship with Indian men becomes an impossibility. His marriage to Stella constitutes both a political and emotional betrayal of Aziz—political because Fielding has thrown his lot in with a community that Aziz and *his* community have sworn to defeat and emotional because the novel is grounded in the belief that love between men of different races is the solution to the problem of international conflict.

But where do Adela and Mrs. Moore fit into the picture, since neither of them are Anglo-Indian wives? Initially, Mrs. Moore appears to be someone who will disrupt the pattern, for she is a woman who maintains a friendship with an Indian man independently of the Englishmen around her. What occurs between her and Aziz—the tender friendship which finds expression first at the mosque, later at Fielding's tea party, and finally at the caves—does not require the presence of an Englishman to give it meaning. But Mrs. Moore's descent into meaninglessness, which turns her into a cranky and petulant old woman, removes her from the stage of interracial friendship altogether. She withdraws so far into herself that she is unable to see any longer the relevance of such friendship, and at Aziz's lowest moment, she leaves both him and India to their respective fates. Her actions just prior to her death at sea cast a shadow back over her earlier pleasant encounters with Aziz. Readers may conclude that she is not capable of participating in the ideal union of nations.

As for Adela, she exists on the margins of this ideal throughout the story, because she seems to lack the ability to enter into friendships with Indians. From the beginning, it is clear that she does not possess the understanding necessary to bridge the gap between these cultures. For instance, in spite of her good will, she repeatedly makes errors in judgment and in feeling during her conversations with Aziz and with other Indians, and the result is she never wins anybody's affection. Her moment of truth in the courtroom, when she courageously retracts her accusation, goes unappreciated by the Indian characters in the novel. The action elicits their hostility, in fact, because of the unemotional way in which it is accomplished:

> For her behaviour rested on cold justice and honesty; she had felt, while she recanted, no passion of love for those whom he had wronged. . . . And the girl's sacrifice—so creditable according to Western notions— was *rightly* rejected, because, though it came from her heart, it did not include her heart. A few garlands from students was all that India ever gave her in return. (245, emphasis mine)

This is the narrator speaking, and it is interesting that he is in complete accord with the Indians' reaction. Indeed the novel seems generally bent on demonstrating the shallowness of Adela's behavior in India. She is well meaning but, unlike Fielding, quite incapable of establishing anything beyond superficial connections with Indians. The fault lies in Adela's deficient vision of India, and this is most apparent in the beginning when she announces her desire to see the 'real India.' Such a goal is shown finally to be pathetically misguided, since one of the main points of the novel is that the 'real India' is unapprehendable; it might not even exist. And Adela never acquires and ultimately does not seem to want the knowledge that Fielding possesses from the start—that Indians themselves are all that anyone can know of 'the real India.' Thus the novel suggests that if Indians gave Adela almost nothing in return for her courage in the courtroom, because of her mistaken notions about India, it was all that she deserved.

Despite her inadequacy, Adela does function as the person through whom Fielding and Aziz meet and whose misfortune causes their friendship to deepen. It is as a result of Adela's desire to see the 'real India' that the two men embark on their cross-cultural relationship. When Fielding organizes a tea party for Mrs. Moore and Adela, Aziz is invited because of Adela's interest in him. He arrives early, before Mrs. Moore and Adela, and immediately strikes up a friendship with Fielding. Once Aziz learns that the two women will be coming to tea as well, he is disappointed, because, as the narrator explains, "he preferred to be alone with his new friend" (84). At the outset of this party, the women are made to seem superfluous.

Adela's frightening experience in the cave serves to cement even further the friendship between the two men, since it is because of Aziz's arrest that Fielding is forced to take a public stand in favor of his friend and against Adela and the Anglo-Indian community. But at the same time that the novel documents their increasing intimacy, it simultaneously invalidates Adela's experience of sexual assault.

Aziz and Fielding grow closer as Adela's memory of the incident seems to blur. Although she is at first certain of what has happened to her in the cave, eventually she is forced to entertain the possibility—an idea implanted by Fielding—that she had hallucinated the entire experience; "the sort of thing," she herself draws the comparison, "that makes some women think they've had an offer of marriage when none was made" (240). Fielding also suggests that it was the Indian guide who entered the cave after Adela and attempted to assault her, but Aziz's friend Hamidullah angrily dismisses that possibility: "I gather you have not done with us yet, and it is now the turn of the poor old guide who conducted you round the caves" (243). Finally, in her last conversation with Fielding, when he presses her to examine the moment in the cave once more, she closes the subject for good by complacently adopting his suggestion about the guide. We are told that "the question had lost interest for her suddenly" (242). Every opinion in the text, even Adela's, conspires to relegate her experience of sexual assault to the edges of the story, and the reason for this resides in something I have mentioned earlier, namely, Forster's indifference to women. I should make it clear that this indifference does not prevent Forster from constructing women as characters with interesting stories and experiences of their own. Mrs. Moore and Adela are both central figures in the novel, and their separate approaches to India in particular and life in general are delineated with careful detail and with sympathy. What Forster is indifferent to are those aspects of these women's characters that exist apart from and even in spite of their roles in patriarchal and imperialist structures.

Although she is not a wife, Adela functions like so many female characters in *A Passage to India,* as a conduit or even a cipher. She provides the opportunity for Fielding and Aziz to meet and later the means through which their friendship is tested and strengthened. It is largely at her expense that they are friends at all, since in order for them to retain their friendship, her account of the event in the cave must be retracted. Once Adela withdraws her accusation of Aziz and his innocence is no longer in question, the incident in the cave moves into a new area of significance. As a personal experience, it recedes into unimportance. In the end, it does not matter to any of the characters what actually happened in the cave. Adela's experience of sexual assault is elided to make way for another reading, a reading that transforms the personal into the transpersonal and the universal. The incident becomes a moment of supreme mystery and represents, therefore, one more testament to the unreality, the "muddle" that the novel posits as India.

Forster's treatment of womanhood is even more fascinating and problematic when analyzed alongside the feminized image of India that the text appears on the surface to affirm. As in much British fiction about India, in Forster's novel the country is depicted as a seductive and alluring female. Various moments throughout the text contribute to this conception of India, particularly the Caves section. This passage follows Adela's contemplation of her future life in British India, but it is evident from both the content, which proclaims its speaker as a person with more than a superficial knowledge of India, and the masculine gaze, which fixes India as a female object, that it is not Adela who is speaking. It is a male voice:

How can the mind take hold of such a country? Generations of invaders have tried, but they remain in exile. The important towns they build are only retreats, their quarrels the malaise of men who cannot find their way home. India knows of their trouble. She knows of the whole world's trouble, to its uttermost depth. She calls "Come" through her hundred mouths, through objects ridiculous and august. But come to what? She has never defined. She is not a promise, only an appeal. (148–49)

Such a construction seems to have been irresistible during the colonial period. Almost every novel and a number of poems written about India by Englishmen in the nineteenth and first half of the twentieth century contain some vision of India or of the East as a magnetically attractive female figure.[5] Forster taps into an Anglo-Indian tradition when he uses this image in his novel. But a close look at Forster's construction reveals something radically different.

In other British writing, this trope is invariably composed of a catalog or lavish descriptions of much-loved Indian things. Kipling's "Mandalay," about a London man pining for his beloved and for her country, contains the best-known example of this discursive practice:

'If you've 'eard the East a-callin', you won't never 'eed naught else.'
No! you won't 'eed nothin' else
But them spicy garlic smells,
An' the sunshine an' the palm-trees an' the tinkly temple-bells;
On the road to Mandalay . . . (189)

But in Forster's construction, there is no catalog because there is nothing to inscribe; India has no substance. "She is not a promise, only an appeal," the narrator tells us, a siren who calls to men and then disappears when they reach her. We can understand why Kipling's Londoner is drawn back to the East because we are given the details of his longing and a list of her attractions. Forster's India, however, is apparently an empty show. If we read Forster against Kipling, we recognize that Forster is implicitly criticizing those who, hearing India call "through objects ridiculous and august," actually believe that she has something to offer. In *A Passage to India,* the otherness of the East, "the sunshine an' the palm-trees an' the tinkly temple-bells," is subsumed by the modern writing mind of the West, which is determined to find not difference but an extension of its exiled self in India.

The male narrator's refusal or inability to see the difference of India has everything to do with the fact that India is constructed as a woman. *A Passage to India* is a narrative in which it is nearly impossible to discern any perspective but a western perspective or any gender but the masculine gender. Thus the women characters and female figures in the novel tend to function as conduits or as obstacles to the friendship of Fielding and Aziz. In a similar manner, when Forster adopts the traditional Anglo-Indian image of India as a seductive female, her magnetism is shown to be a ruse, since she is all appeal and no substance, and her meaning is made dependent on the masculine mind that apprehends her. Images of India as an other who possesses an autonomous existence outside the western writing mind, who is not an extension of that mind nor is fully apprehendable by it, are available in the text, but they are not female images.

As in many western novels written during the colonial period, for example, Joseph Conrad's *Heart of Darkness,* the image of the colonized country is a construction which participates in the mutually constitutive discourses of both exoticism and eroticism. However, while Conrad's Africa comes to be represented most poignantly by the proud and alluring African woman who emerges out of the jungle to bid farewell to Kurtz, Forster's India is a masculine one. It is not the seductress calling to troubled men with her hundred mouths who claims the narrator's most careful and loving attention. It is, rather, the punkah puller described so painstakingly during the scene in the court room and later the servitor whose floating village of Gokul causes the collision of Aziz's and Fielding's boats at the end of the novel. Of all the emblems of India in the text, these portraits of Indian maleness come closest to embodying Forster's conception of and affection for the country. Unlike the female siren figure of the Caves section, the punkah puller and the servitor are not subject to the narrator's philosophical scepticism, which neutralizes otherness through an elaborate and ultimately dismissive analysis. On the contrary, these images somehow cannot be explained away or made to seem nebulous and ungraspable. In their concrete impenetrability, they lead the text out of the discourse of liberal imperialism because they are never subsumed by the western writing mind, which dominates every other Indian image in *A Passage to India.*

The punkah wallah and the temple servitor are notable in the novel because of the control that they, as Indians, are allowed to exercise over their environments. The servitor holds this authority by virtue of "his hereditary office to close the gates of salvation." It is his job during the celebration of Krishna's birthday to bring the festivities to an end by pushing the clay image of the god's village into the lake. At the moment that the clay dolls of Krishna's family begin to collide and sink, the two boats containing Fielding and his wife, Stella, and Aziz and Stella's brother, Ralph, replicate the action. The four outsiders drift "helplessly" toward the servitor, who "awaited them, his beautiful dark face expressionless, and as the last morsels melted on his tray it struck them" (309). This causes the boats to capsize and Aziz and Fielding to become friends once again. "That was the climax, as far as India admits of one," the narrator announces (310). Although the servitor stands outside the story's climax, in that he is not part of the reconciliation, he is responsible for having brought it about. Moreover, in the midst of much confusion and helplessness, he is represented as a figure of calm supremacy, who—depending on how one interprets the word "awaited" quoted above—even seems to have some foreknowledge of the event. The discourse of power and knowledge is more pronounced in the description of the punkah puller. He is officially the least important of all the characters in the court room, yet in Adela's eyes, "he seemed to control the proceedings" (220). Like the servitor, he is depicted as outside the course of the story but as somehow its director: "Pulling the rope towards him, relaxing it rhythmically, sending swirls of air over others, receiving none himself, he seemed apart from human destinies, a male Fate, a winnower of souls" (221). This metaphor of the punkah wallah as a "male Fate" is confirmed when Adela, whose vision of him incites her to question her own sense of self-importance, eventually recognizes the mistake she has made about Aziz, a moment which then serves as the central turning point in the novel. It takes the presence of the punkah puller at one point and the temple servitor at another to provide the necessary plot complications and finally to bring the story to its conclusion.

These two masculine figures function as the embodiment of their author's feelings about India, about India's attractions and its relationship to the West. That these feelings are sexual is evident in the eroticization of both the punkah puller and the servitor. The narrator delineates the servitor as "naked, broad-shouldered, thin-waisted—the Indian body again triumphant" (309), the "again" referring back to the punkah wallah. The narrator's gaze seems homoerotic. Similarly, in the description of the punkah wallah, although it is Adela's eyes that we are following, it is the male narrator's or perhaps the author's desire that we hear:

> Almost naked, and splendidly formed, he sat on a raised platform near the back, in the middle of the central gangway, and he caught her attention as she came in. . . . He had the strength and beauty that sometimes come to flower in Indians of low birth. When that strange race nears the dust and is condemned as untouchable, then nature remembers the physical perfection that she accomplished elsewhere, and throws out a god. . . . This man would have been notable anywhere; among the thin-hammed, flat-chested mediocrities of Chandrapore he stood out as divine. (220)

There is no indication anywhere in the text that Adela has noticed other Indian men in Chandrapore, described here as "thin-hammed, flat-chested mediocrities." Indeed, Adela's own asexuality and her non-sexual approach to the world, both of which are made much of in the novel, would undoubtedly render her incapable of such an erotic perception.

What is remarkable about these eroticized, male images of India is that they seem to emerge out of an Orientalist perspective.[6] Earlier, I examined this perspective at work in Kipling's short stories and even to some extent in Duncan's novel. Orientalism, both in Edward Said's explication of the term in his book of the same name and in older scholarship about imperialism, such as Francis G. Hutchins's *The Illusion of Permanence,* which defines Orientalism—or what he calls "Orientalization"—as a politics standing in opposition to liberalism, is a way of seeing the East entirely as the other, as that which is not the West. In order to preserve this dichotomy, Orientalist or conservative politicians of the colonial period had also to preserve the separateness of the East. Hence, the westernization program, which liberal policy encouraged, was criticized by the Orientalists for much the same reasons that Kipling belittles Wali Dad in "On the City Wall"—because it robbed the colonized of their own culture and replaced it with a watered-down version of the West. Implicit in Orientalism is a certain respect for the indigenous culture. But, as Hutchins observes, this respect was frequently translated into a refusal on the part of the Orientalists to acknowledge or allow change to occur in the East:

> An India of the imagination was created which contained no elements of either social change or political menace. Orientalization was the result of this effort to conceive of Indian society as devoid of elements hostile to the perpetuation of British rule, for it was on the basis of this presumptive India that Orientalizers sought to build a permanent rule. (157)

Fittingly, the predominant Orientalist image of the East is one that emphasizes its timelessness.

The figures of the punkah wallah and the temple servitor in *A Passage to India* are both products of Orientalism, for both are imaged as somehow existing outside time, in that eternal and changeless India that the West cannot and should not touch. As such, they are exempt from the narrator's sceptical analysis, which usually examines the objects, people, and beliefs of India in order to absorb them into a western narrative. Still, it can be argued that the existence of these pristine Orientalist images in a text that tends to flatten out difference does not take us very far. Although they lead us away from the liberal paradigm that dominates the novel, we are, nevertheless, still within an imperialist discourse. Forster has simply switched camps from the liberal to the conservative.[7] I think, however, that we can interpret these glimpses of Orientalism in light of a much more radical thesis. The inappropriateness of their presence in this novel encourages us to do so. Instead of seeing these images as turning us back to an imperialist arena, we can allow them to point us to a perspective that the text obliquely endorses but is completely unable to articulate given the limits of its vision. This is the perspective of the peasant or the subaltern.

A Passage to India is primarily concerned with valorizing the interracial dialogue between men, and those voices which might get in the way of this ideal are either incorporated, that is made to work on its behalf, or rendered irrelevant. Somehow the punkah wallah and the temple servitor escape this treatment. They are, in fact, accorded the deepest respect and admiration that the novel has to offer. The reason that they cannot be recuperated in the interests of the prevailing liberal reformative ideology is that they stand too far outside the novel's ideal. The interracial dialogue toward which the text strives is a closed conversation. Only the ruling Englishmen and the Indian elite, such as the western-trained doctor, Aziz, and the lawyer, Hamidullah, are capable of participating, since they have acquired the language in which the dialogue is conducted. The punkah wallah and the servitor have no access to this language. That the text nevertheless accords a place to these subaltern figures, a place that it does not subsequently colonize, suggests that another kind of dialogue is possible.

The so-called Indian masses—the workers, the peasants, and the untouchables—have been the subject of much elite writing about India, both historiography and literature. Gandhi, imperialists such as ICS officials and viceroys, Anglo-Indian novelists, and most recently the subaltern historians, all have laid claim to the places that these people who apparently do not write are supposed to occupy. All have endeavored to construct their history and to speak on their behalf. Forster does not do this. His male subalterns are silent but still authoritative. If there is a non-imperialist perspective in *A Passage to India,* it is not the women characters who provide it because their voice is entirely appropriated. Nor is it Aziz with his brand of nationalism, which, so far as it is examined at all, is shown to be simply the inverse of imperialism, the other side of an elite dialogue. If there is a passage to India which might be able to take us beyond the novel's imperialist structures, it is through the powerful silences of the punkah wallah and the temple servitor.

4

The High-Caste Hindu Woman as a Site

of Contest in Imperialist/Nationalist India

At the same time that British writers were creating a textual space which would contain their conceptions of India, Indians were engaged in mapping out a discursive area of their own. There was much overlapping as Indian writers tended either to support or disrupt British discourse. However, it could be argued that some of these writers were able to step outside the cognitive and psychological structures established by British imperialism and offer Indian alternatives to or critiques of western ideas and ideals. Whether or not such a practice was possible, given the all-consuming nature of imperialism, is an issue that has received a great deal of attention in contemporary scholarship on colonialism and postcolonialism. This chapter is concerned with investigating that possibility from the perspective of one of the most contested figures in colonial India, the high-caste Hindu woman.

It was the sometimes adversarial, sometimes friendly intercourse between British imperialists and the Indian elite that rendered Indian women visible in colonial discourse. The status of Indian womanhood was first conceived as an issue relevant to both groups in the 1810s and 20s, when Raja Rammohan Roy and his followers in India and Britain petitioned the government to outlaw the practice of *sati* or widow sacrifice. This legislation inaugurated the age of social reform in India. It was followed by the Widow Remarriage Act of 1856, the 1874 Right to Property Act, giving a widow a life interest in her husband's share of property, and the Age of Consent bill of 1891, which raised the legal age for sexual intercourse from ten to twelve for girls. The participants in the nineteenth-century agitation for women's rights were primarily male, although some British women were also involved, and the objects of their solicitude were invariably Indian women.

All four of the above statutes, which initiated some of the most famous controversies in modern Indian history, were specifically concerned with improving the lot of the high-caste Hindu woman. *Sati* was exclusively a high-caste custom, and neither Muslim, Parsee, Christian, Jewish, nor low-caste Hindu widows were debarred from remarriage. Only the high-caste Hindu woman was faced with the possibility of destitution at her husband's death, since all the other religions of India made some kind of provision for widows and since low-caste women were permitted by convention (and often forced by necessity) to work outside the home. Moreover, it was a distinctly Hindu tradition to arrange the marriage of girls before puberty. In the nineteenth century, then, it was the high-caste Hindu woman, more so than any other female figure, who evoked the pity of social reformers in India and abroad. As a consequence of the elaborate attention focused on her, she eventually came to represent the state of her nation in much Indian nationalist and British imperialist discourse.

The textual argument over which group—British, Indian, missionary, or social reformer—could most accurately depict the circumstances and nature of the high-caste Hindu woman continued for over a hundred years. It was still going on at the time of Nehru and Gandhi and was even then dominated by male voices, though many Indian women had, by this era of Indian nationalism, joined in. But it was perhaps most heated at the end of the nineteenth and beginning of the twentieth centuries, when very few Indian women had any kind of public expression at all. The stakes were high. For behind each separate construction of the high-caste Indian woman lay the vested interests of a political approach to India as a whole.

After 1857, British policy in India had moved toward a position of non-interference. Consequently, Indian and English social reformers often found themselves confronted by government aloofness whenever they agitated for change in legislation concerning women.[1] The resistance of the government to social reform and the new policy of non-interference was the result of a general shift in attitude among British officials following the 1857 Revolt. The liberal determination to improve India, which prevailed in the early and middle 1800s, gave way to an Orientalist refusal to change India. The central thesis of Hutchins's book *The Illusion of*

Permanence is that this shift could be traced to the fact that the British government had begun to think of itself as a permanent institution in India: "In pursuing this end, Orientalizers sought out those aspects of the Indian political, religious, and social traditions felt to be compatible with British rule and endeavoured to give them as much encouragement as possible through measures of public policy" (158). Conversely, those aspects of Indian society that threatened the British presence in India were discouraged. Social reform disturbed the status quo. It endangered an Empire that saw itself as permanent because, if taken to its logical conclusion, which would be the full modernization of India, social reform rendered a British government dedicated to the preservation of a traditional society obsolete.

Colonial ideology works on the premise of moral superiority. The rhetoric of the civilizing mission called upon the British to draw a portrait of themselves as morally more advanced and to construct Indians, but especially Hindus, as an effete people, belonging to a culture which had once been strong but was now in a state of decay. The image of the Hindu woman played a particularly important role in maintaining this hierarchy. Uma Chakravarti explains: "The 'higher' morality of the imperial masters could be effectively established by highlighting the low status of women among the subject population as it was an issue by which the moral 'inferiority' of the subject population could simultaneously be demonstrated" (34). So long as Hindu society remained degenerate in the eyes of the British and its women could be shown to exist in a state of degradation, the colonial government could justify its presence in India as a protective and uplifting influence. Once Indian women were freed from their subjection, however, the question of Britain's moral superiority would be open to debate. It is clear, then, that the conservative imperialist bent on holding on to political power in India had a stake in constructions of the Indian woman as oppressed both by her society and her husband but as benefitting from British rule even in her double subjugation. She was a person to be pitied and patronized but was not to be perceived as so victimized that her situation necessitated immediate corrective action.

A book, entitled *Women in India*, written by an English female journalist in 1895 constructs this kind of Indian woman. Mary Frances Billington traveled to India as a member of the staff of an English newspaper. Her purpose was to "penetrate the mysteries which lie beyond the *purdah*" in order to document the life of the Indian woman from the cradle to the grave. She is careful to insist from the beginning that she does not intend to follow the lead of the missionaries and social reformers, who, she implies, generally produce *sensational* accounts of "cruelty, misery . . . or intrigue" when writing about Indian women. Armed with her newspaper training, which she claims "enabled me to grasp facts first and draw conclusions afterwards," Billington is instead determined to "describe life as it really is" among the women of India (xii). She will count her duty done, she says, "if I can only convince some of those who vote away blithely, in a confidence profound as their ignorance . . . that Indian women are not altogether in such pitiful plight as some of their so-called friends come and tell us . . ." (xiii).

It is significant that Billington quotes one of Kipling's most famous Anglo-Indian proverbs, "What should they know of England who only England know," since the Orientalism of Englishmen such as Kipling is the political attitude that informs her book. The approach to India she offers is dispassionate; it purports simply to describe the customs and everyday experiences of Indian women, and hence it assumes a basis of objectivity. Like Kipling's Orde in "The Enlightenments of Pagett, M.P.," she does not regard her own commitment to British imperialism as an obstacle to her objectivity. Obviously a hidden agenda is at work. Cloaked behind a pose of objectivity is Billington's determination to prove that the condition of Indian women is by no means so abject as missionaries and social reformers have encouraged English voters to believe. It certainly does not call for any fundamental alteration of the status quo. At the end of the book, her political orientation clearly emerges as one which is entirely in line with the government's: "The policy of interference and innovation only introduces further items of discord which, under the existing order, it should be our utmost care to avoid" (268). Orientalism is a conservative position; it resists change and for this reason is dedicated to the preservation of "traditional" society in India. Moreover, if, as Hutchins maintains, the British in the last decades of the nineteenth century wanted to see themselves permanently ensconced in India and as a result of this conception were bolstering up those aspects of Indian society which supported this notion, it is hardly surprising that Billington should turn to what she considers her area of expertise, Indian women, and find there the evidence of a stable changelessness necessary to guarantee the continuance of British rule. Her mention of "those who vote away blithely," presumably to alter the status of Indian women, suggests that she conceives of her book as a means of affecting the way some Englishmen vote, of ensuring that they stop voting in "ignorance" and stop fixing lives that do not, in her estimation, need to be fixed.

However, although she does not believe that Indian women require any great change in their lives, beyond what the government has already offered them in terms of education and hospital facilities for childbirth, she is not prepared to admit that Indian and especially Hindu women are emancipated. Her book leaves us with no doubt that they are oppressed by men, and this she presents as if it were hardly a regrettable and certainly an unalterable "fact." In her chapter on the medical aid available to Indian women, she writes,

> It is impossible yet to get away from the fact that female life has no very great value in the East, and there are plenty of men still to be found who argue, why should they pay heavy doctors' bills for their wives when, if they die, they can so easily replace them? It is on this ground that I do not think India offers an unlimited field of work for English lady doctors. (109)

The cold logic of this passage is probably a reaction to the passionate and furious style found in missionary tracts on Indian women. We are supposed to understand this tone as indicative of her objectivity. However, it also points to Billington's acceptance of things as they are (or as she thinks they are) in India and further, and more important, to her tendency to construct Indian women from what she believes is the perspective of their men—as things or objects which are easily replaced and to which one has no emotional attachment. That she feels she must align herself in this way—not with an objective but with an *objectifying* gaze—actually places her in the position she assigns to Indian men in their relationships with Indian women. It is a position of superiority that reinforces the inferiority she says is ascribed to Indian women by their men. Furthermore, readers are surely meant to conclude from this passage and from the example of Billington's own lifestyle as a liberated English woman who is able to hold down a job and travel alone to India that the devaluation of women is a sign of the inferiority of a culture. Billington's Orientalism creates a no-win argument. Implicit in her book is the assumption that Indian culture is inferior, because Indian women are regarded as inferior, but the immense social change that would be required to accord these women equal status threatens the foundations of British rule and is therefore to be discouraged.

Billington also engages in an us-and-them discourse, which is a rhetoric common to Orientalism and which permits her a certain distance from the Indian subjects of her book. This distance is necessary for her to maintain the categories she sets up as Indian and western, which in turn allow her almost to dismiss one of the most controversial issues for the social reformers of the late nineteenth century: the situation of the Hindu widow. Billington does not feel the need to rehearse the plight of the high-caste widow in her own book, since the matter has been given so much attention by a type of writer she identifies as "the sensation-monger" (31). Because she does not want to add her own opinions to a body of writing she finds unseemly, Billington confines herself to making only one declaration about the Hindu widow: "No doubt . . . with a race which places the sexual pleasures in such paramount estimation, a girl would feel that to live life as thousands of European 'old maids' do, her fate was specially hard . . ." (31–32). Rather than embrace this fate, Billington suggests, the Hindu girl would rather marry and take the risk of widowhood, which would leave her a drudge in her dead husband's house. What are we to surmise from such a statement—that, though her sexual drive makes her incapable of doing so, the Hindu woman is better off forgoing the sexual pleasure available through marriage and not marrying at all, or that she is somehow to blame for her oppression as a widow because she had been unable to control her sexuality? And why is the choice of most Hindu women to marry made to seem somehow an affront to those European women who are single and supposedly without a sexual life?

Clearly, Billington is tapping into the binary thinking encouraged by Orientalism, a thinking which though seemingly simple is nevertheless fraught with inconsistencies. Secure in the belief that some characteristics belong to the West and others to the East, she appropriates for herself and her culture the virtue of sexual control, while relegating to the Indian population the defect of unfettered sexual desire. But she cannot do this without allowing some resentment to rise to the surface of her writing. Hindu women are castigated for not being able to endure the single life that "thousands" of European women lead, although the Orientalism implicit in her position denies Hindu women the capacity for the sexual control such a life requires. The logical conclusion of this argument is that Hindu women are doomed to become widows because, by their very nature, they cannot help but choose sexual activity over sexual abstinence. If they were able to forgo the "sexual pleasures" and, like many Englishwomen, remain single, they might escape the fate of the widow. That Billington sees single life as the only answer to the problem of the Hindu widow, an answer, moreover, that she believes Hindu women are incapable of accomplishing, puts her in the ranks of the imperialist 'non-reformers', whose vested interests in maintaining what they viewed as a static society in India prevented them from offering any solutions that might actually have been workable.

The reformers were at the other end of the British imperialist spectrum, the missionaries being the loudest and most vociferous. Unlike the Orientalists, the British missionaries in India saw the Indians as corrupt but redeemable, and the many tracts and books they published on the subject of India were geared toward raising the money necessary to achieve their redemption. The British missionaries shared with the liberal imperialists I examined in the last chapter not only the tendency to see all things English as superior to all things Indian but also the desire to set India right. While Orientalists emphasized the difference of India in an attempt to maintain the status quo, missionaries and liberal imperialists noted the difference in order to argue for change, change which, of course, would accommodate western preconceptions.

Jenny Fuller, a long-time resident of Bombay, published her book *The Wrongs of Indian Womanhood* in 1900 because, she says, "It has been many years since the subject of Indian women's wrongs has been much before the public, and . . . the public is so forgetful . . ." (15). Unlike Billington, she is not so much interested in objectivity as in accuracy, though her notion of accuracy has an emotional as well as a factual component. She ends her preface with the statement that she hopes her readers will "catch the message" contained in her book "and which my heart has burned to give" (16). Fuller's book is the culmination of her own personal mission to convince the British public and the British government in India of the need to reform through legislation the situation of the Indian woman. As such, its argument is founded on intense emotional identification with Indian women, great indignation at the wrongs committed against them by Indian men, and enormous pity.

Fuller's text is based on the assumption that British imperialism is a good thing; it is, according to her, a God-given right. Along with the right, however, comes a duty, which she believes has not been entirely fulfilled in the case of the Indian woman:

> It has not been our desire to do any injustice to government . . . but, at the same time, we dare not ignore the great opportunities and responsi- bilities of government to the millions of oppressed women under them; and we plead with them to rise to the full height of their opportunity and responsibility, and to be true to the trust given them when God allowed India to come under their rule. (188)

Rising "to the full height of their opportunity" means, for Fuller, entirely overriding the desires of the Indian people. She encourages the govern- ment to take the initiative in every reform measure without bothering to wait for any endorsement from the population: "Some of these wrongs are a great iniquity and a scandal to any government. The people would grumble; but when it was done they would acquiesce. Hindu fatalism, if nothing else, would help them to do it" (185). Fuller is so convinced of the righteousness of the British government, the British system, and British values, and of the total degradation of the Indian people that she is pre- pared to see the people further subjugated in order that they be ultimately saved.[2] As the book progresses, we learn that she equates the salvation of India with the annihilation of everything Indian, namely Indian religion, custom, and philosophy. Her conflation of the Indian with the Hindu in the above passage suggests that the details of India's cultures are of little importance to her. This is a far cry from Billington's Orientalism. While Billington carefully documents the differences between the Muslim, the Hindu, the Parsee, and the Christian Indian in an attempt to preserve these differences and the traditional society from which they have sprung, Fuller rides roughshod over India's distinctions because her agenda calls for the elimination of difference altogether. She is committed to the transformation of Indian society into a replica of the West and consequently finds no value in Indianness.

Billington's book consistently uses an Orientalist us-and-them rhetoric whereas Fuller works with a presupposition which can more accurately be described as "they are us," a rhetoric in which British values become a universal standard for Indians and all people. Because she so deeply identifies with the horrors which she believes Indian women and female children face daily, she has no difficulty categorically condemning their customs. The practice of child marriage is presented as something particularly contemptible, for she juxtaposes it with her own motherhood and evokes the protective feelings her children arouse in her. At one point in her book, she recalls how a Hindu friend holding her little girl on his knee playfully asked the child when she would be married. The girl was confused, the parents were appalled, and the subject was changed. What follows this episode is a panegyric to English parenthood:

> The little lass soon forgot the query, but we never did; and many a time as we tucked her in her bed at night, or watched her eager enthusiasm over her studies, or noticed her guardianship over her brother, or felt her loving care that saved us some burden, have we thanked God that no iron custom had power to take her from our sheltering love and care, until she was able to stand alone, or choose for herself. (34–35)

In comparison with the tender affection and care depicted here as coincident with English parenting, Hindu parents emerge in *The Wrongs of Indian Womanhood* as barbarous, unfeeling monsters who are prepared to sacrifice their helpless daughters to marriage in the name of their religion. It is only by constructing Hindus as unthinking followers of their religion and Hinduism as the root of the most serious wrongs committed against Indian women that Fuller is able to dismiss Indian cultures so thoroughly. Even those educated Indian men who are working to reform Hinduism and eradicate the practices most oppressive to women are objects of her derision, for they are depicted as lacking the courage of their convictions. Fuller denounces every possible Indian solution to the problem of Indian women because she is determined that there be only one solution and that it be a western one.

In the last chapter of her book, her purpose becomes clear. Here she outlines certain teachings of Hinduism in regards to women, teachings which require Hindu wives to submit always to their husbands even though such submission may result in their being brutally treated. Fuller concludes, "As long as men and women remain devout Hindus, so long will this estimate of women pervade society. . . . Give her true ideas of salvation, if you want her to find and to fill her true place" (282–83). For Fuller, these "true ideas" are Christian and the "true place" of the Indian woman is something similar to the place of English women. The norm is invariably western in *The Wrongs of Indian Womanhood,* and Hindu women are constituted as deviants in relation to it.

Billington's and Fuller's books represent two nineteenth-century British constructions of the Hindu woman, which, though vastly different in terms of their political allegiances and hidden agendas, can nevertheless be called imperialist in that they share a belief in the importance and efficacy of the western civilizing mission to the East. There were many other imperialist constructions of Hindu womanhood, but I have chosen these two because they seem to embody the major trends in imperialist thought which dominated English texts about India toward the turn of this century.

That Billington and Fuller were women writing about women was another factor in my choice. The textual conversation between Indian and English women during the colonial period has received little attention from historiographers, and, consequently, the standard picture of the nationalist/imperialist confrontation in India depicts two large groups of men, divided by politics, culture, and race, waging a century-long battle over the political status of the Indian subcontinent. If women are present at all, they are usually portrayed as caught in the crossfire. Even the Subaltern historians and most of the post-Orientalist historiographers do not go much beyond this paradigm.[3] I think, however, that women from both countries were more involved in this battle than this picture suggests, and not simply as observers but as constructors of their cultures and of the political climate that characterized their eras. Their emotional investments in imperialism or nationalism, evangelical Christianity or social reform, go as deep as that of the men, and, like the men, they stood to lose or gain according to the outcome of the battle. Billington and Fuller clearly saw themselves as participants and contributors to the British governance of India, and it seems to me that we should see them in this light as well.

The other side of the conversation involves Indian women and their conceptions of the nationalist moment. Here the issue is more complex because Indian women writing during the colonial period were members of a subject population. Imperialist discourse and practice, which constituted them as subordinate, structured what they had to say and the way in which they said it. Their experience as women offered them a potential alternative to the textual space constructed by the dominant male population of both countries, but the question remains whether or not any subjugated voice, even one that might be regarded as an alternative to the ruling discourse, can be authentic enough to speak against imperialism or represent a view outside of imperialism.

Critics are divided on this issue. In an article entitled "Figures of Colonial Resistance," Jenny Sharpe points out the difficulties in trying to retrieve the voice of the "native" under colonialism. One of the most pressing problems for western critics, she suggests, is identifying the speaker. Too often the voice of the "colonial subject" is mistaken for that of the subaltern. The "colonial subject" she delineates as the western-educated Indian who has acquired a subject status "by acceding to the authority of Western knowledge" (f.n. 140). The subaltern, on the other hand, is not permitted such status under imperialism and does not have access to such knowledge. What her argument finally affirms is that although the voice of the colonial subject can be retrieved by western critics, it is invariably spurious and even disingenuous, unavoidably so because of the concessions that the indigenous elite have had to make to imperialism. "Caught within the frame of colonialism, the native voice can only be inauthentic," she concludes. As for the subaltern voice, it is "ultimately irretrievable" (152). One only further subordinates the subaltern by attempting to recover this voice. The most we can do, she seems to argue, is follow Forster's lead and allow the subaltern not to speak.

Sharpe is right in pointing out that figures of colonial resistance are extraordinarily difficult to identify and, further, that the voice of the indigenous elite is too frequently made to represent all of the subject population by critics of the West. The subaltern is effaced by such practices. However, the notion that the voice of the colonial subject or indigenous elite is inevitably inauthentic, a position confirmed by much of the postcolonial scholarship of Gayatri Chakravorty Spivak, jettisons a rarely studied corpus of texts written by authors who should not be so unproblematically dismissed as Sharpe and Spivak seem to do with terms such as "colonial subject" and "native informant" (Spivak, "Can the Subaltern Speak?" 284). Granted that when Sharpe and Spivak use these terms they are generally referring to male writers of the indigenous elite groups in India. But by not even addressing the issue of Indian women writers from the elite class, who are not subaltern but who are nevertheless facing a discursive predicament which cannot be subsumed and explained away by categories designed to delineate western-educated Indian men under colonialism, Sharpe and Spivak are excluding these women as effectively as they claim western critics of imperialism are effacing the subaltern.

In order to examine meaningfully the texts produced by women writers of the elite groups in colonial India, it seems important to get rid of this discourse of authenticity. It is too tautological in its direction. Eventually, after eliminating all inauthentic voices such as British imperialist and Indian nationalist ones, we are left with the subaltern, who cannot speak because s/he ceases to be a subaltern the moment s/he speaks. We cannot retrieve the male or female subaltern; we can only enshrine them in their irreducibility. I distrust this mystification of the subaltern because it necessarily renders inauthentic and dismissable every voice on the very basis that it does speak, with the exception, of course, of the critic's voice.

I am also uneasy about a tendency that I see in much middle-class postcolonial scholarship to make incredibly generalized presumptions about subaltern populations that are literally millions strong. For instance, in Spivak's latest book *Outside in the Teaching Machine,* she describes the "habitat of the *subproletariat* or the *subaltern*" as a space that "had no established agency of traffic with the culture of imperialism. Paradoxically, this space is also outside of organized labor, below the attempted reversals of capital logic." And in the next paragraph, while making the introductory comments to her interpretation of a recently-written short story entitled "Douloti," she says about the author, "Mahasweta [Devi] invites us to realize that, in the context of this fiction, for the subaltern, and especially the subaltern woman, "Empire" and "Nation" are interchangeable names, however hard it might be for us to imagine it" (78). Clearly, here and in many other places in her writing, Spivak uses the subaltern, particularly the gendered subaltern, as a discursive site from which to make often brilliant critiques of middle-class and patriarchal institutions such as nationalism and neo-colonialism. But the subaltern—as the category has been constituted by subalternist historiography to which Spivak has contributed—is not merely a discursive site. Its "discursiveness" stands alongside and points to its other reality: the subaltern and the gendered subaltern are millions of people who have lived and currently live in India—tribal people, agricultural laborers, factory workers, prostitutes, etc. To make such massive, rather than contextual, generalizations about their realities is surely to duplicate the strategies of patriarchy, imperialism, and nationalism. Finally, Spivak's inattention to the constructedness of Mahasweta Devi's subaltern characters—they represent, after all, both Devi's and Spivak's own middle-class conceptions of subaltern realities—transforms the subaltern into a focus to explore primarily middle-class concerns and a fetish to expiate middle-class guilt. I can't help but wonder if the "subaltern" in so much of Spivak's writing is actually a middle-class filter through which we envision the people of India who are not colonial subjects or postcolonial elites.

Hence, while I agree with Spivak and Sharpe about the need to distinguish between the subaltern and the colonial subject (since to ignore the subaltern in our work or confuse its representation with that of another is to replicate the imperialist project) I think that scholars have to be conscious of their own political and personal agendas when writing about subalterns. Furthermore, we must surely acknowledge that analysis of other places of resistance is also worthwhile, even places that are or were much indebted to colonial and national ideologies or subject constitution. Without overlooking the subaltern or subalterns, it is conceivable that *some* colonial subjects have something new to tell us about the workings of imperialism and nationalism.

In pursuit of that difference, I propose to examine two Indian women writers of the indigenous elite, the subject of whose writing is themselves, the high-caste Hindu woman. Pandita Ramabai Sarasvati was a social reformer. Her treatise on the status of Hindu women, published in 1887 and entitled *The High-Caste Hindu Woman,* caused a sensation among Indian nationalists, British imperialists, and Christian missionary organizations and, to some extent, dictated the course that social reform involving the Hindu woman would take over the next few decades. Swarnakumari Devi

Ghosal was a novelist, first in Bengali and later, after the turn of the century, in English. *An Unfinished Song,* a novel published in Bengali in the 1890s, which she translated for an English audience in 1913, is an account of the agonies of a young Hindu woman who tries to hold on to a sense of her self as her family arranges her marriage. Both women were famous in their day, known inside and outside of India. However, although the Pandita is still studied by nationalist historians, Swarnakumari has virtually been forgotten. She was one of the first novelists to have contributed to Indo-Anglian literature, and yet, with the exception of a few feminist histories of Indian women, in which she is only mentioned, her work is ignored. Her name doesn't even appear in the card catalog of the Nehru Memorial Museum and Library in New Delhi. When I speculate on the paucity of attention paid to the fiction of Swarnakumari Devi and contrast it with the unbridled popularity of the pre-independence novels of Mulk Raj Anand, R. K. Narayan, and Raja Rao, most of which continue to win the regard and acclaim of literary critics in India and the West (and deservedly so), I suspect that the neglect of this woman writer is the result of her femaleness. My discovery of her work, however, has convinced me that there is more to be said about the early Indo-Anglian tradition of literature than can be garnered from these three canonized novelists. The roots of Indian fiction in English are by no means exclusively male.[4]

Both Pandita Ramabai and Swarnakumari Devi were Brahmin women, educated initially in Indian languages and later in English, and as such, they were immensely privileged, since few Indian women of any religion or class were educated in the nineteenth century. Had they never committed their ideas to paper, had they never spoken out about the lives of Indian women, they would have been subalterns, according to Spivak's definition of the word. Since they have spoken, we must move them into the category of the "colonial subject," the "native informant." Beyond recognizing that their writing is necessarily conditioned by the "planned epistemic violence of the imperialist project" (Spivak, "Rani" 131), what do we do with them now? To answer this question, we need to come to some understanding of the colonized woman and of the possibilities of resistance implicit in that subject position.

Spivak's concept of the "self-consolidating Other" is a useful starting point.[5] In her article "The Rani of Sirmur" she describes a young Englishman, Captain Geoffrey Birch, riding about the Simla Hills in his capacity as assistant agent of the Governor. The year is 1815, early in the colonialist enterprise. His reason for being there, he explains in a letter to Charles Metcalfe, the Resident at Delhi, is to "acquaint the people who they are subject to." Spivak interprets his activity in another way: "He is actually engaged in consolidating the self of Europe by obliging the native to cathect the space of the Other on his home ground. He is worlding *their own world,* which is far from mere uninscribed earth, anew, by obliging *them* to domesticate the alien as Master" (133). We see the process which creates the "self-consolidating Other" from the point of view of the imperialist ruler in Spivak's work. How the "native" might go about transforming the self into an Other that consolidates the imperial self is another interesting area of investigation. Ashis Nandy in *The Intimate Enemy: Loss and Recovery of Self Under Colonialism* provides a paradigm of this process, which can be applied, although not uncritically, to the texts of Swarnakumari Devi and Pandita Ramabai.

Along with Spivak, Nandy delineates the most dangerous form of colonialism as that which "colonizes minds in addition to bodies" and which "releases forces within the colonized societies to alter their cultural priorities once for all" (xi). The West ceases to be merely a geographical space; it takes on a psychological existence as well. This is the colonialism that survives the death of Empires. Not surprisingly, such colonialism is incredibly all-consuming. Nandy contends that not only does it furnish the colonized people with "models of conformity," which are the non-threatening beliefs and codes of behavior that they are expected to adopt, but it also creates "models of 'official' dissent" (xii), which are equally non-threatening to the colonial rulers because this behavior is controlled and predictable. The colonized, then, are tempted to wage their battles against imperialism on the ground that imperialism has provided, within the psychological limits that imperialism has defined, and using the categories that imperialism has created. Or to put it in Spivak's terms, in order to consolidate the imperial self of Britain, Indians were forced to internalize the British as master and as opponent and cathect the space of the Other. It is possible even today, Nandy argues and Spivak would undoubtedly agree, to be anti-colonial in a manner that has been promoted by colonialism. He adds that most interpretations of colonialism, even his, are informed by colonialism, and therefore he designates his own book not as a history but as a "caution-ary tale." It cautions the reader "that conventional anti-colonialism, too, could be an apologia for the colonization of minds" (xi).

Given the comprehensiveness of colonialism, it is difficult to imagine a way out, a psychological form of resistance which would not simply re-affirm the imperialist system. The colonized seem permanently doomed to play the role of the victim, even if they choose to oppose colonialism. But Nandy asserts repeatedly throughout his book that there is an alterna-tive role. "I reject the model of the gullible, hopeless victim of colonialism caught in the hinges of history," he writes. "I see him as fighting his own battle for survival in his own way, sometimes consciously, sometimes by default." Domesticating the West is his way of fighting that battle and "protect[ing] his society against the White Sahib" (xv). This process is often mistaken for westernization, but it is, in fact, a means of putting the West into an Indian perspective. Nandy believes that Indians in colonial India, particularly those of the indigenous elite, enjoyed one advantage over the English: they could choose to be both Indian and western. The English could not do this without threatening their political status, which was maintained on the Orientalist assumption, shared by English and Indi-ans alike, that the English were different from the Indians and, according to imperialist ideology, that one of the indicators of this difference was their supposed ability to rule. If the English were to adopt what colonial-ism had designated as Indian qualities, this ability to rule would be called into question. Indians, on the other hand, were free to "use the Occi-dent for their own purposes" (77). They could incorporate the West into their psychological make-up without jeopardizing their so-called Indian-ness, (though, of course, the definition of Indianness was constantly being formed and reformed according to various imperialist and nationalist dis-courses). This inclusion of the culture of the West into the psyches of the East could be used as a method of resistance to colonialism. Nandy writes:

> one could perhaps say that in the chaos called India the opposite of thesis is not the antithesis because they exclude each other. The true 'enemy' of the thesis is seen to be in the synthesis because it includes the thesis and ends the latter's reason for being. It is Sankara's Vedanta, carrying the clear impress of Buddhism, which finished Buddhism as

a living faith in India, and not either Brahmanic orthodoxy or any state-sponsored anti-Buddhist ideology. (99)

The West does not overtake the East in the mind of the colonized but resistant Indian. It is simply contextualized, given enough of a place that the West as a separate entity becomes redundant.

Nandy uses the nationalist politics of Gandhi as an example of this strategy of resistance. He describes Gandhi as a non-player who, nevertheless, "beat the colonizers at their own game" (52) by creatively manipulating the rules of that game. One of the demands that colonialism made upon its promoters was that, in order to maintain an illusion of superiority, certain marginalized aspects of the European personality had to be rejected and were subsequently projected onto the colonized population. When the English in India adopted, therefore, their ethos of hyper-masculinity, with its concomitant values of achievement and productivity, they identified the Indians with what they had come to regard as the opposite of the masculine, namely, those qualities associated with femininity. Gandhi resisted the English, Nandy argues, by using their own psychological repressions against them. He exalted non-violence, self-sacrifice, and passive endurance, the "feminine" cultural traits that the English had turned their backs on. In other words, Gandhi refused both the "model of conformity" and the "model of dissent" that imperialism had offered him. The "model of dissent" would have required him to combat English hyper-masculinity with Indian hyper-masculinity. He developed instead an alternative feminine reference within which Indians did not appear degraded or weak. He demonstrated that this feminine way of living and method of political resistance was a valid option which Indians and others should choose instead of imperialist values because these had become disproportionately powerful and therefore unhealthy.

Although this "feminine" form of political dissent came to be associated with Indianness, Nandy asserts that Gandhi, in fact, "always tried to be a living symbol of the other West" (48), the feminine West that the Englishmen in India had repressed in themselves and projected onto the Indians: "Gandhi's partiality for some of the Christian hymns and Biblical texts was more than the symbolic gesture of a Hindu towards a minority religion in India. It was also an affirmation that, at one plane, some of the recessive elements of Christianity were perfectly congruent with elements of Hindu and Buddhist world views and that the battle he was fighting for the minds of men was actually a universal battle to rediscover the softer side of human nature . . ." (49). Gandhi domesticated the West, then, by appropriating the feminine Christian values which had been relegated to the edges of the western psyche and to India, the edges of the Empire. He also insisted that these values belonged not only to the West but were latent in the Indian traditions as well. This method of incorporating the West into the East is, Nandy says, a legitimate and creative response to western imperialism.

Nandy's theory of resistance allows us to appraise and vindicate the texts of the indigenous elite in a way that is contrary to Sharpe's and Spivak's ideas about the insurmountability of the imperialist project. However, Nandy examines the problem and possibility of resistance only from the point of view of Indian men. The efforts of Indian women to combat colonialism are doubly complex because Indian women, such as Pandita Ramabai and Swarnakumari, had to contend with both indigenous patriarchy and western imperialism. If the psychological strategy of colonialism involved the projection of the feminine onto the subject population and if Gandhi's appropriation of the feminine allowed him to develop a form of political resistance, as Nandy argues, how do we assess the resistance to colonialism offered by Indian women who, because of Indian patriarchy, had no choice but the feminine and for whom the feminine could be an extremely oppressive construct? The acceptance of his own and his culture's "femininity" was, for Gandhi, a liberating experience. For Pandita Ramabai writing *The High-Caste Hindu Woman* and for Swarnakumari in *An Unfinished Song,* the codes of conduct associated with Indian femininity were frequently obstacles to them and their countrywomen's liberation. Obviously, any analysis of the texts that these women wrote must be accompanied by an understanding of colonial resistance that takes into account the existence of a patriarchal system in India at the end of the nineteenth and beginning of the twentieth centuries. For we have to be able to comprehend their texts in terms of not one but two oppositional discourses. Nandy's theory of colonial resistance and Spivak's concept of the "Self-consolidating Other" are both extremely useful tools in interpreting *The High-Caste Hindu Woman* and *An Unfinished Song.* Still, we must be careful not to lose sight of the dual enemies of patriarchy and Empire against which these women ranged themselves, their lives, and their texts.

Pandita Ramabai was as much a non-player as Gandhi, though she entirely rejected both the western and Indian ideals of femininity which he so effectively valorized. It is important to remember that she wrote her famous book, *The High-Caste Hindu Woman,* over twenty-five years *before* Gandhi even entered the nationalist political arena, during a period when notions of Hindu womanhood had not yet been codified into the model that Gandhi inherited. It was still very much a matter for debate whether or not Hindu women were indeed the embodiments of such "feminine" virtues as selflessness, passive endurance, and nonviolence, ideals that Gandhi fundamentally took for granted. In the late nineteenth century, the debate was raging over the definition of the high-caste Hindu woman, and Pandita Ramabai, Swarnakumari, Billington, and Fuller were all contributors to that definition. More than a definition, however, what Pandita Ramabai had to offer the cross-continental conversation on Indian womanhood was a critique of the existing patriarchal construction, and an interpretation of this construction which recognized its indebtedness to two patriarchies, the British as well as the Indian.

At the level of readership, she sought to bypass both patriarchies by writing her book for an audience of predominantly American women. Her motive in choosing such an audience was undoubtedly political. American women were more likely to support her cause because they could provide Pandita Ramabai with the money she needed to start a school for Hindu widows—the express purpose behind the writing of *The High-Caste Woman*—without having constantly to measure their allegiance to an imperialist enterprise against their allegiance to their own sex. Conversely, in their writings on Indian womanhood, Billington and Fuller must have felt it mandatory to state their unequivocal support of their country's imperialist policies in India. That this compromises their sympathy for and their "message" (to use Fuller's term) about Indian women is a source of tension in both books. It is also significant that before publishing her book in the United States, Pandita Ramabai had tried and failed to get financial support from the British public and from British organizations dedicated to righting the social wrongs of women in India. The middle-

and upper-class American women to whom *The High-Caste Hindu Woman* is addressed must, on the other hand, have had a clear, or at least a clearer, conscience about supporting social reform for Indian women, for sales of this book managed to raise over the $50,000 that was deemed necessary for Pandita Ramabai to begin her work.

On the surface the Pandita's book seems to share the same basic intentions that prompted Billington and Fuller to write their texts. All three authors openly state their desire to reveal to a non-Indian audience the misunderstood life of the Indian woman. The difference for Pandita Ramabai is that she, herself, is an Indian woman. Consequently, her entrance into the conversation about Indian women is regarded by British and American reformers as a momentous event. In the original introduction to *The High-Caste Hindu Woman*, Rachel L. Bodley dramatically announces, "The silence of a thousand years has been broken, and the reader of this unpretending little volume catches the first utterances of the unfamiliar voice" (i). It is, Bodley claims, a voice of "woe," and its sorrow is the sorrow of millions of Hindu women. Later editions of *The High-Caste Hindu Woman* pick up on this depiction of Pandita Ramabai as a woman who speaks on behalf of her oppressed countrywomen. In the 1901 edition, Judith W. Andrews, Chairman of the Board of Managers of the American Ramabai Association, which was set up to assist the work of the Pandita in India, describes her as a "fearless champion of the rights of her unfortunate sisters," and her book as seeking "to strike from them the chains of ignorance and superstition that for centuries have kept them in cruel bondage" (8-9). This attempt to delineate Ramabai as a sort of Hindu Joan of Arc reaches its florid peak in Helen S. Dyer's 1907 biography of the Pandita, in which the publishing of *The High-Caste Hindu Woman* is represented as a turning point for all Indian women: "But now a voice had arisen from among themselves to tell with intimate knowledge how the iron-bound customs of centuries had ground woman into a position of servitude and ignorance . . ." (23). What all three of the above quotations have in common is their tendency to treat the woman, Pandita Ramabai, as synonymous, even identical, with the population of Hindu women about whom she writes. These three western writers also go one step further than Pandita, herself, does in her book; that is, they constitute her as the representative of all Indian women, from every class, caste, and religion.

This is in spite of the fact that Pandita Ramabai is very careful to point out in the beginning of *The High-Caste Hindu Woman* that her subject will be confined to the parameters of her title. She does not claim to speak for or to recount the experiences of low-caste women or women of different religions.

Spivak sees this particular western tendency to efface the subaltern as an inextricable aspect of the imperialist project, one from which contemporary writing about the third world has not yet freed itself.[6] That Pandita Ramabai does not reproduce this strategic exclusion for her western audience, that she does not pretend to speak for or depict the women outside her own personal orbit is, I think, a testament to the integrity of her book. In *The High-Caste Hindu Woman*, she is concerned only with those lives with which she, as a high-caste Hindu woman, is familiar. The book is principally comprised of incidents of oppression she has personally witnessed as well as interpretations and translations of Sanskrit passages that she herself has read in the original. Muslim, Christian, and Parsee women are not mentioned at all. The sole reference she makes to "women of the working classes" is to admit that they are more self-reliant than "their sisters of high caste in India" (100) because they are permitted to work. Pandita Ramabai seems to think that at least in this freedom they are enviable. Having called attention to this aspect of her work, I must also acknowledge that while the Pandita does not endeavor to define or speak for the subaltern working-class woman, her book does participate in a predominantly Indian discourse (though some European Orientalist scholars were involved as well) that deliberately ignored the lower caste woman in its efforts to construct a new ideal of the high-caste Hindu woman.[7]

Pandita Ramabai was a Sanskrit scholar, one of the few women in nineteenth-century India to have learned this traditionally masculine knowledge. In fact, the titles "Pandita" and "Sarasvati" were accorded her in Calcutta by an assembly of Brahmin pandits who were amazed to meet a woman who had acquired such erudition. ("Sarasvati" is the name of the goddess of learning in the Hindu pantheon.) Considering her unusual training in this ancient language, it is understandable that her critique of the Hindu ideals of womanhood should be grounded in the Sanskrit scriptures. She suggests that these texts, from which women are not allowed "to pronounce a single syllable" (55), are fundamentally responsible for the subordination of the high-caste Hindu woman. The numerous Sanskrit passages she quotes from the laws of Manu, a second-century writer, whom she insists "all Hindus, with few exceptions believe implicitly" (52), condemn women for being heartless, seductive, dishonest, indiscriminate in their sexual choices, and "as impure as falsehood itself" (53), a phrase that the Pandita deplores so much that she quotes it three times. Finally, she concludes with an allusion to the very class of men that sought to pay tribute to her with their titles: "Those who diligently and impartially read Sanscrit literature in the original, cannot fail to recognize the law-giver Manu as one of those hundreds who have done their best to make woman a hateful being in the world's eye" (55). Pandita Ramabai's book implicates these men, the renowned Sanskrit scholars of India, in the oppression of women, for she intimates quite strongly that they have indeed either failed to recognize Manu's contribution to the Hindu woman's subjugation or wantonly supported and abetted this subjugation.

The Pandita recognizes that there is a brighter side to these scriptures, that they also honor women, particularly mothers. This privileging of motherhood over all other female roles is the tradition that, for instance, Swami Vivekananda drew on during his frequent speeches about Indian women in the United States. In a speech delivered in California in 1900, he articulates the image of the Hindu mother that dominated the discourse on Indian women throughout his own and Pandita Ramabai's life:

> No, no! Woman! thou shalt not be coupled with anything connected with the flesh. Thy name has been called holy once and for ever, for what name is there which no lust can ever approach, no carnality ever come near than the word Mother? That is the ideal in India. (11)

Swami Vivekananda and other social reformers and Indian nationalists before and after the turn of the century propagated the deification of the mother as part of the nationalist revival of Hinduism. In her book, Pandita Ramabai shows us the "reverse side" (52) of this rhetoric. She demonstrates that such glorification of the mother ideal masks an insidious and deeply entrenched hatred, which works itself out in the actual lives of high-caste Hindu women.

Hindu mothers in India, Pandita Ramabai tells us, are certainly showered with respect and the devotion of their children. However, this treatment is generally confined to the mothers of sons. Mothers of daughters, she says, unless they are fortunate enough to have borne their sons first, and women who have no children at all are the victims of this glorification rhetoric. Because they have not produced boys, they are not entitled to the respect, honor, and devotion which the Hindu tradition exclusively reserves for the mothers of sons. Instead, they are vilified and held in life-long contempt. In no other country in the world, the Pandita writes, is pregnancy fraught with such anxiety. A woman's entire future life hangs in the balance:

> A lady friend of mine in Calcutta told me that her husband had warned her not to give birth to a girl, the first time, or he would never see her face again. . . . In the same family there was another woman, the sister-in-law of my friend, whose first-born had been a daughter. . . . Poor woman! she had been notified by her husband that if she persisted in bearing daughters she should be superseded by another wife, have coarse clothes to wear and scanty food to eat . . . and she should be made the drudge of the whole household. (15–16)

The underside of Hindu society's deification of the mother, then, is the condemnation of the sonless woman. Moreover, all women pay the price for this rhetoric, since all women are at some time in their lives without sons.

Yet prospective mothers are not the only Hindu women who suffer as a result of living in a society that venerates motherhood at the expense of all other female roles. The possibility of choosing something other than motherhood is virtually eliminated by such a philosophy, and any Hindu woman who makes even a gesture in that direction is made to bear the brunt of her patriarchal community's wrath. To illustrate the point, Pandita Ramabai relates the story of a friend of hers from Bombay. Rakhmabai was, in accordance with Hindu custom, married while she was still a child but permitted to remain in her father's home, where she was educated. After her father died, she refused to live with her husband, who promptly brought a suit against her in the British courts. The young woman defended herself on the grounds that the marriage was not valid since she had not consented to it. A British judge in Bombay initially settled the case in her favor, at which point, Ramabai writes, "the conservative party all over India rose as one man and girded their loins to denounce the helpless woman and her handful of friends" (65). They threatened the British government with public displeasure if it failed to uphold the Hindu law which demanded that a wife live with her husband under any circumstances. An appeal was made, and the case was sent to the lower courts for re-trial. The husband won, and Rakhmabai was told that she must either go live with her husband or face a jail sentence. She was, furthermore, ordered to pay the court costs for both parties. In a letter to Pandita Ramabai, who was in the United States when this case was tried, Rakhmabai confesses that she cannot obey the judge and therefore expects to be jailed. The conclusion she draws from her experience with both the British justice system and Hindu orthodoxy is, "There is no hope for women in India, whether they be under Hindu rule or British rule" (66).

Pandita Ramabai reacts to the judge's decision with outrage. It is interesting to observe how she chooses to focus her anger and the picture she constructs to explain the situation. She declares, somewhat sarcastically,

> Taught by the experience of the past, we are not at all surprised at this decision of the Bombay court. Our only wonder is that a defenseless woman like Rakhmabai dared to raise her voice in the face of the powerful Hindu law, the mighty British government, the one hundred and twenty-nine million men and the three hundred and thirty million gods of the Hindus, all these having conspired together to crush her into nothingness. We cannot blame the English government for not defending a helpless woman; it is only fulfilling its agreement made with the male population of India. (67)

Of all the women's stories recounted in her book, it is this tale of Rakhmabai that elicits the strongest response from the Pandita—perhaps because Rakhmabai is an educated women, like herself, and is, in spite of the strength and independence that such schooling should confer, rendered helpless by a seemingly unconquerable combination of patriarchy and imperialism. In her anger, Pandita Ramabai delivers an interpretation of the political situation in India toward the end of the nineteenth century that is markedly original. For she clearly depicts the problem confronting all Hindu women as the product of *both* the Indian and British systems. The Indian nationalists generally conceived of themselves and their countrymen as occupying a position against British imperialism. The British, on the other hand, constituted the nationalists as their principal enemies in India. Missionary proponents of social reform, such as Fuller, and Orientalists, such as Billington, also tended to construct the situation as one in which most British stood on one side of the political fence and Indians on the other. Pandita Ramabai, however, paints a different picture. In her view the line of demarcation is drawn according to gender rather than race. In other words the battle is waged not between the Indians and the British, as almost every political faction from either country assumed, but between men of both races and Indian women, particularly high-caste Hindu women. The implications of such a perspective are far-reaching.

In Pandita Ramabai's construction, imperialism emerges as a contract that has been entered into by two parties of men, the British and the Indians, for the purposes of subjugating Hindu women. Although she does not suggest that the oppression of Hindu women is the primary motive behind the imperialist enterprise in India, the Pandita demonstrates that women are caught in its trajectory. She states that "British profit and rule" (68) are sustained through the pacification of "the male population in India," and such pacification ultimately means the maintenance of a harsh Indian patriarchy. In Pandita Ramabai's view, English men have no valid excuse for treating Hindu women with less moral justice than that meted out to women in their own country. Nevertheless, they continue to support their Indian government, she declares, "at the sacrifice of the rights and comfort of over one hundred million women" (68). These Hindu women are the necessary victims of an imperialist project which requires the consent of both the British and Indian men in order for it to continue. Thus, it is through the suffering of Hindu women living under Indian patriarchy that imperialism in India is preserved. Rakhmabai's lament that there is no hope for women in India, no matter which party rules, voices the intense desperation that underlies and informs Pandita Ramabai's assessment of imperialism.

The High-Caste Hindu Woman also contains a reading of Indian nationalism, which effectively strips it of its masculine pretensions. Men and women, she says, are "indissolubly united . . . as members of the same body of human society" (95). When one suffers, so does the other. The imposition on Hindu women of purdah, child marriage, and other inventions of Indian patriarchy has succeeded, generation after generation, in weakening their physical, moral, and spiritual fiber. Presupposing a doctrine of pre-natal influence, Pandita Ramabai argues that the children of such "imprisoned" women are bound to inherit these character flaws, and consequently, "we see all around us in India a generation of men least deserving of that exalted appellation" (96). At the time that the Pandita was writing, the most vocal faction of nationalists tended to combat British imperialism with a version of the hyper-masculinity ethos that Nandy discusses in his text. The mark of the English-educated man in India became the degree to which he was committed to the cause of nationalism. Pandita Ramabai undermines this ethos by questioning the patriotic capacity of any men whose mothers are so oppressed: "The men of Hindustan do not when babes, suck from the mother's breast, true patriotism, and in their boyhood, the mother, poor woman, is unable to develope [sic] that divine faculty in them owing to her utter ignorance of the past and present condition of her native land" (97). In effect, she reverses the mother myth, which such renowned speakers as Swami Vivekananda and Sri Aurobindo Ghosh used to promote the cause of Hindu culture and nationalism throughout the world, by contending that, despite the tendency of Hindu men to idealize their own mothers and motherhood in general, Hindu mothers are ignorant and therefore cannot help but raise ignorant sons. She then goes on to attribute the existence of British imperialism in India to the subjugation of Hindu women. She writes, "The complete submission of women under Hindu law has in the lapse of millenniums of years converted them into slavery-loving creatures. They are glad to lean on any one and be altogether dependent, and thus it has come to pass that their sons as a race, desire to depend upon some other nation, and not upon themselves" (98). Through such an argument, she is able to suggest that the achievement of political independence in India is inextricably connected to the emancipation of Hindu women. Indian men will not be able to govern themselves, outside the ambit of British imperialism, until they have relinquished their desire to oppress Indian women. The first cannot occur without the second.

As radical as the Pandita's ideas seem in the context of the political climate of the late nineteenth century, still we must ask ourselves if she has not simply reproduced for an American audience the ideology of colonialism. I referred earlier to this ideology by quoting Chakravarti's observation that the status of the colonized woman is often the vehicle through which colonialism establishes the moral superiority of the colonizer. The colonized woman is depicted as degraded and therefore in need of the protection and civilizing influence of the colonizer, in order to justify the continuation of western imperialist policies. If this is indeed what Pandita Ramabai is doing in *The High-Caste Hindu Woman,* then she certainly fulfills Spivak's conditions for the "self-consolidating Other." The presence of colonial ideology in her book could be used as evidence to indicate that she has, to use Spivak's terms, internalized the alien as Master and cathected the space of the Other.

Under imperialism, an Indian writer who had assumed the role of the Other, thereby consolidating the imperialist self, would undoubtedly begin to see herself and her culture through western eyes. She would judge situations and traditions in India from the vantage point of the West. It is true that the norms present in *The High-Caste Hindu Woman* tend to be western in origin, for Pandita Ramabai consistently measures the status of Hindu womanhood by means of an unspoken comparison to girls and women in western countries. This becomes overt in the final chapter when she asks her readers to "compare the condition of your own sweet darlings at your happy fireside with that of millions of little girls of a corresponding age in India, who have already been sacrificed on the unholy altar of an inhuman social custom" (118). The language here, as well as the encouragement she offers her American readers to identify with the plight of Hindu girls, is highly reminiscent of Fuller's text *The Wrongs of Indian Womanhood.* Can we further assume that the Pandita is also duplicating Fuller's liberal imperialist stance, that, like Fuller, she is committed to a construction of Hindu womanhood which can only recognize it as deviant in relation to western women? Pandita Ramabai was, after all, a Hindu-born Brahmin who later turned Christian. Moreover, throughout her career, she was frequently accused of running a school for Hindu widows for the hidden purpose of converting them to Christianity.[8] Perhaps a Christian point of view in India in the last decades of the nineteenth century was necessarily colored by the agenda of imperialism.

It would be short-sighted of me to suggest that she had somehow escaped the inculcation of colonial ideology or that she had avoided the

realignment of her cultural priorities, which is the inevitable psychological consequence of colonialism in the minds of the indigenous population.
Spivak's and Nandy's warnings about the all-pervasiveness of the colonialist enterprise do not go unheeded. But recognizing the imperialist
pitfalls into which the Pandita's book may have fallen is just not enough.
We must also acknowledge that the subject position which she, probably unwittingly, adopted in writing *The High-Caste Hindu Woman*, the
position of the "self-consolidating Other" who sometimes inadvertently
reinforces imperialism even while resisting it, was the only one available
to her. Centuries of Indian patriarchy and decades of western imperialism
had permanently altered the subjectivity of the Hindu woman, to the point
where, by the time Pandita Ramabai wrote her book, there was no un-
embattled subject position for her to occupy. The resistance to patriarchy
and imperialism which her book offers must be assessed with this in mind.

According to Nandy, Gandhi resisted the Empire with a rhetoric of
nonviolent femininity. Pandita Ramabai also resisted, but her method was
deconstructive rather than constructive. She does not so much offer an
alternative to the West, using the West's own repressions, as Gandhi did, as
she exposes the hidden costs and hidden allegiances behind this rhetoric of
femininity. These costs are exacted on the bodies and paid for by the lives
of Hindu women, and this rhetoric is dependent upon the preservation of
a covert affiliation between an indigenous patriarchy and an alien imperialism, an affiliation which ensures the subjugation of the Hindu woman.
Interestingly enough, however, Pandita Ramabai does not propose a way
out or offer a philosophy which would end the subjugation. In spite of
the pragmatism behind the publishing of *The High-Caste Hindu Woman*,
in spite of the Pandita's clearly expressed hopes that the book would raise
enough American money to fund a Hindu school for child widows, she
does not appear to believe that the situation of the Hindu woman can be
drastically changed. There is, for instance, no suggestion in the book that
her own work to rescue and educate the most downtrodden of all, the
child widow, will affect the lives of other Hindu women. The most she
seems to propose is that a haven for these girls can be made, where they
will temporarily escape the worst of their oppression, and that later when
they are sent back into the world, they will be equipped with the knowledge and strength to bear "the perilous blasts of social persecution" (118).[9]

The Pandita's book is not hopeful; it does not look forward to an auspicious future for Hindu women. The alleviation of the greatest suffering is all it appears to promise. *The High-Caste Hindu Woman* is not a book that advances the nationalist dream of a free India, and it does not subscribe to the twentieth-century feminist ideal of the emancipated Hindu woman. But it does provide a critique of imperialism and patriarchy from which both of these movements drew their inspiration and determination to resist. It is ironically the case that although Ramabai's writing depicts Hindu women as subjugated (a position imperialists appropriated in order to justify their continued rule), her writing still remained in some quarters effective in undermining imperialism, not the least because she pointed out that imperialism benefited from the oppression of Hindu women by Hindu patriarchy.

While Pandita Ramabai depicts the high-caste Hindu woman in such a way as to critique the existing patriarchal and imperialist structures, Swarnakumari Devi, in her fiction, balances some criticism of the cultural expectations foisted on Hindu women in India with a construction of a new ideal of womanhood. Within this new ideal, the Hindu woman moves toward a future in which she is both liberated and self-reliant, though, somewhat paradoxically, still retaining her renowned devotion to her husband. In *An Unfinished Song,* her first novel to be published in English,[10] fate, Hindu tradition, and even Indian patriarchy are enlisted to bring about the realization of this utopian vision. Ultimately, even the West contributes to the growth of Hindu womanhood in India. Swarnakumari's novel demonstrates the validity of Nandy's notion of synthesis as a form of colonial resistance.

Swarnakumari attempted to live this ideal in her own life. Married, while still a child, to a nationalist who encouraged her to continue the education her father had started, she was one of the first women novelists in India, one of the first woman nationalists, one of the first women editors, and yet when her husband died, she took on the role of the traditional Hindu widow, wearing white and maintaining a personal purdah. Her society, which was made up of the Indian elite and a few European residents in India, supported her in this conception of herself. In the 1913 introduction to *An Unfinished Song,* E. M. Lang, an English friend, credits her with qualities that do not suggest a consistent personality. She is applauded, on the one hand, for being "a forerunner, a type of the future woman of India, now that education is becoming general" and, on the other, for her unwillingness to emerge entirely "from the seclusion of the purdah" (6). He remarks, approvingly, that "Mrs. Ghosal, with all her progressive ideas, still preserves the dignified tranquillity of the purdah nashin lady; brilliant as she is in the eyes of her countrymen, flattered as she has been, she never asserts herself nor gives an opinion unasked . . ." (7). In Lang's representation of her, then, Swarnakumari's style emerges as the site of the coalescence of cultures. She is made to personify two different and, arguably, contradictory value systems. At one and the same time, she is the so-called traditional Hindu woman who is distinguishable from other women in the world by her dedication to her husband, dead or alive, as well as the new Indian woman who, following the example set by the women of the West, is able to win international acclaim for herself and her people. We hear in his approval of such a combination in an Indian woman both the Orientalist and liberal strains of imperialist discourse. The former valorizes her efforts to preserve her culture in her own person and the latter applauds her ability to transcend it.

Indian nationalist discourse has memorialized her in a similarly inconsistent way. At her death in 1932, *The Amrita Bazar Patrika,* an English-language newspaper, remembers her as "the pioneer of Bengali woman writers" who "rendered incalculable service to Bengali literature" (July 5), a statement which would seem to draw attention to the progressiveness of her writing. However, in another article two days later she is praised for being a conservative author: "She scorned to stir up the muddy waters of social life" (July 7). Years after her death, in a book entitled *Pioneer Women of India,* Padmini Sen Gupta carries on this rather contradictory construction of Swarnakumari Devi as both a writer and social reformer, way ahead of her time and her sex, and also as a model of the traditional Hindu woman. She states that Swarnakumari discarded the purdah early on in her marriage and thus became "one of the first Bengali ladies courageous enough to mix freely in society" (90) and finishes off the chapter with the observation that she was "the embodiment of the womanhood of Bengal" (93). The question obviously is, how does a woman become "the embodiment of the womanhood of Bengal" while at the same time representing the future ideal of her sex? A slippage has to occur in order for this contradiction to be maintained without the entire construction sliding into absurdity, a slippage between what it means to be traditional and what it means to be progressive in elite Indian society. Swarnakumari Devi lived her life and wrote her novel during a moment in Indian history when such a slippage was necessary for the high-caste Hindu woman to be able to project an image of herself into the future of her rapidly changing country.

Not only in her life but in most everything she wrote, this slippage is apparent. At the surface level of her fiction, Swarnakumari seems determined to uphold the image of the Hindu woman that, by the turn of the century, had come to be regarded as traditional.[11] The Hindu woman, Swarnakumari insists, is, in a world of women, unique and exceptional. She describes her in the preface to her short stories collection:

> a Hindu woman is a complete mystery to the foreigner, is she not? . . . Yet those who know her can realise how sweet and noble she is. . . . Her modesty and simplicity, her intense devotion to her husband and his people, her self-effacement and self-sacrifice, and her constant reliance on a Higher Power—all these rare virtues, as found in her, are too genuine to be imitated by women of other nations. (ii)

That this woman bears a remarkable resemblance to the Victorian angel in the house is not something upon which Swarnakumari chooses to comment. In the last statement quoted above she appears to assume that it is the Hindu ideal of womanhood that has been borrowed by other countries— not the other way around. Her claim to be the source of this traditional model of femininity, made on behalf of her Hindu culture and in a tone which refuses to be gainsaid, points to a tension beneath the surface of her writing. She must establish the Hindu woman as the most authentically traditional of all women because this issue has previously been a matter of some debate. Swarnakumari Devi is undoubtedly engaging in the cross-cultural conversation about Indian womanhood, in which Fuller, Billington, and Pandita Ramabai have also been involved. The fact that this conversation was conducted almost exclusively in English and that she began in 1913 to publish her fiction in English editions, after years of writing only in Bengali, would seem to point to her conscious participation in it. Moreover, her intent in writing about the Hindu woman is surely to rescue her from the discourse that renders her a degraded and deviant person, whose subjugation justifies the governing presence of the British in India.[12] Far from degraded and deviant, for Swarnakumari, the Hindu woman is the inspiration and the mainstay of her community and her nation.

In her work, this tension between the traditional and the progressive plays itself out in the psychology and life choices of her woman protagonists. My analysis will be confined to the character of Moni in *An Unfinished Song,* but I think a similar argument could be made about Shakti from *The Fatal Garland* and about some of the women who figure as the subjects in her short stories. I have chosen to focus on Moni because she is Swarnakumari's best representation of this confluence of apparently-opposing forces. Swarnakumari deliberately places Moni on the edge of historical change, in an age of social reform which is particularly concerned with the cause of women. Moni possesses an incredible drive to be self-reliant and an occasionally aggressive personality—these traits were encouraged by much late nineteenth-century reformist ideology—coupled with a conception of marriage that appears to circumscribe both these qualities. How this tension is treated constitutes the principal movement in Swarnakumari's novel.

From the beginning of *An Unfinished Song,* Moni, the first-person narrator, in order to establish her authenticity as a Hindu woman, calls on a discursive tradition which defines a Hindu female by her immense capacity for love and devotion. She spends the first few chapters documenting the course of her love, as it moves first from her father to a boy named Chotu, whom she meets while in grade school, and later to a cherished ideal of the husband she is certain one day she will have. After meeting Romanath, a friend of her sister and brother-in-law, who awakens in her a memory of the love she felt for the boy Chotu, she begins to entertain thoughts of loving him, knowing that this love will be the culmination of all the others. She explains to her readers why she is so preoccupied with the prospect of her marriage and her future husband. For a Hindu woman, she states, a husband "is the representation of the Divine on earth . . . the object of her worship." This supposition has been inculcated in the Hindu woman to such an extent over the centuries that "it has moulded her nature and is in itself enough to awaken her love and foster it" (45). Moni clearly sees herself as a representative Hindu woman. This is peculiar, since she is nineteen years of age before her family even considers arranging a marriage for her, a detail which, she suggests in the first chapter, makes her unusual. Consequently, she focuses her account of her life on the one trait that nineteenth-century rhetoric about the Hindu woman claims distinguishes her from all other women: her wifely devotion. Moni appears to subscribe wholeheartedly to this depiction and to identify with it unconditionally. However, there are indications in the text that this rhetoric is insufficient to describe the new kind of Hindu woman which the novel is concerned with delineating. It certainly does not go far enough for Moni herself.

What separates Moni from the Hindu women discussed in, for example, Pandita Ramabai's *The High-Caste Hindu Woman* or in Billington and Fuller's texts, is that she is not content for this devotion to be one-sided. She accepts that the wife having found her god in her husband, "surrenders herself in worship to him entirely," but she also demands that the husband live up to the same ideal of marriage that shapes his wife's conduct and belief system. Early on in the novel, she declares, "That man is blessed who, once installed in the shrine of a consecrated heart, dedicates himself to her and thus justifies the end of life" (16). Later, when she learns that Romanath has contracted an engagement of sorts with an English girl, she invokes this treasured and personal conviction to account for her failing interest in him. She is not satisfied, she asserts, to have her husband's love only in her present life. She must believe that she has had it in every past life and in every life to come:

That at any time his life should not have been entirely mine, that his affections should ever have belonged to another—I could not tolerate the idea. In this respect I expected of man what man expects of woman. As a man wants undivided devotion from the woman he marries, as she is not allowed ever to give a thought to any man but him, so did I want my husband's whole existence to be mine. (67)

This creed, which she hangs on to in the face of severe trials throughout the course of her story and which is finally justified at the end, constitutes Moni's rebellion against the Hindu patriarchy that dictates her behavior in marriage. It is an implicit rather than an explicit criticism of the system because Swarnakumari is concerned in this novel more with establishing a new image of Hindu womanhood than with condemning the old. Her loyalty is to Indian nationalism and to the nationalist method of social reform, which was very careful, especially when it came to agitation for women's rights, not to sound too much like the western missionaries. The nationalists during the last decade of the nineteenth century and the beginning of the twentieth had to tread a fine line between pursuing social reform piecemeal and largely ineffectively for the sake of their future political independence and openly denouncing certain aspects of their society and religion which might call their entire culture into question. Because of her commitment to the nationalist movement, Swarnakumari's critique of the system is of the subtlest variety.

Nevertheless, criticism of Indian patriarchy is present, though in a somewhat attenuated form in the novel. It seems to stem from fear, which she generally keeps to the edges of the text, but which haunts Moni throughout the recounting of her story. This is the fear of choosing or being forced to choose the wrong husband. The wrong husband is a man who is not worthy of a virtuous woman's love and is not capable of returning it. Romanath functions as the model of this figure. According to the Hindu society in the novel, he is an eligible bachelor because he is handsome, is of "good social standing" (109), and because he will be able to provide for Moni. His sole flaw is that prior to meeting Moni, he has had another relationship with an English woman who continues to believe she is engaged to him and waits in England for word from him concerning their marriage and her passage out to India. With the exception of Moni, however, the Hindu people that comprise the elite society depicted in the novel do not regard this previous attachment as a valid excuse for Moni's refusal to marry him. Moni's sister, in fact, tries to exonerate Romanath by pointing out the impropriety of a marriage between a Hindu man and an English woman. Further, both she and Romanath trivialize the English woman's feelings for him. But Moni identifies with her anguish and refuses to be her competitor for Romanath's love. She tells him, "I will not place myself as a barrier in the way of the girl who loves you" (75). Behind Moni's courage lies her deep horror that the Indian patriarchal system, which demands that she worship her husband for all of her life, will fail her if she marries Romanath. She knows that the system makes no provisions for the ignoble husband, the one who does not deserve a wife's devotion. It presupposes that all men deserve this.

This fear comes out in the novel through Moni's repeated attacks of anxiety, one of which requires medical attention, through her mental and emotional confusion, and through the nervous strain that plagues her as she struggles to accommodate her family's wishes without renouncing her own ideal of marriage. At one point, she describes the pressure to conform as a "great danger" and imagines herself "standing alone in the dark while sharp weapons were aimed at me from every direction" (177). Despite the enormity of her fear, however, Moni continually offers verbal support of the Hindu custom of arranged marriage. The closest she comes to questioning the custom openly occurs at that point in the text when she is unable to make her sister understand why she will not marry Romanath. In her sister's eyes, she says, she is wantonly throwing away a bright future. In her own eyes, she is living up to her most cherished values. Suddenly, the reader hears her frustration with a custom and a society that does not consider the potential for a woman's unhappiness in marriage:

> The one object of a maiden's life is matrimony; she must be given to a desirable bridegroom, that is the goal of her existence. If she finds a worthy man who professes to love and is willing to marry her, she must consider that her future is assured, she has all that can make life dear. A husband's love truly is sufficient to counter-balance all the miseries that life can bring, but when that love is wanting what will constitute a woman's life? (109)

There are no examples of bad marriages in *An Unfinished Song*. It is only a possibility that hovers unpleasantly at the rim of the story.

At the end of the novel, Moni is finally rescued from an unhappy alliance by a combination of forces—her own intuition which enables her to recognize her true love in the person of Binoy Kumar Chaudhury, her father who sweeps down on her sister's home in Calcutta to put an end to any marriage negotiations with Romanath, and fate which reveals that the bridegroom her father has chosen for her is actually Chaudhury. In the character of the father, Swarnakumari enlists the help of Indian patriarchy to ensure a happy ending for her protagonist. The father arrives in Calcutta angry that Moni's reputation has been damaged by her association with

Romanath and determined to set things right for his daughter. He tells Moni's older sister, "I will myself secure a bridegroom for her, one whom I can trust. I want no more of your English courtships" (179). Unknown to Moni, her father has already arranged her betrothal. Moni initially protests, refusing to marry any man because she believes that she has given her heart to someone she cannot have. But her father dismisses her feelings, sounding every inch the patriarch when he states, "For both the temporal and spiritual well-being of woman marriage is the best road ... be prepared to receive your husband with a joyful heart" (190–91). Swarnakumari Devi is playing India against England here. By having the father, the representative of Indian patriarchy in the novel, demarcate Moni's first alliance as "English," she associates Romanath's deceit and the confusion it produces with England, thereby projecting onto the colonizers the undesirable aspects of courtship. The Indian custom of arranging marriages through the father is therefore freed of all negative connotations, since these connotations are depicted as one consequence of the English imperialist invasion of Hindu culture. The father's intervention, which, through a twist of fate, brings about the successful conclusion to her search for her ideal mate, thus effectively establishes the ascendency of Indian patriarchy at the close of the story. But Swarnakumari Devi manages to demonstrate the superiority of the traditional Indian marriage system over a marriage the wife chooses only by suppressing the elements in the text that have previously called that system into question. The balance between the traditional and the modern, which Swarnakumari tried to maintain in her fiction and in her life, breaks down at this point, and the traditional is permitted to hold sway at the cost of the modern.

Swarnakumari's answer to the problem of how a Hindu woman can retain her traditional customs and values without giving up her desire for self-reliance and liberty is figured through the character of Chaudhury, the embodiment of Moni's ideal. He functions as her ideal in the novel because he combines adherence to Hindu tradition with a respect for certain facets of the English conception of womanhood. For instance, he appreciates the "genius" (126) of George Eliot, daring to compare her to Shakespeare, though this elicits a charge of "blasphemy" (127) from Moni's brother-in-law. He also enthusiastically admires the "liberty and self-reliance" of English women. He describes them for the benefit of Moni and her sister who, unlike him, have never been to England and who have had little opportunity of observing English women in India:

> Day by day their sphere of activity expands until they have begun to invade the realms of politics. . . . It is impossible for us to realise here what influence those women exercise on their country and on the individual, and how beneficent that influence is. Our life seems purposeless compared with it. (141)

In Chaudhury's estimation, English women provide an example for anyone in India, male or female, who wants to change his or her society. As the wife of a man who admires independent and politically active women and who is able to recognize and pay tribute to genius in a woman, Moni can look forward to a future in which she is allowed to pursue these virtues in her own personality. Furthermore, Swarnakumari ensures that Moni's ideals in marriage will be fulfilled as well, for Moni has found a husband whose devotion to her will equal her devotion to him, and as a result she will be able to worship him as the Hindu tradition demands.

The resistance to colonialism in *An Unfinished Song* lies in Chaudhury's role as the husband of Moni and in his idealization of those qualities which he designates as belonging to English women. Swarnakumari Devi borrows from the West in an attempt to realize her utopian vision of the future for Hindu women. In this future she envisions an Indian woman who is able to combine in her person the traditionalism which the Hindu culture expects of her with the self-reliance associated with English notions of femininity. Recalling Nandy's assertion that in India the "true 'enemy' of the thesis is seen to be in the synthesis because it includes the thesis and ends the latter's reason for being" (99), we can begin to comprehend Swarnakumari Devi's method of resistance. It draws from the culture of the West only that which will advance Hindu womanhood generally and that which can be incorporated into the psychology of the Hindu woman without entirely altering her cultural priorities. Significantly, it does not relinquish what Swarnakumari believes is the distinguishing feature of the Hindu woman, her marriage ideal and her dedication to her husband. Indian patriarchy, she further suggests, must learn to accommodate this new image of the Hindu woman, a woman who is both traditional and progressive but who is nevertheless authentically Indian. Yet nowhere in the novel does she advocate the overthrow of the patriarchal system altogether. In *An Unfinished Song,* Swarnakumari ultimately constructs a resistance to western colonialism which is at the same time supportive of Indian patriarchy.

For Swarnakumari Devi and Pandita Ramabai—Indian women writing within the confines of imperialism and patriarchy—it comes down to a precarious balancing act, as they strive to maintain some measure of allegiance to their indigenous systems, while continuing to criticize those aspects of their social and cultural situations that they have found intolerable. In my efforts to find a better place for these women among writers of the colonial period, I have done my own balancing act. I have steered a course between Spivak's and Nandy's theories, neither wanting to renounce these critics, who have worked hard to dismantle the abiding effect of imperialism, nor entirely wanting to support them. It is true that the Pandita and Swarnakumari are "self-consolidating Others," as Spivak would suspect. The norms in both of their texts tend to be western, and both authors are frequently forced to adopt defensive postures in their confrontations with the West. Earlier, I suggested that this term, "self-consolidating Other," is a masculine delineation, but it can be altered to accommodate the distinct experience of Indian elite women writing during the colonial period. Still, we must recognize that, as Others, Indian women had to consolidate two selves, the self constructed by British imperialism and the self engendered by Indian patriarchy. This makes their writing much more complicated than writing by Indian men under colonialism and much more dangerous. They should correspondingly be that much more difficult for critics to dismiss.

5

Gandhi, Ambedkar, and *Untouchable*

Of all the issues that came to the forefront during the Indian nationalist movement, untouchability was seemingly the least contentious. For with the exception of a small group of orthodox Hindus, everyone who spoke publicly on the subject appeared to be on the same side. And that side believed in the necessity of change. By the 1930s and 40s, politicized Indians had come to view the age-old practice of untouchability as a stain, tarnishing the increasingly favorable reputation of India. It was identified as archaic, backward, and hardly conducive to the cause of nationalism, especially in a country claiming the inalienable rights promised by democracy. This growing and highly publicized desire on the part of many Indians to put an end to untouchability led to a situation in which change began to seem imminent. Indian and English language newspapers, for example, were full of accounts of temples being thrown open to outcastes, of fasts undertaken for their sake, and of speeches delivered for the express purpose of heightening public awareness about the evils of the custom. Factions as diverse as the Congress, the communists, men's and women's associations dedicated to social reform, and some untouchables themselves believed that its eradication was under way. Yet in spite of the apparent straightforwardness of their expectations, untouchability proved to be a more complicated issue than originally imagined. It was, moreover, anything but a simple issue in its evolution as a national cause.

The problem with the construction of untouchability at this moment in Indian history was that in most nationalist and imperialist discourse, and certainly in that which received international attention, untouchables were invisible. Their discursive representation was almost entirely in the hands of the elite. Thus we see and hear untouchables created by non-untouchable writers—Gandhi's reconstitution of untouchables as "harijan" or "children of God," for instance—but rarely do we see them from their own points of view and hear their own voices.[1] Granting that their voices are inevitably mediated by nationalist rhetoric, by the circumstances of imperialism, or by western expectations, we must, nevertheless, be struck by the fact that untouchables do not seem to speak in pre-independence Indian texts except through the lips of their self-appointed saviors. Unlike high-caste Hindu women, who, as we saw in the previous chapter, were vocal participants in a debate about themselves, untouchables remained virtually silent in the public narratives about them, as more privileged Indians and westerners took over their representation in the interests of nationalist and/or imperialist agendas. In elite constructions of untouchables, therefore, we can trace the dominant politics of the time.

I say "virtually silent" because, of course, there were untouchables writing and speaking about untouchability prior to 1947. One of the most famous of them, Bhimrao Ramji Ambedkar, figures prominently in this chapter. But their own accounts of the historical situation in the thirties and forties are, even today, often ignored or co-opted by the cause of Congress nationalism in historiography concerned with the nationalist movement of the Gandhian era. Bipan Chandra's history of the Indian independence struggle offers us a prime example of such treatment. In his brief discussion of the politics of the untouchability movement in the early 1930s, he skims over the Round Table Conference, an event which some historians have interpreted as the emergence of India's untouchables and the issue of untouchability into the broader political arena of nationalism. The Round Table Conference was a meeting place for various Indian interest groups and was designed by the British government in an attempt to gather opinion for the purpose of framing a new constitution for India. Delegates from these groups, such as the Muslims, women, the princes, and the untouchables, were invited to London by the government to participate in the creation of the constitution. Bipan Chandra dismisses the Conference and its non-Congress delegates with the following observation:

Apart from a few able individuals, the overwhelming majority of Indian delegates to the Round Table Conference (RTC), hand-picked by the Government, were loyalists, communalists, careerists, and place-hunters, big landlords and representatives of the princes. They were used by the Government to claim that the Congress did not represent the interests of all Indians vis-a-vis imperialism, and to neutralize Gandhiji and all his efforts to confront the imperialist rulers with the basic question of freedom. (285)

According to Bipan Chandra, British intentions in organizing the Conference were highly questionable. Their primary motive, he implies, was to create a number of communalist factions, which would then stand against Congress and slow the course of the nationalist movement. However, the picture we get of the Round Table Conference in the writings of Ambedkar, an untouchable leader chosen by the British to attend, is significantly different.

Ambedkar maintains that the Conference held great potential for the untouchables of India. It gave them, for the first time in Indian history, the right to determine their own future apart from the Hindu majority which, he says, had done little for the untouchables except to humiliate and persecute them. When Gandhi arrived at the second session of the Conference in 1931—Gandhi and the Congress had boycotted the 1930 session because of the government's refusal to promise that India would be granted Dominion Status, like Canada and Australia, in the near future—the debate over who was the proper untouchable delegate began. Ambedkar was outraged at Gandhi's insistence that only he, the Mahatma, could speak on their behalf, a right he claimed to have earned as a result of his experience living among the untouchables and his public identification with their plight. In a speech to the Conference, Ambedkar points out Gandhi's unfitness for the role. He argues that "Gandhism" can offer no hope to the untouchables because it does not represent a radical enough departure from the very institution, Hinduism, which is responsible for the oppression of its outcastes. Hinduism has created a "veritable chamber of horrors" for the untouchables (quoted in Dobbin 112) because the Hindu scriptures sanction and encourage their mistreatment. In light of this other side to the story, Bipan Chandra's assertion that the Conference was something of a decoy to draw attention away from the "basic question of freedom" shows a marked Congress bias, for it assumes that freedom from imperialism was a "basic" issue for every Indian. Far more "basic" and more immediately necessary, from the point of view of Ambedkar's untouchability, was freedom from Hindu and other elite dominance. His explanation to the Conference about the principal political interests of the untouchable communities makes this position clear:

> The Depressed Classes are not anxious, they are not clamorous, they have not started any movement for claiming that there shall be an immediate transfer of power from the British to the Indian people . . . but if the British Government is unable to resist the forces that have been set up in the country which do clamour for transference of political power—and we know the Depressed Classes in their present circumstances are not in a position to resist that—then our submission is that if you make that transfer, that transfer will be accompanied by such conditions and by such provisions that the power shall not fall into the hands of a clique, into the hands of an oligarchy, or into the hands of a group of people, whether Muhammadans or Hindus; but that the solution shall be such that the power shall be shared by all communities in their respective proportions." (*What Congress* 66)

This is an important statement, for it posits untouchability as a force outside of Indian nationalism and nationalist aspirations. Obviously, there was more to be said about untouchability than the simple declaration that it had to end. How it was to end, who was to bring about its demise, and who would profit in the process—these questions surrounded this issue throughout the thirties and forties in India.

Mulk Raj Anand's famous first novel *Untouchable,* published in 1935, deserves to be considered in the context of this moment in Indian history because, unlike other Indo-Anglian fiction from the thirties, it foregrounds these questions and investigates their possible answers. I would even go so far as to contend that his novel allows us to see what much Indian historiography chooses to elide—the immense complexity of untouchability as a political construct in pre-independence India and its distance from, rather than its affinity with, the Indian nationalist movement. On the pages of *Untouchable,* Gandhi's ideas are enacted and found wanting. Later, another more practical solution is offered in its stead. But this other solution has its own problems, of which the novel is not aware. Ultimately Anand is conditioned by the same historical shortsightedness that made Gandhi incapable of seeing the limits of his own stance in regards to the untouchables. Neither is able to imagine a world without themselves, the elite, to lead the despised and the downtrodden out of their subjugation.

The courage and tenacity with which Gandhi attacked untouchability has been well documented in the various historical narratives which have endeavored to analyze and remember the Indian nationalist movement. Suffice it to say that it was largely because of his persistence that the problem of untouchability in India became a serious nationalist issue in the first place and later one of the strongest planks in the Congress platform.[2] Gandhi insisted from the moment of his advent into Indian politics in 1915 that India's independence was dependent upon the erasure of the practice in Hindu society. Swaraj (self-government) and the abolition of untouchability were ontologically linked in his discourse, so much so that the one could not occur without the other. He constantly reminded Hindus that "being slave-holders themselves, they could not fight against their own slavery if they did not unconditionally liberate the untouchables," to quote Trilok Nath (225). Moreover, Gandhi's personal battle against untouchability was unprecedented at the time. He invited untouchables to live in his ashram, ate with them, worked with them at cleaning latrines, and demanded that anyone who wished to belong to his community should do the same. He even adopted an untouchable daughter. All of these actions placed him at odds with the orthodox Hindu population who constituted his principal financial supporters. Although untouchability was not outlawed in India until months after Gandhi's assassination in 1948, there is no doubt that he was instrumental in bringing about this achievement. Gandhi's greatest success on behalf of the untouchable people, however, was not in legal terms, since such solutions were hardly his forte. It was that he managed to convince the devoutly Hindu population that untouchability, once thought to have been ordained by God, was an ethically wrong and socially backward custom, which had to be eradicated for the good of the nation and the religion. It is debatable whether anyone else in India in Gandhi's time would have been able to accomplish this feat.

Still, Gandhi's approach to untouchability was characterized by a distinct tone of territoriality. He claimed the right to champion the cause of the untouchables as his and his alone. In a statement made to the press in 1932, he justifies his appropriation of the issue: "The 'depressed' classes question being predominantly a religious matter, I regard it as specially my own by reason of my life-long concentration on it. It is a sacred personal trust which I may not shirk" (*Select Writings* 293–94). Gandhi's reaction to the government's proposal of separate electorates for the untouchables, a decision based on the findings of the Round Table Conference, perhaps evolved from his tendency to identify so personally with the problem.

The government announced in August 1932 that it would allot separate electorates to the untouchables in its soon-to-be-compiled Indian constitution. This meant that untouchables would be able to vote for their own candidates in their own, exclusive constituency as well as with the general Hindu electorate. The government intended that this double vote be a stopgap measure, which would come to an end after twenty years, or earlier through the general process of electoral revision. Gandhi opposed the idea of separate electorates for the untouchables on the grounds that such a system would "ensure them bondage in perpetuity" (quoted in Ambedkar *What Congress* 71). Untouchables, he insists, should not be considered a distinct community, apart from the Hindu majority: "my intimate acquaintance with every shade of untouchability convinces me that their lives, such as they are, are so intimately mixed with those of the caste Hindus in whose midst and for whom they live, that it is impossible to separate them. They are part of an indivisible family . . ." (*Select Writings* 293). Gandhi was confident that untouchables wanted to remain members of this great Hindu family, in spite of their traditional position of disadvantage in it.

Not merely for the sake of the untouchables, however, did Gandhi set himself against the government's proposal. He also saw separate electorates as a threat to Hinduism generally. If implemented, they would form the untouchables into a class which would then function as "a standing and living reproach to Hinduism" (*Select Writings* 291). Such a possibility was, to him, intolerable. All of Gandhi's writings indicate that he was determined to see Hinduism survive the independence struggle. Consequently, on certain issues that he deemed religious—the role of women, untouchability, and the structure of Hindu society—his judgment was conservative; in these areas he would not encourage radical change. Yet despite this conservatism, the Hinduism he envisioned for the future of India was a reformed religion, from which the "sin of untouchability" had been purged. Exactly who was responsible for purging Hinduism of its sin was the crux of his position.

He believed that caste Hindus should carry out the task of eradicating untouchability. It was for them, and not the untouchables themselves, to "atone" (298) for the custom that, according to Gandhi, constituted "the greatest blot on Hinduism" (295). In his Christianized construction of the situation, then, caste Hindus dedicated to the cause of untouchability were engaged in a kind of "penance" (298). The sin being theirs, the repentance and reparation had also to come from them. Gandhi's harijan campaign involved the untouchables to some degree but primarily in a passive manner. They were to be educated, taught to improve their personal hygiene, and encouraged to stop eating carrion. But they were not expected to break caste taboos, go on strike, fast, or participate in any other form of protest against untouchability. The honored role of the *satyagrahi* or truth fighter was reserved for caste Hindus, since it was they who had benefited from the practice of untouchability and had propagated it.[3] Thus, the struggle to end their own oppression was taken out of the hands of the untouchable people by means of Gandhi's rhetoric of atonement. The untouchables were asked to remain nonresistant at the very moment when their resistance might have effected profound change within Hindu society. Undoubtedly, it could be argued that Gandhi's approach to untouchability was not merely the product of his humanitarian feeling for a subjugated people. It was certainly this, but it also served as a control. Gandhi's solution kept the untouchables from securing their own freedom in ways that would have been unacceptable to him—with violence or under the rubric of some nationalist organization other than the Congress.

Gandhi's puzzling attitude about the responsibility for the amelioration of the untouchable condition has prompted a few scholars—the few who have actually investigated the issue of untouchability from some perspective other than that of the Congress—to question his motives. Trilok Nath states,

> None had been more courageous in the demand for removal of untouchability from Hindu society. None had been more energetic in personal efforts for relief. But his demand that Depressed Classes should rely on

the Congress rather than seek for uplift through their own efforts was beyond comprehension. It was against all political experience and his own sound doctrine that progress could come only through personal efforts. (134)

Although Trilok Nath's book exhibits some of the same problems in representation present in more traditional nationalist histories—namely, the tendency to construct untouchables as if their essences were somehow recoverable solely through their leaders—he nevertheless provides us with an unusual account of the pre-1947 untouchable movement, an account which stresses the significance of the politics practiced by untouchables themselves. Gandhi is seen in relation to Ambedkar and to the other Indian politicians who claimed the support of various communities of untouchable people. Regarding the issue of untouchability, Gandhi's ideas in particular seem strange to Trilok Nath because they contradict much of what he had come to symbolize. From the beginning of his career in politics, he had emphasized the need for all Indians to earn their own freedom by participating in non-violent struggles which were designed to reveal to the oppressor his complicity in an immoral system and to the oppressed his inner strength. Thus, swaraj to Gandhi did not simply mean the achievement of independence, as it did for many less farsighted politicians. It meant the achievement of independence in a way that elevated the moral and spiritual character of the protestors. Gandhi was able to galvanize a huge segment of the people of India in his national movement for swaraj in part because he offered them the opportunity to overthrow imperialism and to effect their own spiritual transformation in the process. It was the means that was all-important in Gandhian thought.

In view of his overall program, Gandhi's attitude toward the abolition of untouchability seems at best confused and at worst morally objectionable. For it raises the suspicion that in asking the untouchables to refrain from practicing the kind of spiritual and political action he generally advocated, Gandhi was at least as concerned with maintaining Congress control as with defending the interests of the untouchables. Untouchability could remain exclusively a Congress issue only if the untouchables themselves stepped back and allowed Congress politicians to fight for them. Otherwise—if, for example, the untouchables insisted on engaging in the battle without the leadership of Congress (which is exactly what many untouchable groups did)—the Congress's claim to represent this huge population of Indian people would be called into question along with Congress's status as an all-India nationalist organization. Congress authority and influence would thus be enormously eroded.

Gandhi's notion of caste Hindus doing penance also looked forward only to the elimination of untouchability from the Hindu social structure. It did not promote or point to the eventual sharing of political power by the untouchable people. In none of his writings does Gandhi imagine an India in which untouchables hold at least some of the positions of power. On the contrary, untouchables are expected to continue the pursuit of their various ancestral callings, sweeping streets, cleaning latrines, making shoes, working in agriculture, etc. They are not depicted sitting on committees, occupying government positions, or making political decisions that might affect the entire nation. Such undertakings are the province of the upper castes. Gandhi firmly believed in the *varnavyavastha* or system of inherited vocations, according to which a man was duty-bound to do the same job as his father and forefathers. In an independent India, therefore, untouchables would fulfill their traditional roles, but they would no longer be valued less than the Brahmin, Kshatriya, Vaisya or Shudra castes.

This insistence on the retention of the *varnavyavastha* hampered the potentially revolutionary transformation that might have been introduced into Hindu society through the abandonment of untouchability. It produced a dissonance in Gandhi's politics, which left him wide open to attack from all those who sought more systemic change. Gandhi rejected untouchability as anathema to Hinduism, but he countenanced the *varna* structure from which the notion of the *avarna* or outcaste originated. He did not, however, condone the hierarchizing of professions, which he believed was the fault of the caste system. Caste and *varna* were different in his eyes and even incompatible, at least in his later writings. While he considered the custom of observing caste as "harmful both to spiritual and national growth" (quoted in Ambedkar *Writings and Speeches* 83), the institution of *varna* was, for him, a method of social rejuvenation.

The problem with Gandhi's convictions about the *varnavyavastha* was that the oppression of the untouchables had everything to do with their ancestral vocations. Because untouchables were sweepers who cleaned up the excrement of others or leather makers who worked with the skins of dead animals or workers engaged in some other profession regarded as 'unclean' by caste Hindus, physical contact with them was prohibited by certain Hindu scriptures and customs: hence the name untouchable. It was thought that the touch of these people transmitted their 'impurity' to others. Gandhi worked to rid the untouchable professions of their so-called impurity by insisting that the law of *varna* was a democratic one in which all occupations were of equal value. At the same time, however, he expected untouchables to abstain from eating carrion and to improve their personal hygiene, in other words, to behave in a manner that would make them more acceptable to caste Hindus. The two ideas contradict one another. If all jobs are equal, and therefore equally pure or impure, then one's eating habits and hygiene are irrelevant, since they cannot affect the purity or impurity of one's profession. But what Gandhi was suggesting by enjoining the untouchables to lead a 'cleaner' life was that the popular belief in their defilement, as a result of their work, had some basis in truth. He was, in effect, reinforcing the negative stereotypes of the untouchable by articulating the old upper-caste prejudices about them. As Barbara R. Joshi has observed, "Gandhi's comments on the subject, like those of several other higher caste reformers of the period, are simultaneously practical and myopically patronizing" (44). Clearly, there were other beliefs involved in the practice of untouchability—beliefs concerning notions of pollution, sanitation, and even karma—which Gandhi's arguments do not take into account. His construction of untouchability, then, stops short of being radical because it does not extend far enough into the religious system that gave birth to the concept of the outcaste.

In the thirties, Gandhi's critics generally found fault with his affirmation of *varna*. Shri Sant Ramji, a member of the Jat-Pat-Todak Mandel, which was an organization of caste Hindus dedicated to the abolition of caste, urged Gandhi in 1936 to renounce his belief in the *varnavyavastha* because it was likely to cause more harm than good. He writes, "Hindus are slaves to caste and do not want to destroy it. So when you advocate your ideal of imaginary *varnavyavastha* they find justification for clinging to caste" (quoted in Ambedkar *Writings* 84). Some untouchable leaders were a little more caustic in their criticism. The Mahars of western India, for instance, believed that Gandhi's civil disobedience movement of 1930, because it concentrated solely on the issue of independence, relegated the more important question of temple entry for untouchables to the sidelines. In consequence, the Mahars announced that they had decided to establish the "Indian National Anti-Revolutionary Army" in opposition to Gandhi, whom they refer to as the "Dictator of the Indian National Congress." Their 1930 statement reveals not only their disillusionment with Gandhian and Congress politics but their determination that such politics be opposed even at the cost of swaraj. In their delineation of the project of the Anti-Revolutionary Army, they state that the "Party will regard British rule as absolutely necessary until the complete removal of untouchability and the overthrow of 'Chaturvarna' [the four-*varna* system]" (quoted in Rudolph, n. 142). For many untouchables, then, Gandhi's commitment to the doctrine of *varna* precluded their commitment to Gandhi.

Ambedkar shared the Mahars' doubt concerning the Mahatma. (He was, in fact, a Mahar himself and was instrumental in politicizing his community.) He argues that his distinction between caste and *varna* is fallacious. In Gandhian ideology, he states, *varna* is caste in disguise (see *Writings* 92). Moreover, Ambedkar maintains that Gandhi's refusal to repudiate *varna* was not, as some believed, an attempt to recapture the meaning of an ancient Hindu institution. Gandhi was simply playing politics. The weaknesses in his argument concerning *varna* and caste arise from

> the double role which the Mahatma wants to play—of a Mahatma and a Politician. As a Mahatma he may be trying to spiritualize Politics. Whether he has succeeded in it or not Politics have certainly commercialized him. . . . The reason why the Mahatma is always supporting caste and *varna* is because he is afraid that if he opposed them he will lose his place in politics. (*Writings* 93)

In Ambedkar's assessment, then, the moral and spiritual obligations implicit in Gandhi's status as Mahatma, or great soul, gave way to his need and desire to retain power as a nationalist politician at a crucial time in India's history. Ambedkar suggests as well that Gandhi's ideas about untouchability were to some extent dictated and encumbered by his adherence to the nationalist/Congress objective of ousting the British.

Ambedkar was Gandhi's angriest, loudest, and most forceful opponent on the issue of untouchability. His 1946 book *What Congress and Gandhi*

Have Done to the Untouchables is a testament to the rage and helplessness he felt as an untouchable leader in the thirties and forties, whose position, political stance, and opinions were constantly undermined by Congress nationalism. The book documents the course of events and the decisions made concerning the outcastes of India in the twenty-five years or so since Congress and Gandhi took on untouchability as part of their agenda. Ambedkar does not depict the Indian National Congress in a favorable light. But his importance as a contemporary critic of Gandhi and the Congress increases when we consider that he was one of the few Indians active in the politics of the time who dared to offer a consistent and thoughtful critique of this central nationalist organization and its powerful leaders.[4]

Because he was involved in the making of it, Ambedkar was a strong supporter of the government's 1932 communal award, in which untouchables were granted separate electorates. He believed that the political severance of the 'Depressed Classes' from the rest of the Hindu community was supremely necessary if these classes were to escape their subjugation in either a colonial or an independent India. One of the assumptions of Ambedkar's book is that the desires of the untouchables and the Congress, which, according to him, comprised mostly the Hindu elite, were not, in fact, coincident. Any merging of the two groups, would, he was convinced, result in the absorption of the untouchable issue into the Congress platform and the continued suppression of his community. For Ambedkar, the untouchables would gain politically only by constant vigilance against just such an occurrence. At the 1930 Nagpur Conference of Depressed Classes, he told his audience of untouchables, "Nobody can remove your grievances as well as you can and you cannot remove them unless you get political power in your hands" (quoted in Trilok Nath 255). The primary aim of his career was to secure power for his community, so that they would not have to continue to depend on caste Hindus for their livelihoods. His advice to untouchables was that they could not afford to allow their cause to be excluded from the realm of the political, which is what he believed Gandhi did by deeming untouchability a religious issue, nor should they get caught up in the nationalist drive to achieve independence. Skepticism permeates Ambedkar's book, skepticism about Congress and Gandhi and their nationalist enthusiasm for a free India, purchased perhaps at the expense of the untouchables.

His tone of skepticism is even stronger in a speech he wrote but did not deliver to the Jat-Pat-Todak Mandel. The speech, entitled "Annihilation of Caste," was rejected by the Mandel because its views were not considered acceptable to the strongly Hindu organization, in spite of the fact that this organization was dedicated to the abolition of the caste system. He nevertheless published it in 1936, and because of its popularity, republished it in 1937 and 1944. In this speech Ambedkar delineates his objections concerning caste and the untouchables. The Hindus, he asserts, are not "fit for political power" (*Writings* 41) so long as they continue to oppress a large class of their countrymen, not permitting them the use of public wells, of public schools, of public roads, not permitting them even to eat and dress in a manner they themselves have chosen. He recounts one incident after another in which caste Hindus beat or ostracized untouchables for not following the rules set out for them by Hindu custom or scripture. Caste, and not just untouchability, should be destroyed, Ambedkar states, and this must be accomplished *before* India achieves swaraj because a nation built on the foundations of caste and untouchability "will crack and never be whole" (66). Contrary to what Bipan Chandra and other historians of nationalism regard as the "basic question of freedom," freedom from imperialism being intended by such a statement, Ambedkar is clearly relegating the goal of India's independence from British imperial power to the edges. The problems of untouchability and caste take precedence over swaraj and must be addressed first, despite the difficulty in tackling such deeply ingrained and fervently defended customs:

> In the fight for Swaraj you fight with the whole nation on your side. In this, you have to fight against the whole nation and that too, your own. But it is more important than Swaraj. There is no use having Swaraj, if you cannot defend it. More important than the question of defending Swaraj is the question of defending the Hindus under the Swaraj. In my opinion it is only when the Hindu Society becomes a casteless society that it can have strength enough to defend itself. Without such internal strength, Swaraj for Hindus may turn out to be only a step towards slavery. (80)

It was to avoid the inscribing of caste thinking into the new India, which Ambedkar knew would eventually replace the colonized country in which he was presently speaking, that he was so adamant about the eradication of caste and untouchability. His charge against Gandhi and the Congress is that they were not adamant enough. By privileging the ideal of swaraj to such a degree that all other issues took a back seat, Congress nationalists such as Gandhi ran the risk of transplanting the elitist structures of Hinduism into a politically independent India, a possibility which, to Ambedkar, would be even more dangerous than the imperialism that was currently in place. As a victim of Hindu elitism, Ambedkar was prepared to support a continued imperialism rather than encourage the pursuit of a swaraj which would preserve the status quo.

Ambedkar went further in his appraisal and condemnation of Hinduism than any other Hindu critic of Gandhi and Congress nationalism.[5] His recommendation to the members of the Jat-Pat-Todak Mandel at the conclusion of his speech is that they discard Hinduism altogether. For, in Ambedkar's estimation, it is Hinduism that is ultimately responsible for the most serious problems of the country. He argues that Hindus do not observe caste and propagate untouchability because they are cruel or inhuman; they observe caste and propagate untouchability because they are religious. Speaking to the Hindu audience for which his speech was originally intended, he declares,

> Reformers working for the removal of untouchability including Mahatma Gandhi, do not seem to realize that the acts of the people are merely the results of their beliefs inculcated upon their minds by the *Shastras* [Hindu scriptures] and the people will not change their conduct until they cease to believe in the sanctity of the *Shastras* on which their conduct is founded. . . . You must have the courage to tell the Hindus, that what is wrong with them is their religion. . . . (68–69)

However, Ambedkar does not believe that the destruction of Hinduism or even of the caste system is possible in the 1930s social and political climate from which he is speaking; and his reasoning here is, strangely enough, elitist in its assumptions. He contends that "the entire destiny of a country depends upon its intellectual class" (71). Since Brahmins largely comprise that intellectual class in India, and since Brahmins are the traditional purveyors of Hinduism and the principal benefactors of the caste system, he cannot imagine them putting aside their own interests in order either entirely to denounce Hinduism or to reform it so as to produce a more egalitarian structure, one in which caste and untouchability have no place and Brahmins have no special status. But Ambedkar's pessimism here confounds his argument, for it is rooted in the presupposition that elite populations, such as an "intellectual class," are a nation's sole source of change. If this were the case, then untouchables could not hope to effect their own transformation and the subsequent alteration of their social and political system, unless they were to get access to that intellectual class. Ambedkar himself had, of course, done exactly this. Although born into an untouchable family, he received an M.A. and Ph.D. from Columbia University in New York and a D.Sc. from London University. The vast majority of untouchables in the 1930s and 40s, however, were uneducated at even the most basic levels. Because of the caste restrictions, they were frequently not permitted to attend school with other Hindus. For Ambedkar, an untouchable with connections to that "intellectual class," to suggest that change can only proceed from this area of the population is to deny that uneducated untouchables have any real power. Even in Ambedkar's construction, then, untouchables seem doomed to the status of followers. They must rely on an educated community member, like Ambedkar himself, to end their subjection.

Into the midst of this discourse on untouchability came Anand's *Untouchable*. It is often regarded by critics as a pivotal work in Indo-Anglian literature because it introduced a new politicized tone into a tradition that had, until this point, been occupied with mystical, spiritual, and domestic matters. Generally, critics who celebrate the revolutionary quality of Anand's *Untouchable* tend to assume that mystical, spiritual, and domestic matters are not also political. I think they are and would hope that my reading of Swarnakumari Devi's *An Unfinished Song,* in the previous chapter, has demonstrated this. While I would acknowledge that Anand's first novel introduced something into the Anglo-Indian literary tradition which had not hitherto been present, I would hesitate to identify this something as politics. I am more inclined to see Anand as changing the focus somewhat. In accordance with the increased attention paid to the lower castes or classes in the nationalist/imperialist arena of the 1920s, 30s, and 40s, Anand has adopted the poor and the socially depressed as his protagonists. Undoubtedly, this choice represents a shift in the tradition, since middle- and upper-class protagonists tended to be the norm prior to the publication of *Untouchable* in 1935.

Yet there is no question that Anand's novel is overtly, even enthusiastically political. Gandhi actually appears as a character in the story, and the novel walks a path between Gandhi's and Ambedkar's perspectives on untouchability. Though Anand is not himself an untouchable, his text takes on the cause of the outcaste, as Gandhi did, and shares with Gandhian thought a belief in the necessity of trusteeship. Consequently, a distinct sense of the helplessness of untouchables in the face of frequently overwhelming persecution pervades the novel in much the same way that it is present in Gandhi's writings. However, another voice interrogates this political stance, finding it desperately inadequate and even harmful to the untouchable community. This voice is not located in any one character or in the narrator, nor can it be unproblematically identified as belonging to Ambedkar, but it replicates his insistence that, in the pre-independence field of Indian politics, emphasis needed to be shifted from the confrontation between Indian nationalism and British imperialism to the situation of the poor and the outcaste in a country that empowers only its elites.

Asha Kaushik, a literary scholar and political scientist, observes that the portrayal of all of Anand's characters—Bakha the untouchable included—is "rooted in radical consciousness" (146). While I fundamentally agree with Kaushik's statement and with her optimistic reading of *Untouchable*, I am more inclined to see the novel as an invention very much of its time and therefore subject to the same historical limitations that beset the work of Gandhi and Ambedkar. *Untouchable* is a novel that promotes elite leadership. Its "radical consciousness" must be investigated within the frame of that picture.

Kaushik is convinced of the political efficacy of the Indo-Anglian novel. In her interdisciplinary analysis of the prevalent "politico-aesthetic vision" found in Indo-Anglian writing, she contends that Indian novelists advance the politics of their day by imagining a future or even a present which is an improvement of the past:

> By virtue of artistic mediation and selection, the creative writers . . . move ahead of the prevailing socio-political assumptions in quest of innovative consciousness, which may ultimately prove to be of lasting relevance. At that level of creative realization, politico-aesthetic vision

is, indeed, capable of paving the way for an active, protesting and liberating role of political imagination in society. (152)

Anand's *Untouchable* is one of many novels that, in Kaushik's view, actually produced a change in the Indian political and intellectual climate by remaining one step ahead of it. But by identifying this tendency—she calls it "innovative consciousness"—in the English fiction of Indian writers, Kaushik is herself taping into a Indo-Anglian convention, which began around the time of Anand's first novel. According to this literary convention, novels offer a particularly fertile ground for political ideas, fertile because what is initially only envisioned on paper is capable of being translated into reality. Many Indo-Anglian novelists clearly see themselves as politicians of sorts and their novels as harbingers of change. Anand is perhaps the best known and most outspoken of these writers. I would further suggest that it is his determination to engage the dominant politics of his times coupled with this legacy of the nationalist movement, which defines Indo-Anglian literature as a political (read "nationalist") tradition, that has contributed to the continued canonization of Anand's *Untouchable*. As Aijaz Ahmad writes in his book *In Theory,* "The subordinating or even foreclosing of certain kinds of questions, the foregrounding of others, is the essential canonizing gesture" (124).

In an article entitled, "The Sources of Protest in my Novels," Anand describes his stories as "new myths," which are meant to replace the old myths of the Hindu epics and puranas. Bakha and Sohini of *Untouchable* displace Sita and Rama of the *Ramayana,* and in this manner Indian culture is renewed. That Indian culture is capable of renewal, Anand has no doubt. "Renaissance," he declares, "is the cue for all human passion, the freedom to grow, ever, to higher consciousness" (31). Nor does he question his role as novelist and hence creator of change. For him, the novel and the novelist are inevitably driven to correct the errors of previous generations: "The novel is for the word's continuance. It is urged to express itself in uneasy syntax, in dim perspectives, and from the urges of those, who seek to break the shackles of serfdom imposed by the past. . . . The protest novel is the source of renewal of the human person" (33). Anand, it seems, wrote *Untouchable* confident that it would effect transformation in his society.

But what kind of transformation is he advocating in the novel? Certainly Bakha is a protagonist desperate for change. Unlike his father, who has learned after years of suffering in Hindu society, to accept things as they are, Bakha finds the mistreatment accorded him by Hindu custom and doctrine barely tolerable. Still, he tolerates it. Throughout the novel Bakha endures one incident of oppression after another, and although his reaction is initially outrage mixed with a desire for revenge, he eventually adopts the submissive demeanor expected of him and ends up affirming the very values and customs that demand his subservience. For instance, the central event of the novel occurs when Bakha accidentally touches a caste Hindu. The man insults him, calls together the nearby caste Hindus to witness Bakha's humiliation, and then slaps Bakha's face. In the course of this event, a particularly powerful one in the novel, Bakha moves from polite regret to anger and then to something like despair. Finally, he comes to a full recognition of his position as an untouchable in a touchable community. He clearly sees himself as the oppressed and the high caste man who slapped him as the oppressor—and more important, as morally wrong. Instead of repudiating the custom that requires his servility, however, he begins to identify with it: " 'I am an Untouchable!' he said to himself, 'an Untouchable!' . . . Then, aware of his position, he began to shout aloud the warning word, to announce his approach: 'Posh, posh, sweeper coming' " (59). Bakha does here what every 'good' untouchable is expected to do—he calls out the name of his profession, thereby warding off caste Hindus and affirming his status as an outcaste.

The pattern of Bakha's reaction to humiliation, in which rage invariably gives way to resignation and weakness, is worth noting and investigating simply because it is so prevalent in the novel. When his sister, Sohini, is sexually assaulted by a Brahmin priest, Bakha repeats the pattern once again. For this event, the narrator articulates the moment:

> A superb specimen of humanity he seemed whenever he made the high resolve to say something, to go and do something, his fine form rising like a tiger at bay. And yet there was a futility written on his face. He could not overstep the barriers which the conventions of his superiors had built up to protect their weakness against him. . . . So, in the highest moment of his strength, the slave in him asserted itself and he lapsed back, wild with torture, biting his lips, ruminating his grievances. (73)

Throughout the text the narrator constantly curtails Bakha's physical, mental, and emotional power. Hence he is depicted as someone who is capable of great strength and potency but prone to weakness because of heredity (he is said to possess a "spirit of resignation which he had inherited through the long centuries" [74]), inability ("He could not reach out from the narrow confines of his soul to his yearnings" [105]), and fear ("But he couldn't do anything. . . . He was deliberately trying to hide his stature in his stoop, as if he were afraid of being seen at all" [110]). Furthermore, Bakha's powerlessness is represented as a condition of untouchability in general. The numerous illustrations of the outcastes' colony in the novel confirm this overall image of communal emasculation. The narrator at one point describes the untouchables moving out of their huts and into the morning sunshine. Such activity, though daily and habitual, is for these people an "act of liberation," and yet their liberation is attenuated by the narrator's insistence on seeing them as inevitably, even inescapably, restricted. He tells us, "The taint of the little prison cells of their one-roomed homes lurked in them, even in the outdoor air" (40). Bakha, like his neighbors in the outcastes' colony, is bound by his untouchability, and Anand's narrator seems determined to keep him that way.

Kaushik would undoubtedly disagree with this reading. She maintains that Anand purposely does not represent Bakha as a "pioneer of violent protest" because of his authorial dedication to the dictates of realism: "He realizes the futility of such an alternative in view of the organized power of the high castes compounded by the frustrating despair, almost immobilizing the depressed classes. The sweeper boy, therefore, is confined to ideational protest and, in his failure to act, one might discern the fidelity if not the strength of the novel . . ." (129). Much of the novel's strength does lie in its stark and painful realism. Prior to Anand's entrance into Indo-Anglian literature, Indian novels did not dwell on the humiliation inherent in the untouchable world. By drawing the 1930s reader's attention to the incredibly pathetic lives untouchables in India were forced to lead, he is therefore committing himself and his writing to an unquestionably political end. He is suggesting, of course, that untouchability is a product of touchability, that Hindus are cruel to propagate the practice, and that consequently a change is necessary. Moreover, he is daring to portray an untouchable as a deep feeling and proud individual, whose subjugation hurts him as severely as it would hurt any other. The "innovative" or "radical" consciousness that Kaushik sees in the novel has its foundations in this angry empathy and in this political commitment to realism.

But realism does not simply depict, it also prescribes. It prescribes by implying that the life and perspective inscribed in novels are simply the way things are. They may be open to some alteration, as *Untouchable* seems to hope, but for the moment they are reality. Ian Watt writes that the primary task of the novel is to "convey the impression of fidelity to human experience" (13). The fundamental premise behind this task is that the narrative mode most often associated with the novel genre, what he calls "formal realism," has the capacity to present a "full and authentic report of human experience." He goes on to speak of "the novel's air of total authenticity" (32) as earlier he had referred to "the novel's mode of imitating reality" (31). Watt's analysis of the novel shares some of the assumptions underlying Anand's *Untouchable*—that the realistic novel is able to copy reality seamlessly. The idea that one reality might have been selected over numerous other possible realities or that every reality is constructed from a specific viewpoint, which makes it prone to certain insights as well as to certain blind spots because of the writer's various political and cultural allegiances, goes unacknowledged in both Watt's discussion of formal realism and in Anand's novel. The danger of not acknowledging the constitutive nature of the realistic novel is that its version of reality will be taken for granted and eventually perhaps will petrify. The political consequences of accepting one reality at the expense of others and of not recognizing that all discursive realities are constructed are particularly serious in the case of a novel like *Untouchable,* because it is about India's most unfortunate and oppressed economic community, whose access to national and international discourse was and is limited by their position of disadvantage. I am not criticizing Anand here for choosing realism, or even Kaushik for praising this aspect of his novel. *Untouchable* was certainly radical at the time of its first publication precisely because of its unflinching realism. What I wish to point out, however, is that Anand's text pulls back at the same time that it pushes forward. The place of its revolutionary consciousness is also the place of its conservatism.

Realism is as problematic a narrative mode as any, and the last few generations of literary scholars, who can be loosely associated with the periods we tend to label the 'modern' and the 'postmodern', have written a great deal of scholarship outlining its inherent weaknesses. But it was not always subject to such criticism. In the nineteenth century, at the height of Victoria's reign when English imperialism was perhaps its most secure, realism represented a severe departure from such dominant literary movements as romanticism and classicism. Instead of seeking after archetypes or the unique, realism ventured to articulate the ordinary, "the real average, the common, essentially animal man," who apparently offered the writer the "lowest common denominator of human experience," as George J. Becker describes realism in 1963, years after it had first fallen into disrepute. He adds, "Realism seems to contain a kind of implicit Benthamite assumption that the life lived by the greatest number is somehow the most real" (25–26).

George Eliot's work is a model of nineteenth-century English realist writing. Not only does she seem to fulfill the requirements of realism with the least amount of dubiousness, but she also composed one of the most eloquent defenses of the movement. In Chapter 17 of *Adam Bede,* she writes,

> So I am content to tell my simple story, without trying to make things seem better than they were; dreading nothing, indeed, but falsity, which, in spite of one's best efforts, there is reason to dread. Falsehood is so easy, truth so difficult. . . . Paint us an angel, if you can . . . but do not impose on us any aesthetic rules which shall banish from the region of Art those old women scraping carrots with their work-worn hands, those heavy clowns taking holiday in a dingy pot-house. . . . In this world there are so many of these common, coarse people, who have no picturesque sentimental wretchedness! It is so needful we should remember their existence, else we may happen to leave them quite out of our religion and philosophy, and frame lofty theories which only fit a world of extremes. Therefore let Art always remind us of them. . . .
> (223–24)

The primary assumption about realism in this passage is that the realists are striving after truth, whereas those who write novels which "make things seem better than they were" are telling falsehoods. Because realist writers could claim such access to 'truth,' pointing to some contemporary historical reality as proof that their work was simply an imitation rather than a fabrication, they could disguise the very aspect of their fiction that supposedly distinguished it from other modes of writing, its fictionality. And if their work no longer seemed like fiction but could be understood rather as a 'slice of life,' the reader would not have to trouble him or herself with acquiring any kind of knowledge about the depicted situation except that provided by the novel. Realism, therefore, especially the nineteenth-century variety, has a tendency to bring to a halt any further inquiry because of its claim to speak the truth.

This would probably not be much of a problem if realism confined its subject to the 'slice of life' with which most of its readers and its authors were familiar, namely the world of the middle class. But, in fact, although the realist novel is "the predominant art form of modern *bourgeois* culture" (Lukacs 2), its subject matter and many of its characters are frequently culled from the working or peasant class. As Becker has observed, for the realists the "most real" is that which is lived by the most people. The passage from *Adam Bede* demonstrates this supposition beautifully. The "old women scraping carrots," the "heavy clowns," the "common coarse people" with whom Eliot's narrator empathizes so feelingly function as a mean for her, by which she is able to judge the extremes in life. However, these extremes are not considered part of the reality in which her "coarse people" participate. What we have, then, in most realist novels is a middle-class author and narrator looking for truth, which is understood as the average, among working-class people. In that search for truth, the author frequently brings with him or her middle-class ideas about life and middle-class guilt and pity.

To suggest that realism can be, but is not always, a form of imperialism and that its motivating emotion is sympathy is hardly going out on a limb. One of the most telling facts in support of this theory is that the height of imperialism and the height of narrative realism coincided in English history. As English imperialists expanded their dominions through conquest and commerce, so too did many English authors colonize the experiences of others—either the working class in their own country or subject populations in the colonies. This is what Erich Heller is hinting at in his 1955 essay "The Realistic Fallacy." He writes, "To describe reality? To mirror it? Artistically to represent it? This is nothing but the innocently respectable surface of realistic literature. Somewhere in its heart quivers the hatred of reality and the lust for conquest" (597). I am sure George Eliot did not think of herself as a conqueror any more than the missionaries did. Her desire was to awaken in her readers the "deep human sympathy" (224) that has come to be considered the special property of her novels. But sympathy is a complex emotion which more often than not elicits charity, and charity does not usually empower the receiver but the one who offers it. Middle-class narrative realism that endeavored merely to describe the class immediately below it in the social hierarchy, though frequently benevolent and compassionate in its intentions, usually succeeded in sustaining the status quo. The workers remained workers and the writers remained middle class.

There are, of course, huge complexities in transferring the paradigm of literary imperialism mentioned above from the center to the periphery, from England to India, from George Eliot to Mulk Raj Anand. Although a member of the middle class, with much educational experience in England, Anand was also one of the colonized in India. When he appropriates English narrative realism for the purposes of exposing the plight of the untouchable communities in India, he is, therefore, engaged in a potentially subversive task. An author writing from the margins, using a mode invented at the center, stands poised in a unique position for analysis. He or she potentially possesses the capacity to interrogate the mode, and the center with which it is complicit, from a perspective not yet articulated. Moreover, Anand's novel, because it was published at a particularly vibrant political moment in the history of the untouchable communities in India, held great promise. It could choose to alter dramatically the way his English and Indian readers viewed these most oppressed people and could conceivably change the conditions of their existence. On the other hand, it could also replicate the pattern established by some earlier English realist writers and colonize the experience of the untouchable in the interests of middle- or upper-class politics. This latter possibility would be realized if the text were not conscious of the imperialist tendency in narrative realism, proven most often by the presence of an omniscient narrator, and if it were not conscious of itself as a middle-class production of lower-class life. In her critique of the Subaltern Studies project, Rosalind O'Hanlon warns scholars about the difficulty inherent in attempting to restore the subjectivity of a long-silenced people. While we may think we are creating a place where an oppressed subject can speak and be heard, the process in which *Untouchable* would appear to be engaged, we might actually be constructing the disadvantaged as a mirror of ourselves and of our political interests, making "their words address our own concerns . . . and render[ing] their figures in our own self image" (210–11). *Untouchable*, I would argue, shows just such a tendency. The novel seems to demonstrate the necessity of elite leadership in the 1930s movement for untouchable uplift. It does not, moreover, endeavor to be conscious of the 'middle-classness' of its nationalism. This is particularly evident in the narrator's occasionally condescending omniscience. Thus, although we must applaud *Untouchable* for its detailed realism and sympathetic portrayal of Bakha's life, we must also recognize the effect of sympathy and the susceptibility of realism to the dictates of middle-class advantage.

This argument is perhaps best substantiated by charting the course of Anand's treatment of Gandhian thought and of Gandhi as a character, because his inclusion of this historical personage is surely a means of augmenting the realism of his story and because in this area of the novel, Anand appears to be acutely aware of the pitfalls of the sympathetic approach. Before we even meet Gandhi, toward the close of Bakha's day and the end of the story, the novel demonstrates the underlying impracticality of Gandhian ideology regarding the untouchables. Charat Singh, a caste Hindu who befriends Bakha, provides the model for Gandhi's image of the penitent Hindu who is willing to atone for the centuries of untouchability. Charat Singh appears early in the text. As Bakha is cleaning the latrines, he arrives complaining of his piles and Bakha's tardiness. He is pleasant to the younger man and gently chides him for his pretensions in wearing English military dress. But the narrator does not allow us to assume that Charat Singh is free of caste prejudice. On the contrary, he simply has the upper hand in any exchange with the untouchable man. This becomes especially clear when the narrator remarks, "Charat Singh was feeling kind, he did not relax the grin which symbolised two thousand years of racial and caste superiority" (19). Behind Charat Singh's congenial grin lies the fact that he can afford to be kind, since he loses nothing by it. As the narrator's comment makes clear, his kindness is actually a sign of his "caste superiority."

Charat Singh turns up later in the novel, bestowing on Bakha more kindnesses. He allows him to retrieve coal for his hookah, an act which an untouchable would not generally be permitted to perform because his touch might defile the pipe. Bakha's response to the privilege is characteristically servile: "his soul was full of love and adoration and worship for the man who had thought it fit to entrust him, an unclean menial, with the job . . ." (119). When Charat Singh subsequently gives him a new hockey stick, Bakha is overcome by feelings of gratitude:

> He was grateful, grateful, haltingly grateful, falteringly grateful, stumblingly grateful, so grateful that he didn't know how he could walk the ten yards to the corner to be out of the sight of his benevolent and generous host. The whole atmosphere was charged with embarrassment. He felt uncomfortable as he walked away. (122)

For all his generosity, Charat Singh only succeeds in treating Bakha like a servant or a child. More important, however, is how this treatment affects Bakha. It entirely disarms him. It makes him dependent because he must rely on the kindness of a caste Hindu before the caste taboo can be broken. There is no empowerment for Bakha in such actions; there is only confirmation of his impotence. Through the character of Charat Singh, then, the novel manages to demonstrate the ineffectiveness of Gandhi's ideas.

Untouchable continues to reveal the problems inherent in the Gandhian solution to untouchability in this manner; that is, it does not openly criticize him, but it gives us the leeway to do so. While waiting for the Mahatma to arrive and address the crowd into which he has suddenly been swept, Bakha recalls that Gandhi had once fasted "for the sake of the bhangis and chamars [untouchable groups]" (157). Gandhi himself refers to this fast a few pages later, using virtually the same terminology. "When I undertook to fast unto death for their sake, it was in obedience to the call of my conscience" (163), he informs the crowd. This notion that Gandhi is fasting "for the sake of" his community is lost on Bakha. He is unable to understand how this behavior might make any difference to the untouchables. The most he can surmise is that the Mahatma is trying to identify with the poverty of his people: "Probably he thinks we are poor and can't get food . . . so he tries to show that even he doesn't have food for days" (157). Bakha's inability to comprehend the Mahatma's fast leads us to interrogate Gandhi's historical statements concerning this famous political act.

This particular fast was undertaken in 1932, after the government announced that it would grant the untouchables separate electorates in the 1935 constitution. In a September issue of *The Bombay Chronicle*, Gandhi affirmed that he was opposed to the separate electorates and was willing to die rather than see them implemented. Moreover, he indicated that this fast was not directed at the untouchables, nor was it necessarily on their behalf. Its aim was to convince caste Hindu leaders of the need to pacify untouchable leaders—and Ambedkar was one—in order that a new agreement might be arrived at which did not divide the touchable and untouchable Hindu community. When Gandhi therefore writes, "If the Hindu mass mind is not yet prepared to banish untouchability root and branch, it must sacrifice me without the slightest hesitation" (*Select Writings* 291), he is obviously speaking to caste Hindus whom he believed had the sole power and right to abolish the practice. The fast, then, was not undertaken to prove anything to or about the untouchables, as Bakha mistakenly assumes; its purpose was to persuade caste Hindus to cease oppressing their fellow Indians. Bakha cannot apprehend the meaning of Gandhi's fast because it does not fundamentally involve him.

In Gandhi's paradigm the untouchable emerges as a pawn or a symbol, victimized by the erasure of his political will. *Untouchable* seems to be aware of this Gandhian construction of untouchability. The speech that Gandhi delivers to the crowd toward the novel's conclusion incorporates the basics of his perspective on the issue, replete with the blind spots implicit in such a view. At one point, Gandhi speaks of a Brahmin boy who lives in his ashram and is engaged in the work of cleaning latrines alongside an untouchable or a scavenger, as Gandhi calls him. The apparent reason behind the Brahmin's willingness to do the work traditionally assigned to untouchables is to "teach the ashram scavenger cleanliness." Approving of the Brahmin's gesture, Gandhi states, "He felt that if he wanted the ashram sweeper to do his work well he must do it himself and set an example" (164). Although Gandhi's comment "thrills" Bakha, we are surely encouraged to question the assumptions here. Is there nothing an untouchable can teach a caste Hindu, not even if both are doing the untouchable's job? In Gandhi's delineation of untouchability, the untouchable is always constructed as dirty, powerless, and in need of help from the same portions of the community that have persecuted him in the past.

Despite his admiration for the Mahatma, Bakha nevertheless manages to recognize this tendency in Gandhi's discourse to support popular conceptions about the impurity of the untouchables. When Gandhi declares that the untouchables' role in their own emancipation is to "rid themselves of evil habits, like drinking liquor and eating carrion," Bakha's answer is, "That is not fair!" (165). He seems to realize that by insisting that untouchables have "evil habits," Gandhi is aligning himself with the Hindu tradition that equates untouchables with the jobs they do. Bakha's earlier assertion, "They think we are mere dirt, because we clean their dirt" (89), apparently applies to the Mahatma, too.

In the end what Gandhi has to offer Bakha is the same thing that Charat Singh gave him—pity: "Bakha visualised himself pitied by the Mahatma and consoled by him. It was such a balm, it was so comforting, the great man's sympathy" (166). But a great man's sympathy does not automatically eradicate a poor man's oppression. The novel posits another solution because Gandhi's paternalism is shown to be insufficient to the problem.

It is not a politician or a Mahatma who voices the novel's most positive approach to untouchability but a poet with distinct Marxist leanings. Iqbal Nath Sarashar trumpets the cause of the downtrodden in India, the peasant and the untouchable, and proclaims their dignity. His solution is more radical than Gandhi's, because it involves a drastic alteration to the social structure of Hinduism. Unlike Gandhi, he insists that caste and *varna*, "those inequalities of birth and unalterable vocations," must be abolished in order to make way for a system based on a total equality of rights, privileges, and opportunities. This system would, moreover, accommodate the introduction of the machine into Indian agriculture and industry. What Sarashar predicts for sweepers such as Bakha is a change in profession, since, according to his program, the first machine to be adopted in India will be the flushed toilet. When the sweepers cease to handle other people's excrement, they will, he says, cease to be untouchable: "Then the sweepers can be free from the stigma of untouchability and assume the dignity of status that is their right as useful members of a casteless and classless society" (173). Sarashar's ideas about the elimination of untouchability are simple and practical, but they are not addressed to Bakha any more than Gandhi's solution was. The poet's message, in fact, decisively excludes Bakha because it is couched in language he cannot understand. The novel knows this. It depicts Bakha standing alone, beyond the elite crowd grouped around Sarashar, and vaguely wondering about the workings of a toilet. The narrator explains that Bakha "felt that the poet would have been answering the most intimate questions in his soul, if he had not used such big words" (174). *Untouchable* is critical even of Sarashar in spite of the fact that the poet advocates the kind of socialism that Anand himself was pursuing in the thirties.

But though conscious of the poet's exclusionary language, Anand, perhaps inevitably, replicates it in his novel. *Untouchable* was written in English. Its 1930s readers, by and large, would not have been untouchables because, with the exception of a select few such as Ambedkar, the vast majority of untouchables were at that time either illiterate or they would not have understood English. As Suresht Renjen Bald observes, Anand's appeal in *Untouchable* was to the "small class of privileged educated Indians" (115) who comprised the elite in pre-independence India. Through his effective use of the narrative mode of realism, Anand is surely calling upon these elites to pity the untouchables and lend their support to the growing movement which sought to free them from their subjugated status. By making that call in English, he is also contributing to the conversation about untouchability which in the thirties was conducted predominantly in that language. But the use of the very language through which untouchability was made an issue of national importance in India ensures that the untouchable is left out of the conversation.[6] At the same time that we should recognize the problems implicit in any 1930s English construction of untouchability, however, we must also give Anand his due. Including untouchables in the discursive formation of themselves and their lives might have been an impossible task for the Indo-Anglian novel of the thirties.

That the call is to the Iqbal Nath Sarashars of this world and not to the Bakhas is evident not only in the fact that Anand has chosen the English language in which to get his message across but also in the passive role he assigns to Bakha in the end. We last see him emerging from the garden in which Gandhi and the poet have spoken after having made the "tentative decision" to pass on what he has heard: " 'I shall go and tell father all that Gandhi said about us,' he whispered to himself, 'and what that clever poet said. Perhaps I can find the poet on the way and ask him about his machine' " (175–76). If any political activism is implicit in these last sentences, it is projected far into the future when Bakha is able to figure out the emancipatory potential in the words of Gandhi and the poet and in the workings of the toilet. What we are more likely to conclude is that the untouchable in this novel needs change, rather than to be an agent of change. This latter role is reserved for Gandhi and the poet. Although the text rejects the Gandhian approach to the problem of untouchability, it simultaneously inscribes it because it leaves Bakha unable to effect his own liberation. It leaves him dependent upon Gandhi, or Charat Singh, or the poet, or on anyone else who has the power and the education to imagine and implement the reform of Indian society. Bakha cannot do this himself because, though physically strong as well as angry enough to demand change, his personal power and the power of all untouchables in India is, the novel suggests, unavoidably curtailed by the subservience of centuries. How can a person who carries a "prison cell" within destroy the social barriers erected by others? There are undoubtedly ways to do this, but *Untouchable* does not provide them. Instead it valorizes the ideal of revolutionary leadership, and, more important, it envisions such leadership coming from outside the untouchable world. Referring to a number of Anand's other novels, Bald comments, "Not only do Mulk Raj's peasants respect authority too much, they accept it in the traditional manner of *mai-bapism.* They cannot repudiate one *mai-bap* (mother-father) without the security of another" (125). Similarly, in *Untouchable,* Bakha is perhaps ready to repudiate the Hindu authority that insists on his degradation, but he does not go so far as to question the very notion of authority itself. On the contrary, he seeks another patron—this time the savior politician in the form of the poet or of Gandhi—in which to place his trust. So long as he remains bound to *any* structures of authority and does not embrace that authority for himself, as Ambedkar recommended to all untouchables seeking political redress for their problems but which Anand's *Untouchable* stops short of suggesting, Bakha will continue to serve someone else's interests rather than his own and, consequently, will perpetuate the system that dictates his or another's oppression. Systemic change is possible when Bakha begins to write himself, instead of having his subjectivity *exclusively* written by others.

The problem is not that Anand, or the poet or Gandhi or any other member of the elite, cannot authentically write about untouchables or take up their cause. As I mentioned in the last chapter, the discourse of authenticity is a dubious one. It inevitably silences everyone but those who are, paradoxically, unable to speak. Even Ambedkar, though an untouchable himself, would be rendered inauthentic by this discourse because of his education, which allowed him access to elite circles and elite ways of thinking and therefore changed his political status as a victimized and underprivileged citizen of India. Spivak occasionally seems to engage in this discourse, but she also repudiates it, more effectively and consistently, I think, than most other postcolonial critics writing today. In "A Literary Representation of The Subaltern: A Woman's Text From the Third World," she interrogates the assumptions often made by elite critics approaching subaltern material. She states,

> Resisting "elite" methodology for "subaltern" material involves an epistemological/ontological confusion. The confusion is held in an unacknowledged analogy: just as the subaltern *is* not elite (ontology), so must the historian not *know* through elite method (epistemology).
>
> This is part of a much larger confusion: can men theorize feminism, can whites theorize racism, can the bourgeois theorize revolution and so on. It is when *only* the former groups theorize that the situation is politically intolerable. Therefore it is crucial that members of these groups are kept vigilant about their assigned subject-positions. It is disingenuous, however, to forget that, as the collectivities implied by the second group of nouns start participating in the production of knowledge about themselves, they must have a share in some of the structures of privileges that contaminate the first group. (253)

Spivak's ideas here seem to me to be extraordinarily important, since they point us in a direction away from the discourse of authenticity, which has consumed so much feminist and postcolonial scholarship in the last few years, and into a more fruitful and interesting area. The question becomes, then, not does one have the right or the appropriate knowledge to portray a people other than one's own, but rather how one goes about doing it and who else is participating. Thus emphasis is placed on the creator and on his or her investment in that which is created. Whether or not Bakha or Gandhi's harijans are realistically depicted is entirely beside the point. What is or is not at stake, is hidden, is displaced in the construction of the other. These questions are far more relevant than the issue concerning the property rights to a collectivity such as the untouchables of pre-independent India. In *Untouchable* the answer to these questions is privilege. Privilege is never sacrificed to the cause of untouchable uplift, not by Anand and certainly not by Gandhi. The privilege of leadership belongs to them even in the end.

So as not to inscribe the same structures of privilege in this chapter, which endeavors to make visible a section of the Indian population rendered invisible by much nationalist discourse, I choose to close on another note, a note about Ambedkar and the untouchable communities across India he hoped to see liberated during his lifetime. He did not see this happen. He died in 1956 after laboriously assisting in the creation of a constitution for independent India that would not permit untouchability. In article 17 of the 1950 Indian constitution, untouchability is outlawed. However, the alteration in Hindu society made possible by this statutory abolition of untouchability was apparently not sufficient for Ambedkar. Just prior to his death, he and literally thousands of his followers publicly converted to Buddhism, a move he had been contemplating since the 1930s. The fact that Ambedkar did not actually take the step toward Buddhism until after he had tried, for years, to reform the predominantly Hindu society of 'free' India suggests that his conversion was, in part, an act of hopelessness, that his disillusionment with caste Hindus had reached a point of no return.

Dynamic and angry in life, in death Ambedkar has been memorialized by the untouchables of India as a "cultural hero and demigod" (Khare 143). His posthumous influence has been so profound that anthropologist D. S. Khare, in his 1984 study of three untouchable communities in Lucknow, is able to establish an epistemological paradigm that divides Indian history into "pre-Ambedkar" and "post-Ambedkar India." Though Ambedkar is fiercely remembered by Indian untouchables across the country (a group of whom in 1964 demanded that a portrait of him be placed in the Central Hall of Parliament alongside the *other* founding fathers of modern India [see Rudolph 145]), his historical importance has barely been acknowledged and certainly not analyzed by mainstream nationalist historians.

Ambedkar's marginalization in history is coincident with the marginalization meted out to untouchables in India at the time this book is being written. It is sad that in 1984 Khare—not an untouchable himself—can still describe the untouchable as a "social enigma" who is "too readily stereotyped by others while he himself remains remote and silent" (1). Refusing to enshrine the silence of the Indian untouchable and yet recognizing that my study cannot presume to elucidate an essential untouchable subjecthood I offer as my concluding statement a quotation from an untouchable whom Khare identifies as a schoolteacher from Modernganj: "We are studied to no end; it is a part of being the disadvantaged in the society. Your job is to inquire, so inquire" (Khare 12).

6 Nostalgia and 1947

The last chapter of British imperialism in India and the Indian nationalist movement saw the emergence on both sides of a new attitude, which changed the tenor of almost every public document that stood witness to the events occurring in the final ten years of conflict. This new attitude, shared increasingly by virtually all the contemporary chroniclers of the Indian/British confrontation (with the exception of a few very conservative Englishmen who, during the war years, clung to the hope that the Empire would continue indefinitely) can be articulated as the fundamental recognition that the end was in sight—the end of the nationalist struggle and the end of the Raj. Scholars cannot point to any particular person or happening as the source of this growing conviction, though we can chronologically list the incidents, constitutional and actual, which served to heighten the impression of an ending being near—the India Act of 1935, which imagined a future Indian Federation, the elections of 1937 and the two to eight years that followed of Indian government in the provinces, the Second World War which exhausted the British emotionally and financially, the August 1942 rebellion, the Bengal famine of 1943-44, the 1946 elections, the Indian Navy mutiny, and the communal riots which ravaged the country and made the leaders on both sides seek a hasty finish. As the final decade of British imperialism in India and Indian nationalism played itself out, it became more and more apparent and was more and more believed that English power in India was ebbing and that the nationalists' control of the political situation was steadily on the rise. For many novelists writing during this period, such knowledge produced nostalgia on the one side for the lost glory of the Empire and on the other for the already bygone golden age of the nationalist movement.

Nostalgia among British writers might perhaps be expected. After all, a great deal of international prestige went along with the possession of the British Empire, a point that William Golant makes in his own nostalgic reconstruction of the Raj, entitled *The Long Afternoon: British India 1601-1947.* He writes,

> India contributed to Britain's image of herself as a great power and world leader. The Indian Empire enlarged the scale and purpose of affairs of state, providing a place to tour with style, a colourful addition to any pageant, and a mission worthy of effort. Even Britain's enemies believed India gave Britain a world view and therefore a reason for respect. (xvii)

In giving up India, the British not only had to renounce power, preeminence, and a playground in which to carry out their fantasies of grandeur, they also had to relinquish a certain way of thinking about themselves. Once India became independent, no longer could they wax eloquent about the hardships and glories of their civilizing mission. No longer could that particular facet of their collective experience—an experience memorialized in so many English texts that a British person did not even have to spend time in India to be able to participate in it—be exploited as a defining characteristic, as it was in the Victorian and Edwardian years when British rule in India was at its most secure. Nor could they be confident that anything they said about India and about Empire would be accepted as truth by other western nations. Their credibility as a world power and as a superior people was profoundly at stake.

So much of the British self-image was predicated upon their historical conquest of India and their perennial pose as its rulers that the loss of India could be seen by some writers as the loss of identity altogether. Edward Thompson, in his 1938 novel *An End of the Hours,* makes an attempt to come to terms with this national bereavement but is unable to imagine an England without an India to define its purpose. His angst-ridden protagonist Alden speaks of "this English civilisation which is dying out, with every nation of the world apparently willing to hasten our dying" (24), as if the political ascendancy of the Indian nationalists necessarily signifies the demise of the English nation. That England might be able to fashion an alternative national identity which would not be indebted to imperialistic notions of territorial expansion and rulership is not an idea Thompson even entertains.

The loss of India on a national scale can be compared to the less grandiose dispossessions that happened every time an English person retired from service in India. India gave individual Englishmen and women an experience they would never be able to duplicate 'back home' in Britain. Often, the happiest and healthiest years of their lives were spent there, in a situation they would frequently describe as exile but which would, nevertheless, be the subject of whimsical reminiscences and yearning. Although most Anglo-Indian authors refused to regard the country as their own, their nostalgic descriptions of it would suggest that they had learned to shape their identities around their Indian experiences. Sara Jeannette Duncan, in *The Simple Adventures of a Memsahib*, voices her community's pessimism at the thought of life-after-India particularly bleakly: "The satisfactions of retirement are obscure, and the prospect of devoting a shrunken end of existence to the solicitous avoidance of bronchitis is not inviting" (306). There is a sad irony here. Duncan herself died in England of bronchitis in 1922, seven years after she had left India for good. In contrast to this unavoidably ugly future stand memories of the past in India, memories which dot almost every novel written by English men and women about India, to such a degree that nostalgia must be recognized as a convention of the Anglo-Indian novel. The narrator of Duncan's *Simple Adventures,* preparing for her own departure on the next ship out to England, poignantly recalls the day "when the spell of India was strong upon my youth, when I saw romance under a turban and soft magic behind a palm, and found the most fascinating occupation in life to be the wasting of my husband's substance among the gabbling thieves of the China bazar" (307). The fact that Anglo-Indians knew they would someday have to leave India forever, knew this the moment they first stepped into the country, renders nostalgic even those novels, such as Duncan's *Simple Adventures,* which were written while the author was still residing on the subcontinent. Susanne Howe's much-quoted observation that Anglo-Indian novels are among the "unhappiest" in the English language obviously stems from some perception of this melancholy enshrined in so many of these texts (32).

The final and irrevocable loss of India to the forces of Indian nationalism meant the permanent retirement of the British. Their textual responses to this ousting were similar to those of the earlier Anglo-Indian retirees. Those who did not want to leave felt compelled to by circumstances. One young ICS officer, after the 1947 transfer of power, would construct his departure as the inevitable outcome of his adherence to an ethics of duty: "I will not dilate upon the personal distress of this uprooting. . . . Enough that though I felt it my duty to leave India, I shall never cease to yearn for another glimpse of a land that gave me so much happiness" (quoted in *Guardians* 344). That Philip Mason could in his 1954 history of the ICS describe the political relationship of the British government with the Indian people as being of "essentially [a] family nature" (348), with the ICS officers often depicted as "fathers" to "wards" and occasionally as husbands or lovers, suggests that the feelings the British had for India as an abstract idea were intensely personal. Certainly it was on the personal rather than the political level that the emotional costs of the leavetaking were paid.[1]

It is perhaps a more difficult task to demonstrate that this mood of sadness is also prevalent in late pre-independence Indian discourse. With complete self-government within their grasp, Indian nationalists were hardly in a position to grieve. And, in fact, few of them did. Nevertheless, a strain of nostalgia similar to that found more prominently in English literature about the end of Empire does thread its way through many of the novels, speeches, and other public texts written in the last decade of British imperialism in India. In the case of the Indian writers, however, what underlies the nostalgia is, I would argue, a fear of corruption.

There was much talk of corruption among Indian nationalists after the 1937 elections, when Indian politicians were elected by the largest yet public franchise to provincial government. Such talk, moreover, continued throughout the war, the Bengal famine, and the 1946 election of Indian politicians, this time to the central as well as the provincial governments. The final few years of British rule also saw the gradual decline of Gandhi and his doctrine of nonviolence as the dominant political influence in the country.[2] A change was underway. The concerns of many Indian nationalists, particularly Congress members after the 1942 Quit India movement, were changing from protest against the government to building up support, patronage, and acquiring experience in preparation for government office. This shift in priorities was indicative of the new image the nationalists were, consciously or unconsciously, generating. Throughout the 1920s and 30s Indian nationalists were typically depicted by the international and national press as occupying the moral high ground in their confrontation with imperialism. Though this status was not substantially lost in the forties, it was subjected to a more stringent scrutiny primarily by the nationalists themselves. The questioning of their intentions and their morality helped to create the impression that something had been lost even as India approached its moment of freedom. It is this impression, I would argue, that some Indian texts of the forties seek either to investigate or to disguise.

In this last chapter, I discuss two novels in relation to the issues I have outlined above, Philip Mason's *The Wild Sweet Witch* and Bhabani Bhattacharya's *So Many Hungers!*. One of the reasons I selected these over other Indo-Anglian and Anglo-Indian works of fiction from the 1940s is because both were published in 1947, the year of the transfer of power, and had been written months before the August 15th separation. I was interested in learning how novelists like Mason and Bhattacharya who had such huge emotional investments in British imperialism and Indian nationalism would construct their worlds on the eve of that portentous event. Interestingly, although these novels were written at a time when it was a foregone conclusion that India would soon be self-governing, that the British would soon depart for good, neither text actually foregrounds this information. On the contrary, both the English and the Indian novel are silent about India's imminent independence. It is, in other words, present in the text but only as a conspicuous absence which the readers of the period would have recognized as such. I have come to conclude that the suppression of knowledge about the fast-approaching moment of separation cloaks each text's attempt to retain the upper hand for its own cause—the ICS in *The Wild Sweet Witch* and the Congress in *So Many Hungers!* By inscribing into their novels a feigned ignorance about the transfer of power, these authors are able to construct a past for their respective politics that is worthy of nostalgia. In Mason's book, written in 1946, India's independence seems unimaginably distant, since the Indian characters are entirely unable to govern themselves and the British are all-powerful. The righteousness of the Indian fight for freedom being the principal theme of Bhattacharya's novel, a ferocious British enemy must be posited, against whom patriotic

Bengalis can demonstrate their solidarity. That the ferociousness of the British and the solidarity of the Bengalis was open to question by the time he wrote *So Many Hungers!* compels Bhattacharya to evoke nostalgia in order to make his point. But it is actually the nostalgia in these novels that alerts us to the details of their particular constructions. For nostalgia implies a certain dissatisfaction with the present, and the present for *The Wild Sweet Witch* and *So Many Hungers!* is not an evolutionary step forward, as politicians on both sides of the Indian/British conflict chose to represent the transfer of power, but an inevitable decline.

The Wild Sweet Witch is, above all, a eulogy of the ICS. Written within a year of this long-standing administrative service becoming entirely defunct, the novel charts its steady withdrawal from India. It features three English protagonists, ICS officers posted to the Garhwal district of the Himalayas during three separate historical periods—1875, when the district officer is at the height of his power, 1923, after nationalist agitation begins to be felt in such rural areas as Garhwal, and 1938, when the British are convinced that they will soon have to leave India, though their departure seems far from immediate. The novel is nostalgic throughout; it yearns for that era in British imperialist history when the district officer ruled over vast numbers of Indian people, and it laments the transfer of that power to growing nationalist factions. It is a defense of the ICS and an attack on Indian nationalist aspirations.

The novel's first chapter is a depiction of life as a district officer in the ICS before nationalist agitation began. Mr. Bennett, the Deputy Commissioner of Garhwal, is a hard-working man "who believed with no shadow of doubt that he was where he was for the good of the people he ruled" (40–41). Bennett's certainty about the rightness of his service enables him to act, with the approval of the narrator, in such a way as to ensure the safety of the people under him without necessarily taking their wishes into consideration. When he rescues a low-caste man from a ritualized death at the hand of his fellow villagers by threatening to execute the village headman, sympathizers are expected to applaud his paternalistic actions because they stem from an "essential goodness of heart" (40) and are based on an accurate assessment and knowledge of Indian custom and society. The narrator assures readers that Mr. Bennett, in his dealings with the Garhwal peasants, "made no attempt to change their way of life beyond putting an end so far as he could to certain practices which were repugnant to Christian morality and which orthodox Hinduism would have disowned" (41). His rule is solidly grounded in the highly questionable and thoroughly arrogant assumption that he is able to determine which practices belong to "orthodox Hinduism" and which do not. What saves Bennett from a charge of authoritarianism, the narrator encourages us to believe, is just this enlightened objectivity—he knows the natives but is not one of them. Mason's Bennett has much in common with Kipling's Orde in "The Enlightenments of Pagett, M.P.," despite the fifty years or so that stretch between their moments of origin. Both justify their positions of domination through an unexamined ideal of enlightened objectivity, reliance on which allows them to disguise their personal stake and participation in the power they wield.

This notion of power as a means of doing good, frequently against the will of the person over whom the power is exercised, recurs in Mason's writing. The Guardians, Mason's history of the ICS, is full of accounts of district officers who felt compelled to override the will of Indians in order to get some 'good' deed done or some 'good' law enacted. Mason apparently put this belief into practice during his own career in the ICS. In his 1989 introduction to The Wild Sweet Witch, Saros Cowasjee recounts an incident that occurred when Mason himself was Deputy Commissioner of the Garhwal district: "Once he had a woman with a putrefying leg placed under arrest so that she could be forcibly sent to a hospital. He admits he had no right to do so, but the people told him he was a king in Garhwal and it was no use being a king if he could sometimes not break the law." Mason's action is justified in Cowasjee's eyes by his motive: "He wanted to help the people—to provide the rough and ready justice on the spot which the Garhwalis sought above all else" (9). But the point is not whether he had a "right" to take this liberty, since he certainly did under the terms of the imperialist government at the time. The question is, if this was the kind of justice "the Garhwalis sought above all else," then why was there resistance to it? Why did the woman have to be forcibly sent to the hospital? Doubtless in order to construct the style of liberal rulership Mason idealizes in both The Wild Sweet Witch and The Guardians, the consent of the people has to be taken for granted and when it cannot be taken for granted, as in the above situation, then its absence has to be strategically ignored. That both the woman with the putrefying leg and the villagers in the novel stand in opposition to their district officer are details that must be swept aside, their ramifications overlooked, if Mason is to succeed in creating an image of the ICS that champions its 'essential goodness' and its universal acceptance by peasant India, the two beliefs on which Mason's eulogy is founded.

The pattern of power evident in these particular incidents is replicated throughout Mason's novel and his history. Indeed a fundamental supposition of both texts is that it was the unresistant consensus of the people—the 'people' being construed solely as the peasant class—that allowed the ICS to rule in India as long as it did. During the time of Bennett in the novel, the late Victorian period, this consensus is depicted as something akin to adoration. Hence the narrator can say of Kalyanu, the representative peasant in the first section, "If it is love to wish ardently for an opportunity to serve and be near the object of one's devotion, then Kalyanu loved Mr. Bennett" (38). Even in the last section of the story, which is set in 1938, district officer Christopher Tregard can assert with confidence that the ICS still has the loyalty of the peasants behind it, though British duty now is to step down as a gesture of trust on behalf of the "vocal classes" of India. He tells his wife Susan,

> it seems to me wrong for us, the English, as a people, to take refuge behind the peasant and say we must stay because he wants us. Every people must express itself through its vocal classes . . . and the vocal classes in India want us to go. It's true they're out of touch with the peasant, but that is just because we're here. It's a thing which can't right itself so long as we are. (199)[3]

For Mason in *The Wild Sweet Witch*, the predominant issue is supremacy. Regardless of the historical period he invokes, Bennett's 1875, Hugh Upton's 1923, or even Tregard's 1938, Mason is concerned with establishing that the ICS never lost control over the Indians. Power was never wrested from the British by the nationalist "vocal classes." On the contrary, they willingly relinquished their hold on the peasants because it was the right thing to do when (and only when) they finally chose to do it. Mason is perpetuating the same liberal imperialist myth at work in Schuster and Wint's 1941 history *India and Democracy,* namely the myth that Indian independence was the implicit purpose of British imperialism. While Schuster and Wint tend to focus that myth on the constitutional reforms that preceded independence, Mason tries to draw the ICS into it, to suggest that the actual men who ruled India, the district officers, were continuously cognizant of their roles as transitional rulers and ready to transfer the power into Indian hands. To perpetuate the myth, however, not only must Mason underplay any indigenous resistance to ICS rule, which he nevertheless feels obliged to document in his novel, he must also paint a picture of ICS control that cannot be substantiated even in his own history of the institution.

Simon Epstein's portrait of the ICS, in his article "District Officers in Decline: The Erosion of British Authority in the Bombay Countryside, 1919 to 1947," delineates the cautiously slow attenuation of the British administrative officer in India over the course of the thirty years that constitute the apex of the twentieth-century nationalist movement. According to Epstein, the ICS, when it was functioning at its peak, was the principal representative of the British government in India. It was its practical arm, and, because of the special status accorded to the man in the field in Anglo-Indian discourse, it was also "the creator as much as the executor of British policy" across the Indian countryside (493). Using Mason's *The Guardians* as one of his source texts, Epstein constructs an image of ICS district officers at the "high noon of empire" (495), when the foundations of British power in India rested on the everyday actions and decisions of these men. All prestige aside—and for the 'Heaven-Born' members of the British administration in India, prestige was a considerable aspect of the job—the district officer's powers extended over the local police and judiciary, the revenue services, which included the appointment of village headmen, accountants, and tax collectors, and the more mundane local district board, where as chairman he ordered and supervised the construction and maintenance of roads, schools, wells, meeting-halls, and most of the other municipal appurtenances that contributed to village life in India. For much of the imperial period, the reins of local government were almost entirely in the hands of the British ICS officer who ruled the district.

Both Epstein and Mason locate the beginning of the end for the ICS in the implementation of the 1919 reforms, which brought dyarchy to the Indian provincial governments. Dyarchy is often treated in nationalist histories as a reform with little or no value to the independence movement because it involved the transfer of insignificant amounts of power from the central to the provincial governments (see Sarkar 166–68 and Bipan Chandra 241). Certain departments previously under the control of the imperial state were handed over to Indian ministers who had been elected by a small franchise. But, as Sarkar notes, the innovation of dyarchy permitted the devolution of only those departments with "less political weight and little funds to ministers responsible to provincial legislatures, skillfully drawing Indian politicians into a patronage rat-race which would probably also discredit them, as real improvements in education, health, agriculture, and local bodies required far more money than the British would be willing to assign to these branches" (167).

Questionable and insufficient as the 1919 reforms were from the point of view of Indian nationalists at the time as well as later historians, they nevertheless succeeded in changing forever the status of the British district officer. For the first time in the history of the British in India, district officers were made subordinate and answerable to Indian ministers. Mason is cynical about this change, claiming that it added one more duty to the list of responsibilities of the already overworked district officer, a duty he alternately describes as "the maddening and infructuous business of answering questions, whether put down for formal answer in the House or sent informally direct" and as "the labour of persuading where he [the district officer] had been used to command" (303). More important, however, was the loss of personal influence and power as a result of the concomitant transfer of many of the chief offices to local bodies of non-officials. District officers, for instance, were no longer permitted to serve as chairman of local district boards. Instead, this position was filled by prominent Indians from the community. Not having the right to assume the district officer's traditional role as chairman seems to have been particularly galling for Mason, since he mentions it in both the history and the novel. In *The Wild Sweet Witch,* Upton, the 1923 Deputy Commissioner for Garhwal, complains to Jodh Singh, the local Indian nationalist, about the laxity of the district board under indigenous chairmanship, allowing schools to fall into disrepair and teachers to go without pay. Had education still been the responsibility of the deputy commissioner, Upton assumes, such neglect would never have been permitted to occur. Finally, he concludes, "No, Jodh Singh, I'll believe in your new India when I see you getting down to something practical" (137). The conduct of the district board without an Englishman to chair it becomes emblematic, in Upton's view (which the novel never questions), of an India ruled by Indians, and the novel seems determined to convince us that such a state cannot succeed.

If the above comments by Upton are the novel's somewhat backhanded way of deploring the 1919 reforms and the small retreat from power they demanded from the district officers, in *The Guardians* Mason is much more explicit about the connection between British authority in rural India and the chairmanship of local boards. Despite the fact that the author himself insists that the reforms were not an attempt to pacify Indian nationalists but were a voluntary renunciation of ICS supremacy, he recognizes how this constitutional event was perceived when translated into practical terms:

> No one—reasoned the peasant—gives up power unless he is forced to. . . . Therefore if the District Board runs a school which the district officer used to run, it is a concession forced from him, a victory for the nationalists. . . . And that Indians thought it a blow made it very difficult for the district officer not to think the same. (246)

According to Mason, the effect of the 1919 reforms was personally experienced by the district officers as an immediate and important displacement of their authority. Though the central government might ascribe another meaning to this transfer of power into Indian hands, preferring to see it as the inevitable and acceptable consequence of their "trusteeship" in India, the district officers felt their control of local government and the local population slipping, and they objected to the situation.

Their objections often took the form of debunking the efforts of the Indians who occupied the newly created positions in local government, as Upton frequently does in *The Wild Sweet Witch*. Mason, in *The Guardians*, seems particularly intent on depicting the Indian politicians, and especially those from the Congress, as bumbling and corrupt "scoundrels" (251). When he writes, "We, the former Guardians, could not forbear some rejoicing at the difficulties in which the Congress were placed; we laughed at their misfortunes and some of us delighted in pointing out mistakes" (280), readers are expected to understand and sympathize with the plight of the district officer under inept nationalist government.[4]

Mason's depiction of the nationalists was in line with the Congressbashing that Winston Churchill, Lord Linlithgow, the Viceroy of India from 1936–43, and Secretary of State L. S. Amery made popular among the conservative element of the British during the war years. All three men seemed determined to use their status to slow or even stop entirely the course of the nationalist movement, and for them, this meant calling the character of prominent Congressmen into question and publicly declaring that the Congress claim to represent all of India was fallacious (see Moore 100–101). I am drawing this connection between Mason and the most renowned arch conservatives of his day, recognizing that it complicates my earlier suggestion that the novelist belongs in the liberal imperialist camp, because I wish to point out just how *acceptable,* at every level of the British administrative machinery, such obviously biased and acrimonious constructions of Indian nationalists were at the time. No doubt there was much bitterness on the part of many Englishmen throughout the last years of the Raj in India and even into the 1950s. Mason could therefore write his history of the ICS in the early fifties, complete with its malicious statements about nationalists, confident that this view was still sanctioned by enough of his readers that his publisher would not hesitate to print it.

In his history, Mason charts the growing dissatisfaction of the ICS officers with their declining status during the final three decades of British rule in India, as Indians began to take over more and more of the administrative and governmental positions available at the local and provincial levels. According to Epstein, the steady deterioration of ICS influence was linked to the overall erosion of British control on the subcontinent, which culminated in the 1946 confession by Viceroy Wavell that "on administrative grounds we could not govern the whole of India for more than a year and a half from now" (quoted in Epstein 515). The conclusion that Epstein draws is that long before the final declaration of the transfer of power, "the possibility of reinstating direct British authority through the district administration had already disappeared in the Indian countryside" (518). The district officers had gradually lost or renounced so much of their authority and prestige that by August 15, 1947 there was nothing left to give up.

This is the picture that Mason, and Epstein quoting Mason, paint in their respective histories. It is a story of ebbing ascendancy. Yet Mason affirms almost the opposite in his novel. Throughout *The Wild Sweet Witch* the narrator seems determined to demonstrate the unquestionable sovereignty of the district officer. From Bennett to Upton to Tregard, the Garhwal deputy commissioner is shown reigning supreme in his district. His authority is rarely, if ever, seriously undermined, not even by the histrionics of the Congressman, Jodh Singh (whose unstable behavior is meant as a critique of Indian nationalism generally). There are numerous incidents in the text that affirm the almost overwhelming power that the ICS officers enjoy in Garhwal, for example, Bennett's capacity to alter forever the way of life of the Singh family, simply by promising to make Kalyanu's son a patwari or minor revenue officer (68), and Upton's deft handling of Jodh Singh, who, in spite of being a fervent anti-imperialist, can say to the deputy commissioner on parting from him, "I do not want any foreign rulers, but I thank God that He has sent us such a ruler as you" (179), an admission of defeat if ever there was one. The most telling expression of ICS power appears in the third section of the novel when Tregard takes over office in 1938, inheriting from Upton the problem of managing Jodh Singh.

Because of his flagrant emotionalism and tendency to speak without weighing the consequences, Jodh Singh is implicated in a murder. We, the readers, witness the event and thus know for certain that he is not guilty, but Tregard can only speculate about what really happened. Despite a rather complicated plot, involving some of Jodh Singh's enemies and at least one witness who is reputedly tortured, Tregard is able to sift through the lies and reconstruct the event exactly as it occurred. It is a feat worthy of Sherlock Holmes, and it is a testament to Tregard's absolute command of the situation and of the subject population. This district officer, speaking within the Orientalist tradition established years before by Bennett, is able to use his superior knowledge of the Garhwali people to ascertain their hidden desires and motives and eventually to come up with an explanation for every anomaly the story about Jodh Singh contains. Without possessing any external proof that his assertions are true, he can therefore announce to his wife with bristling confidence, "I told you something would happen. This is just the kind of thing I imagined" (227). The mystery is solved because any mystery is a threat to the district officer's control.

That ICS authority has not been undermined is assuredly the unstated purpose of *The Wild Sweet Witch*. Furthermore, Mason's hidden agenda would remain as muted and elusive a detail as the villager's resistance to Bennett in the earlier section if it were not for the novel's nostalgia. Its very presence in the text suggests that ICS domination is already a thing of the past in rural India. We first hear the strain of nostalgia in the second section, when Upton, after a long day's work accompanies his wife Margaret on an evening stroll. A landscape of hills, pines and distant snows prompts the following exchange:

> "Hugh, do you think we shall be able to remember it? The lovely things we've seen and the fun we've had?"
>
> "When we're playing golf at Cheltenham, d'you mean? We shall be able to remember that we've had a good time, but you can't live it over again. Memory's a poor thing." (87)

In the last section, the scene is repeated between Tregard and his wife.[5] They, too, believe that the "fun" (197) is over and the time fast approaching when they "must go" (199), a realization which provokes yet another discussion of the nature of memory. A passage from a Francis Thompson poem about a mysterious woman and her lover is cited as somehow emblematic of "the loveliness we've seen here" (201). This passage is one of the cornerstones of the novel:

> But unlike those feigned temptress-ladies who
> In guerdon of a night the lover slew,
> When the embrace has failed, the rapture fled,
> Not he, not he, the wild sweet witch is dead!
>   And though he cherisheth
> The babe most strangely born from out her death—
> Some tender trick of her it hath, maybe—
>   It is not she! (202)

Again it is the wife Susan who articulates the novel's nostalgia, strangely made to identify with the male lover in the above passage and his loss of the wild sweet witch, who, in her mystery and rapturous beauty, symbolizes India. And like Margaret fifteen years earlier, she looks to the most stable and unchanging sight in her environment, the Himalayan range, as the inspiration for her memory when she suggests, "Let's try very hard not to forget" (203).

Nostalgia implies that something has been irretrievably lost. When Upton, Tregard, and their wives express tender affection for India, speaking as though they were already gone from the land and their lives there over, I cannot help but wonder if the nostalgia within the text stands in for the nostalgia which must have surrounded the novel's production. Is it the author's personal nostalgia, or do the feelings of the characters communicate the collective bereavement of the English ICS officers generally, who in 1946, at the time the novel was written, were in the process of conceding the last remnants of their power to Indian officials and of leaving forever the British India they had ruled? Only by recourse to such possibilities can I explain the mood of imminent loss that informs the novel and causes me to suspect the ICS authority the narrator seems so bent on celebrating. The question is, if the district officer's rule is as stable and secure as the text claims, why does Mason evoke nostalgia at all? Obviously the presence of nostalgia in any text is a primary indicator of someone's, probably the author's, dissatisfaction with the present. In *The Wild Sweet Witch,* this dissatisfaction can hardly be located in the main characters, since the novel allows no room for reading discontent into their feelings and actions. On the contrary, readers are encouraged to believe that the three deputy commissioners, though often fatigued from overwork, are fundamentally happy with their jobs and with the imperialist government that lends them power. Furthermore, the two English women characters, Margaret Upton and Susan Tregard not only share the daily satisfactions that their husbands experience but consistently occupy virtually the same paternal position in their relationship to the land and the people. This is why Susan can identify with the role of the male lover in Thompson's verse. The inappropriateness of the characters' expressions of nostalgia suggests that its origins are outside the text. Recognizing this, we can interpret the text in light of the nostalgic atmosphere that heralded the transfer of power in 1947, in which case it becomes apparent that the novel is mourning, not the individual dispossessions that Upton, Tregard, and their wives will inevitably encounter when they retire, but the final and irredeemable forfeiture of ICS authority. The seemingly unassailable office of the deputy commissioner, delineated so painstakingly in *The Wild Sweet Witch,* masks the increasing lack of control that the men of the ICS, including Mason himself, actually experienced in the field of rural India. Hence this novel represents Mason's quite hopeless protest against the British retreat from India. To borrow an image from the American frontier, it is the ICS's last stand.

Having established the source of the novel's sorrow, readers can begin to come to terms with what this evocation of nostalgia struggles to exclude from our reading. Speaking of imperialist nostalgia generally, Renato Rosaldo writes, "In any of its versions, imperialist nostalgia uses a pose of 'innocent yearning' both to capture people's imaginations and to conceal its complicity with often brutal domination." By way of explanation, he adds, "The relatively benign character of most nostalgia facilitates imperialist nostalgia's capacity to transform the responsible colonial agent into an innocent bystander" (108). The nostalgia in *The Wild Sweet Witch* works toward this end. It serves to conceal the participation of Bennett, Upton, and Tregard in a form of government that depends on the silencing of indigenous resistance. Such incidents as the villagers' refusal to follow Bennett's dictates concerning ritualized killing and the attempts at local self-government of which Upton is so dismissive must be either underplayed or rationalized in order for the imperialist state to maintain its pretence of ruling by the consensus of the people. Any violent suppression of anti-imperialism by British administrative forces, which history documents in India throughout the long period of nationalist uprising, is left out of Mason's picture altogether. The massacre at Jallianwalla Bagh constitutes a marked absence in the text.

The nostalgia produced by this construct of hegemony usually envisages an era during which resistance simply did not exist, or if it did, its slight presence could be attributed to indigenous primitivism. In *The Wild Sweet Witch,* Bennett's golden-age rule is notable for its ease, which can be directly traced to the speedy and unquestioning obedience of the peasants. The villagers' attempt to circumvent authority is made to seem childishly devious and is therefore almost effortlessly put down. Readers are not supposed to interpret Bennett's actions as domination; he is merely correcting the villagers and ending a rather unpleasant custom. In *The Guardians,* there is a similar construction of the past. Mason, in the midst of describing nationalist protest, suddenly imagines a time when the English governed a trusting people: "They [the English] had been incorruptible, their word had been synonymous with truth. It had once been assumed on all hands that they were just and, within reason, benevolent. Now everything they did was questioned" (251). This statement makes resistance seem irrational, the product of anarchic forces beyond English control. Englishmen are therefore absolved of any responsibility for creating the conditions that produced resistance to their government. They are made to appear as the 'innocent bystanders' Rosaldo mentions above. The fact of their imperial supremacy is shunted to the side of the picture, where it can be strategically overlooked both by the author and the reader.

Mason's nostalgic novel and history, then, contain a series of exclusions, which must be maintained if the basic premise underlying both texts is to be upheld. This premise is that the British district officers in India were fundamentally benevolent rulers. Implicit in his writing is the assumption that the men of the ICS loved India and wanted what was best for its people. Hence Mason can describe the Indian/British relationship as "an affair of the heart" and its ending as an inevitably poignant "divorce" (*Guard* 347). I have no doubt at all that many Englishmen did, in fact, love India, but the problem with allowing the metaphor of a love affair to represent the truth about British imperialism in India is that as a truth it is extraordinarily limited. It tells only one version of a many-sided story. Because this version of British imperialism in India is grounded in such a tender and seemingly benign emotion as love, moreover, readers are lulled into accepting this single perspective as the whole story.

I doubt that the whole story is or ever will be available. The most that history and literature provide is various, often contradictory perspectives on the British presence in India, perspectives with some insights into what individual English men and women thought they were doing there and how their thinking contributed to the collective imagining of their imperialist experience. We therefore pick up the pieces of their story and hope that the present has given us the eyes to see that which was invisible to them or which they did not want to see. Confronting their illusions, misrepresentations, and their truths helps advance an understanding of the cultural constructs that perpetuated imperialism in India until its demise in 1947.

From the point of view of the Indian National Congress on the other side of the transfer of power, there is a similar story of faded glory, ebbing control, and nostalgic longings after a simpler past. This is in spite of the fact that the Congress was on the verge of seeing the fulfillment of its purpose, namely the ousting of British power. Of all the novels written by Indians in the last decade of the national movement, Bhattacharya's *So Many Hungers!* offers perhaps the most transparent portrait of Congress politics because it seems so desperately determined to promote an image of supremacy and strength. But in order to do so, like *The Wild Sweet Witch,* it must encourage us to overlook certain troubling issues, which might possibly call into question the text's fundamental assertion of Congress/peasant unity. Where the two novels differ, however, is in their manipulation of the nostalgic. While Mason's *The Wild Sweet Witch* makes nostalgia at least partially an aspect of its surface text, *So Many Hungers!* suppresses all knowledge of its own nostalgia. That the novel is nostalgic becomes apparent when it is placed in its historical moment. Published within months of independence day, August 15, 1947, and composed between the years 1944–46, *So Many Hungers!* looks back to the 1943 Bengal famine and imagines an era of Indian nationalism when the enemy was easily located in the government, and the movement itself was free of incongruities and internal strife. Bhattacharya's work is at its heart an expression of the nostalgic desire for an age of simple morality and effective action, neither of which was much in evidence during the chaotic, violence-ridden months that *So Many Hungers!* was written.

The strongest indication of the novel's nostalgic base is its depiction of the British/Indian political encounter. Drawing the simplest paradigm possible, the text posits two mutually exclusive polities poised in a struggle of epic proportions. Both groups are homogeneous and universalized. The novel simply refuses to be specific. Only toward the end are the Indian protagonists even identified as Congress nationalists. Prior to this, Rahoul, his famous freedom-fighting grandfather Devata, and the peasant family of which Kajoli is the principal member are portrayed as participants in a vague, monolithic "national movement" (44)—monolithic because it seems to involve every Indian who has not sold his or her soul to the British, either to acquire regular employment or to take advantage of British power for the purposes of rampant material gain, and vague because its parameters are studiously undefined. We are encouraged to believe that its influence stretches almost boundlessly throughout Bengal and other parts of India.

By the same token the amorphous regime against which the national movement has stationed itself is never precisely described. Instead, readers are permitted only impressions of India's domination by a dangerous and indeterminate bureaucracy. This disavowal of specificity allows the narrator to produce such mysterious statements as "lynx-eyed authority had watched every step of the national movement" (58) and obliquely to refer to "authority's bitter hatred of the people on whose bones Empire had been built" (59) without actually having to name the enemy. By painting his political canvas with such broad strokes, Bhattacharya avoids the complexities of both British imperialism and the Indian nationalist response to it. The nostalgia that *So Many Hungers!* represents cannot work, however, *unless* the paradigms on which the novel is grounded remain polarized and unsophisticated. For nostalgia is inherently a 'simplifying' emotion.

One of the complexities that the novel circumvents involves the Congress itself. We are told that Indians, being basically harmonious in their attitudes to imperialism, stand behind "that one personage whom India knew to be her man of destiny" (37), a personage later identified as the Congressman Jawaharlal Nehru. Bhattacharya sees him as the undisputed champion of the people and the predominant national leader of his time. His famous statement, made during his trial at Gorakhpur prison, in which he calls himself "a symbol of Indian nationalism" and insists that in condemning him, the British judiciary condemns the "hundreds of millions of the people of India" (38) is quoted in the text and goes unchallenged. We are, in fact, expected wholeheartedly to agree that this one man represents the whole of India. The reason he is able to do so is that the masses for whom Nehru speaks are consistently depicted as a "voiceless people" (21), a people entirely incapable of defending themselves or even of airing their grievances and hence in need of spokesmen from the intellectual classes. Clearly Bhattacharya is speaking from within the same belief system that contributed to the writing of Anand's *Untouchable*. Following in Nehru's footsteps, Rahoul and Devata assume this speaking role in *So Many Hungers!* This novel is therefore a product of the Nehru tradition exemplified in his *A Discovery of India*. This tradition *requires* the silence of the masses and their mute cooperation with the Congress. What this means is that the "struggle of the common people to break their chains" (86), to use the language of the novel, must remain strictly anti-imperialist in its scope. The possibility of a class struggle is strenuously evaded in Bhattacharya's text.

I use the word 'strenuously' because the overall setting of *So Many*

Hungers! is the Bengal famine of 1943, indisputably an event in Indian history that contains elements of class conflict. One class, predominantly the landless peasants, found itself pitted against the foreign central administration and the Bengali upper classes who were in control of the rice market. Millions of peasants died during the famine, in part as a result of the hoarding of rice and black-marketeering in which Bengal's upper classes participated. The Famine Inquiry Commission, set up by the Central Government in 1944 after the worst of the hunger was over, came to some interesting conclusions about the causes of the famine. Because it operated under the auspices of a still-imperialist British government in India, the Commission in its 1945 report tends to shy away from assigning too much blame to the central administration. It chooses instead to cite the incompetence of the precarious Indian government of Bengal as the primary contributing factor to the food shortages and consequent mass starvation. By using B. M. Bhatia's 1963 book *Famines in India,* however, as a corrective to the Commissions report, we can surmise that it was in the interests of the imperialist administration—which had become surprisingly conservative by this period—to *ensure* the precariousness of the Indian government in the province of Bengal. After quoting a passage from a letter written by the Viceroy, Lord Linlithgow, in which he absolves his government of all blame in the matter, preferring to see the Indian provincial administration as entirely responsible, Bhatia suggests that such British callousness in regards to the famine may have been born "out of deep-seated hostility on the part of most British officials at the time in India . . . towards the working of Provincial Autonomy" (339).

Both Bhatia and the Famine Inquiry Commission, nevertheless, seem to agree that the Bengal famine constituted a betrayal of the peasants not only by the two governments but by the middle- and upper-class Bengali communities as well. The Commission's report contains the following statement: "the public in Bengal, or at least certain sections of it, have also their share of blame. . . . Enormous profits were made out of the calamity, and in the circumstances, profits for some meant death for others. A large part of the community lived in plenty while others starved, and there was much indifference in the face of suffering. Corruption was widespread throughout the province and in many classes of society" (106–107).[6]

In his more recent *Prosperity and Misery in Modern Bengal: The Famine of 1943-1944,* Paul R. Greenough confirms much of Bhatia's earlier interpretation. He points out, for instance, that the bulk of Bengal's landlords opted out of the traditional responsibilities they were required to assume during times of famine. Instead of distributing food to the people who worked for them, an obligation that was implicit in the unspoken contract between the landlord and the peasants who cultivated his land and provided the necessary services to maintain his household, upper-class landlords as a group tended to make financial contributions to the middle-class run relief organizations, all the while hoarding their private rice and paddy stocks either for their own consumption or in the hopes that they could increase their profits when the prices of those stocks skyrocketed, as they inevitably did during the famine (163). Nor were the poor and peasant classes adequately served by these same relief organizations, which, having been established by middle-class Bengal, went on to rescue middle-class Bengal. As Greenough explains, these organizations operated alongside the government relief dispensed by gruel kitchens. The kitchens catered mostly to those Bengalis who occupied the lowest ranks of society—the poor, the low caste, and the untouchables—because, although they were open to everybody, the more impoverished members of Bengal's middle class often refused to patronize them for fear of losing caste and/or respectability. By directing their attentions exclusively to the middle class, the relief organizations actually managed to set themselves up in competition with the government-sponsored kitchens:

> Most "middle-class" food relief during the famine was in the form of rice, and most of this rice came from the stores of the Civil Supplies Department. . . . it is clear that rice taken from government stocks for private relief was at the expense of the official gruel kitchens and, hence, at the expense of the rural poor. To some extent, then, "middle-class" relief was a form of privilege. (135)

At least one of the implications of that privilege was the overall survival of the Bengali middle class. Of the 3.5 to 3.8 million people who died of famine between 1943 and 1946, the majority by far were from the peasant and labor classes.[7]

That Bhattacharya can construct the Bengal famine as a moment of great political cohesiveness for Bengalis, a time when they were able to unite against imperialism, attests to the existence in *So Many Hungers!* of a personal agenda, which insists on using the peasants' experiences of starvation and death for the purposes of glorifying the national movement. Many of the above historical details are available in some fashion in *So Many Hungers!* and yet Bhattacharya still manages to avoid suggesting that the tragic deaths of so many rural people during the Bengal famine can be traced to the middle- and upper-class alliances that ensured the preservation of the elite and the sacrifice of the poor. Instead we are meant to view the suffering of peasant Bengalis in 1943 as somehow congruent with the suffering, supposedly on their behalf, that the predominantly upper-class Hindu men and women of the Congress endured as a result of their anti-imperialism. This construct is problematic in the extreme because it leads to an appropriation on the part of the *bhadralok,* or Hindu upper classes, of the peasants' great tragedy and a concomitant abdication of responsibility.

Rahoul and his wife Monju are the two upper-middle-class characters whose growth toward political and spiritual enlightenment is charted in the course of the story. But while Rahoul's allegiance to the Congress national movement is a given at the beginning of the novel, we actually observe Monju's conversion, the moment when she ceases to think of herself as an individual and starts to define her identity in terms of an Indian nation. It occurs when a starving pregnant woman stumbles into the family household and in the process of giving birth dies with only Monju nearby as a witness. At this point the woman is revealed to her not as "a pauper ever whining for morsels" (148) but as another mother. Monju recognizes the essential oneness of humankind and comes finally to understand "the glory of service" (148) which has fuelled her husband's search "for a happier life for the common man." In the final comment the novel makes on the event, the woman, as a peasant separate from the *bhadralok* who have watched her death, is forgotten. She is subsumed into the epithet "our womenfolk" and made a pawn in the patriarchally motivated and anti-imperialist struggle of the upper classes: " 'Excellencies and Hon'bles,' said Rahoul later when the night had ended and the corpse-disposal squad had come and gone, 'they have killed one more of our womenfolk. They shall pay—pay hard for everything' " (149). With this statement Rahoul effectively erases the otherness of the starving peasant woman. She virtually becomes one of his family members, analogous to his mother or sister and belonging to him, the eldest son and heir, in the same way that they might. Consequently, he is able to usurp the grief of the peasant woman's son or brother. This tendency in Rahoul and in other upper-middle-class Bengali characters in the text to align themselves with the peasants, proclaiming a family tie to them, serves the added purpose of effacing any blame in which they might participate as a result of the famine. For certainly it is not family members who have brought about the peasants' starvation, readers are supposed to surmise, but someone external to the community. The Congressmen and women who identify with the lower class are, therefore, permitted to occupy a position of victimization similar to that of the dying peasant population at the same time that they are idealized as its rescuers.

Although Bhattacharya depicts the Congress in 1943 at the height of its influence and righteousness, some of his contemporaries have drawn a different picture. Most of the 1940s writers who critique the performance of the Congress usually cite 1937 as the start of its moral decline, since this year saw the creation and functioning of Congress ministries in various provinces throughout India. The Congress swept the 1937 elections, winning 711 out of 1585 provincial assembly seats, with an absolute majority in five out of eleven provinces. Pressed into forming ministries, against the advice of its socialist members who demanded the total repudiation of office, the Congress soon found itself operating as a government for the first time in its history. Initially, the Congress ministries were able to bring about some progressive change, in the areas of civil liberties and agrarian legislation, and they did make somewhat limited attempts to introduce educational and health reforms, limited because these reforms could not reach the main causes of the poverty of the masses of Indian people. But within a relatively short period, Congress policies began to show an increasingly anti-labor and anti-peasant bent.

C. R. Rajagopalachari, who was the head of a Congress government in Madras, began as early as October 1937 to prosecute nationalists from other anti-imperialist organizations for delivering seditious speeches. Furthermore, the police, an institution that had oppressed Congress itself for years, were called out by Congress governments to suppress certain communal riots and Left-led labor and peasant revolts (see Sarkar 352).

Congress's critics found such actions enormously telling. R. Palme Dutt, in his 1940 *India To-Day*, writes that the Congress Ministries actually acted as "organs of imperialist administration" (463). He adds,

> The experience of the two years of Congress Ministries demonstrated with growing acuteness the dangers implicit in entanglement in imperialist administration under a leadership already inclined to compromise. The dominant moderate leadership in effective control of the Congress machinery and of the Ministries was in practice developing to increasing co-operation with imperialism, was acting more and more openly in the interests of the upper-class landlords and industrialists, and was showing an increasingly marked hostility to all militant expression and forms of mass struggle. (469)

Dutt repeatedly describes the Congress as an organization whose interests remained closely connected to those of the landlord class. The functioning of the ministries made this particularly apparent. He also argues that it was fear that kept the Congress from championing the cause of the peasant to the extent that an abolition of landlordism would be the logical outcome, fear of the social forces of agrarian revolution that might arise in consequence of such a step. An agrarian revolution "would sweep away their own class privileges," he observes (524).

D. F. Karaka in *I've Shed My Tears: A Candid View of Resurgent India*, written a few months before independence day, shares Dutt's belief that Congress had, by 1940, fallen from its moral pedestal. However, he locates the source of the corruption not so much in its bad faith regarding the problems of the peasant as in the general arrogance and hypocrisy that had crept into the Congress ranks once they had a taste of the power available through the holding of governmental office. While Dutt seems to believe that the Congress approach was always enormously flawed, Karaka was at one time its avid supporter and well-wisher. His book is a record of his growing disillusionment with the Congress and its members.

Karaka contends that the Indian National Congress was fundamentally a sound political organization whose personnel and leaders had grown "smug and complacent" as a result of its burgeoning influence over the Indian people (199). Its success in the 1937 elections, demonstrating that it was the foremost Indian nationalist party, led the Congress to believe,

Karaka writes, "that it had the exclusive right to represent every sect and community in the country" (199–200). This attitude infuriated the Muslim League and its leader, Mohammed Ali Jinnah, who claimed that the Muslims in India required a party of their own, distinct and separate from what he—and Karaka—saw as the predominantly Hindu Congress.

This new high-handedness became particularly apparent in Karaka's home province of Bombay when, in spite of the fact that the Congress had not achieved a majority in the 1937 election and ended up forming a minority government, it refused to set up a coalition and "share the spoils with the Muslim League": "Instead, to appease those who criticized the Congress for its refusal to adopt coalitions, the Congress adopted what might be called the 'stooge system.' It took into its ministries, Moslems willing to sign the Congress pledge in return for a seat in the cabinet" (203). Such dismissive treatment of the Muslim League served to buttress Jinnah's contention that the Congress was committed to the interests of the Hindus and would, when freedom came, allow the Muslims to play only a secondary role in the affairs of the country. By 1946, when the next round of elections took place, Congress had lost much of its Muslim support; the League won 442 out of 509 Muslim seats in the provinces and all 30 reserved Muslim constituencies in the center. Karaka contends that Congress had itself to blame for the alienation of the greater part of the Muslim population. By neglecting the issue of Muslim minority status in Congress circles and by minimizing the importance of Jinnah as the voice of Muslim dissatisfaction with the Congress, it was unable to "counteract the effect of Jinnah's growing popularity" (204). Writing before Pakistan was a reality, Karaka suggests that it was primarily the Congress's failure substantially to engage the Muslims in its struggle for independence that brought Partition closer than it had ever been before.

Not only Karaka but virtually every text that documents 1940s nationalism makes some reference to the rising tide of India's communalism, which set the stage for what was to become the crowning calamity of the independence struggle, the Partition. This piece of nationalism, however, is omitted in Bhattacharya's *So Many Hungers!*, though the novel purports to be about the "national movement," albeit from the point of view of Bengal. Not one character in the novel is Muslim, neither among the upper classes nor the peasants. Consequently, no communalist disunity is possible within the context of the world posited in the novel. The Congress, which the text so unrestrainedly valorizes, is also distinctly Hindu in its make up. Such a homogeneous image of the Congress in Bengal eliminates the need for any questioning on the part of the reader of the party's policy concerning the Muslims.

The absence of the Muslim perspective from Bhattacharya's construction of the Bengal Congress finds some justification in other histories of Indian nationalism. D. A. Low points out that the Bengal Provincial Congress Committee was "*bhadralok*-dominated": "As early as 1923, moreover, Congress in Bengal, dominated by its Hindu elite, had already lost the support it had earlier had amongst Bengal's Muslim Jotedars [petty landlords]" (23). According to a 1964 essay written by Humayun Kabir, a well-known Muslim activist, Bengal's earlier history—the era toward the end of the eighteenth and beginning of the nineteenth centuries—was responsible for the later Muslim/Hindu divide. British imperialism had settled in Bengal first and, in establishing itself, had favored the Hindus over the recently-ousted and more politically powerful Muslims. The British created a situation in which the propertied class was almost exclusively Hindu, while Muslims largely comprised the peasant and laborer population (15).[8] In another essay he wrote in 1943, Kabir further states that the Congress in Bengal traditionally appealed to the Hindu minority and more specifically to its middle and upper classes. However, though Congress was able to capture the imagination of the Hindus, it was unable to implement an effective mass action because it lacked the support of Bengal's majority community, the Muslims. Kabir writes, "Bengal shows perhaps more clearly than elsewhere the consequences of Congress dependence on sentiment rather than organisation, on middle class allegiance rather than awakened mass consciousness" (22). That Bhattacharya's novel leaves Muslims out of its picture of Congress seems understandable given the divisive political atmosphere in Bengal in 1943. Nevertheless, the text does repress the reason behind the Congress's inability to recruit Muslims in large numbers, and obviously it does so in order to lend credence to its evocation of nationalist unity. To maintain the ideal of a united Bengal ranged in nationalist agitation against a foreign power, Muslim dissent must be invisible in *So Many Hungers!* Bhattacharya's exclusion of the Muslim peasant from the Bengal famine of 1943 is another matter altogether.

So Many Hungers! displaces the Muslim peasant in its reconstruction of the Bengal famine first at a tangible level. Millions of people lost their land, their possessions, watched their families die, and finally died themselves in the 1943 famine. Among the dead and dying were many, many Muslims. Greenough observes that although there was some attempt at the time to minimize the extent of Muslim hardship, "there is no evidence to suggest that Muslims as a whole were less affected by the famine than Hindus" (189).[9] Since no Muslims appear in the novel, the famine seems to be exclusively a Hindu tragedy. By writing the Muslims out of the picture, Bhattacharya also writes out the issue of Hindu responsibility for both Hindu and Muslim deaths. If, as Kabir insists, Muslims constituted the greater part of the peasant population and Hindus the largest proportion of the upper and middle classes, then the rice hoarding and black-marketeering, which contributed to the food shortage, was largely Hindu-controlled.[10]

Muslims are excluded from the story of the 1943 famine in Bengal at a symbolic level as well. Their rituals and religion are erased from Bhattacharya's portrait. At one point in the text, Rahoul ponders the passivity of the peasants in the face of death by starvation. Both the event to which he alludes as an example of peasant revolution and the conclusion he comes to about the peasants' refusal to act show marked Hindu biases:

> Barely a year had passed since these men, or their brethren, had risen in anger against the tyrants, the robbers of freedom, who had swept the people's leaders into prison without even a pretence of trial. But they would not rise in revolt that their stomachs could be soothed—a selfish personal end! They would fight and die over a moral issue. But hunger was their fate, an expiation of the sins of past lives. The peasants' hands were manacled with their antique moral tradition. (95–96)

It was the Quit India movement which saw the arrest and imprisonment of the major Congress leaders in 1942, a movement from which Indian Muslims largely remained aloof (see Sarkar 399). When Rahoul speaks of the "people's leaders," therefore, he is effacing Muslims from the category of the 'people.' Nor can these men be unproblematically identified as the "people's leaders," since the majority of the people in Bengal in 1942–1943 were unwilling to be led by them. Furthermore, Rahoul's representation

of Bengali peasants as a fatalistic folk who embrace hunger as "an expia-
tion of the sins of past lives" strategically ignores Muslim religious belief,
which does not hold to the doctrine of *samsara* or the cycle of lives. The
"moral tradition" mentioned in the above passage is a Hindu practice
masquerading as a pan-Bengali culture.

The Hindu hegemony that Bhattacharya tries to establish in *So Many
Hungers!* is thus constantly fractured by the gaps it must leave in order to
construct its version of events in Bengal in the early forties. These gaps lead
us to an understanding of the dynamics of the text as a three-way discourse.
British imperialism in India—what the novel obliquely refers to as "authority"—contends not only with the "national movement," symbolized
by the Congress, but also with Muslim interrogation of that movement.
Although this interrogation must be read into the text, it nevertheless
exists as a potential voice and therefore as a definite site of resistance to
the dominant Hindu construction of reality that Bhattacharya promotes.

While Bhattacharya was writing his novel, Bengalis were murdering
each other in the streets of Calcutta. From August 16 to August 19, 1946,
an estimated four thousand people were killed and ten thousand injured.
It was predominantly a mutual massacre carried out by the Hindu and
Muslim communities, with Muslims in the end dying in greater numbers
than the Hindus. Between March 26 and April 1, 1947, a second round of
riots occurred, "followed by chronic disturbances and stabbing incidents
till the very eve of independence" (Sarkar 433). The communal violence
spread to other parts of India, to Bombay in September 1946, to Bihar in
October, and finally to the Punjab in January 1947, which proved to be
"the greatest holocaust of all" (Sarkar 434). In just over a year, 180,000
people were killed in the Punjab, while six million Muslims and four and
a half million Hindus and Sikhs had the questionable distinction of becoming what journalists and historians would describe as the largest refu-
gee population in the known history of the world.[11] That in the midst of
this carnage Bhattacharya could write a novel about the peaceful unity between Congress and the peasants of Bengal, implying that such harmony
existed throughout India, indicates his powerfully nostalgic vision. Unable
to discover a golden age around him, he creates an era when there was
one. He is looking for innocence and solidarity, and he turns to a famine
to find these virtues because famines—with their disastrous urgency and

enormous need—seem to strip issues of their complexities. But innocence and solidarity exist in his Bengal of 1943 only if readers, following Bhatta-charya's paradigm, narrowly define conflict in pre-1947 India as purely anti-imperialist in scope. His golden age is therefore a mask, behind which the face of India's independence struggle was violently changing, preparing itself for the transfer of power that would finally bring nationalist Indi-ans the autonomy they had demanded for over fifty years. Bhattacharya's literary blindness—his refusal to write about the violence around him—is comparable to the political blindness of Nehru and other nationalist leaders, whose inability or unwillingness to confront the problem of com-munalism contributed to the disaster of Partition (see Sucheta Mahajan's analysis in Chandra 500–503).

This 1940s suppression and undervaluation of knowledge about com-munalist violence has had far-reaching consequences. In the realm of Indian historiography, it has, according to Gyanendra Pandey, created something of a trend. He argues in a 1992 article that the history of sectar-ian conflict in India is generally told as a "secondary story": " 'Hindu' poli-tics, 'Muslim' politics, and Hindu-Muslim strife appear as minor elements in the main drama of India's struggle for independence from colonial rule . . ." (29). The demands of a nationalist discourse, which constructs Indians as fundamentally secular, peace-loving people who are concerned with nation-building, have overwhelmed the other stories in twentieth-century Indian history to such an extent that Partition and all its violence is represented by historians, journalists, filmmakers, and novelists as an "aberration," "an accident, a 'mistake.' " Pandey understands the reasons for the collective avoidance of this very difficult subject. He writes, "We have no means of representing such tragic loss, nor of pinning down—or rather, owning—responsibility for it" (33). Partition, including the hor-rors that preceded and followed it, constitutes a traumatic event in India's history. Its suppression or deflection into categories of meaninglessness—such as those implicit in words like 'aberration,' 'accident' and 'mistake'—ensures the continuance of a dominant and state-supported nationalist narrative. It is the heterogeneity of India's histories that is at stake here.

But there are writers who have, as witnesses, recorded the violence of those days. Writing in 1946, around the same time that Bhattacharya com-pleted his book, Karaka delineates the communal furies erupting around him as a "force of unrest" which "has now become the most outstanding fact in India today." He adds, "There is nothing else in the whole political pattern which is so clearly discernible" (277). The violence had gone beyond ideology and beyond the nationalist leaders' ability to contain it. But Karaka attaches a positive significance to the rioting and destruction. It denotes, for him, a "spirit of revolt," "a new consciousness," "a new nation." He sees in the future of his land and people more "dead bodies unidentified in our morgues . . . more riots, more disturbances, more strikes and more innocent blood shed." In his eyes, this is the price, in the end, of India's political independence.

I conclude this chapter and this book with Karaka's last comment, rather than with intimations about the brutalities that would precede, coincide with, and follow the transfer of power. Because it seems to me that the state of mind that Karaka believes he is on the verge of achieving was the goal of all the pre-independence Indian writers whose work has contributed to these pages: Dutt, Kabir, Swarnakumari Devi, Bhattacharya, Pandita Ramabai, and Anand. Karaka writes, "But whatever may be the boundaries of my land, I know I shall have my freedom soon and I shall have my self-respect" (280). These are important things to have, and so many Indians ushered in August 15, 1947 with hopes that these were what they were getting. Out of respect for these authors and with the humility of someone who was born with a good share of political freedom, I choose to remain on the side of those hopes.

Notes

Introduction

1 See particularly the introduction and first chapter of Brantlinger's *Rule of Darkness*. Hutchins and Morris's books, *The Illusion of Permanence: British Imperialism in India* and *Pax Britannica: The Climax of an Empire* respectively, throughout offer examples of the noisiness of the British as they proceeded to consolidate their empire in India as well as in other countries around the world.

2 I am referring here to feminist writings about the colonial period, the work of the *Subaltern Studies* historians, and recent analyses of India's low caste and untouchable peoples, all of which tend to challenge the belief propagated in mainstream histories of the nationalist movement that the Indian National Congress and its predominantly male, upper- and middle-class leaders brought about massive change on behalf of India's downtrodden people. Scholars such as Kumari Jayawardena in *Feminism and Nationalism in the Third World*, Rosalind O'Hanlon in *Caste, Conflict, and Ideology*, Trilok Nath in *Politics of the Depressed Classes*, and Malavika Karlekar in *Voices from Within*, to name only a few, not only contest the traditional supposition made by many historians that the Congress alone was responsible for reforming Indian society but also point out that whatever change the Congress did introduce, it was generally circumscribed by its allegiance to capitalist and patriarchal forces.

3 "Anglo-Indian" is a term that in India today refers to persons of mixed European and Indian racial background. Because the term was adopted by the British in India to designate themselves, I am using it in my discussion of imperialist literature to avoid confusion. "Indo-Anglian" is the adjective used to describe the body of literature written by Indians in English.

4 Although Tennyson's poetry is generally featured in university English classes, for instance, we do not study either his "To the Marquis of Dufferin and Ava" or "The Defence of Lucknow" or "On the Jubilee of Queen Victoria," all of which—and more besides—are as imperialist as anything Kipling wrote.

1 Containing Indian Nationalism: Kipling's Struggle

1 See chapter 1, "The First Major Challenge: The Revolt of 1857," written by K. N. Pannikar, and Bipan Chandra's chapter 2, "Civil Rebellions and Tribal Uprising," in *India's Struggle for Independence*.

2 In *India Today: The Background of Indian Nationalism*, Duffett, Hicks, and

Parkin, writing their history in 1942, five years before political independence was achieved, assert, "It is important that Canadian or American readers, accustomed to thinking of the word Congress as referring to a constitutionally established legislature, should remember that in India the term Congress refers merely to a political party" (63).

3   Although in the early nineteenth century India was commonly referred to as an "Indian nation" or as several Indian nations in the imperialist tracts of the time, by the close of the century Indian nationality was fervently denied by British imperialist writers. Speaking to a Cambridge undergraduate class in the 1910s, Sir John Strachey argued, "India is a name which we give to a great region including a multitude of different countries . . . there is not, and never was an India, or even a country of India, possessing, according to European ideas, any sort of unity, physical, political, social, or religious; no Indian nation, no 'people of India,' of which we hear so much" (quoted in Hutchins 142).

4   Kipling's later fiction about Anglo-India, those works written after he had left the country in 1889, shows less critical detachment. However, in his first two collections of short stories, *Plain Tales From the Hills* (1888) and *Life's Handicap* (1891), the role he assumes is predominantly that of the sardonic observer.

2   A Memsahib and Her Not-So-Simple Adventures

1   Darling served as an Anglo-Indian official in the Punjab for over thirty-five years, from 1904 to 1940. He wrote several books about India but is probably best known for his writings on Punjabi peasants. One book in particular, *The Punjab Peasant in Prosperity and Debt* (1925), earned him international acclaim.

2   Not surprisingly, Kipling's infamous poem "The White Man's Burden" was published during this period, in 1899, as were many of his most fiercely imperialist short stories, such as "The Tomb of His Ancestors" and "The Head of the District," both of which congratulate the white man on a job well done.

3   E. M. Forster was applauded by Indians and Englishmen alike when he suggested some of the same things fifteen years later in *A Passage to India*. Forster is frequently written about as if he were the first British novelist to take the Indian desire for self-government seriously. This is in spite of the fact that he barely acknowledges the existence of the nationalist movement in his novel. It is interesting that Darling, in his autobiography, repeatedly aligns himself with Forster and Forster's views on India. In the 1960s when Darling wrote about his early experiences as an ICS officer, these views had taken on the mantle of authority.

4   See "An Interesting Condition" and The Burden of Nineveh," respectively

published in *The Pioneer* and *The Civil and Military Gazette* in 1888. Kipling's journalism has been reproduced in *The Readers' Guide to Rudyard Kipling's Work,* ed. R. E. Harbord.

5 I have examined this in more detail in an article entitled, " 'The Bride of His Country': Love, Marriage, and the Imperialist Paradox in the Indian Fiction of Sara Jeannette Duncan and Rudyard Kipling," published in *Ariel,* January 1990.

6 To give Darling credit, we should acknowledge that he at least is sympathetic to the predicament of educated Indians under British rule, which is more than can be said of most of the other writers of this period, both of fiction and nonfiction. Some of the fiercest attacks on the Indian character in Anglo-Indian literature come in the form of ridiculous portraits of Bengali *babus* or clerks. They are frequently shown to be cunning, cowardly, and effeminate men whose English is the object of much humor on the part of the narrator. See Kipling's short story, "The Head of the District" and Thomas Anstey Guthrie's two novels, *A Barnyard for Bengal* (1902) and *Baboo Hurry Bungsho Jabberjee, B.A.* (1897).

7 This is one of the cornerstones of Kipling's metaphor. Kipling's love for India is apparent everywhere in his fiction, as is his seemingly contradictory conviction that it must continue to be governed by the British. For Kipling, love and subjugation go hand in hand. The conventional Victorian marriage, with its strict hierarchy along gender lines and its idealization of love, is particularly appropriate in Kipling's work as a metaphor of the colonial relationship between India and Britain.

8 In her 1992 book *The Rhetoric of English India,* Sara Suleri has come up with a wonderfully insightful and subtle interpretation not only of Fanny Parks's journal, *Wanderings of a Pilgrim in Search of the Picturesque,* but of a number of autobiographical texts written by 'ordinary' (read middle class, not extraordinary) Memsahibs. Her basic argument is that, because of the terror, the panic, and the patriarchal ideals implicit in the project of British imperialism, white women in India demonstrated a "very different sense of colonial possession, in which to rule was simultaneously to be dispossessed; to be forced to evolve an aesthetic in which the working of such power became synonymous with the metaphorical redundancy of femininity" (77). The aesthetic that documented both their diminution under British patriarchy and their collusion with its imperialism Suleri calls the feminine picturesque, a mode of writing and painting that was particularly practiced by middle-class memsahibs.

9 In *The Memsahibs,* Barr briefly describes the lives of the British women who lived in barracks with their soldier husbands and raised their children there. She calls them "the wretched Englishwomen, the lowest in rank and least remembered of all the 'mems.', who chose, or were obliged, to accompany their menfolk for the ten-year stint on the hot hell of the Indian plains. . . . Arrived

at a new post, the soldier's wives went off to haggle in the native bazaars and the officers' wives shuddered to see them—as they did to hear them carolling drunkenly from the canteen occasionally, or keening over their dying children" (95). The lives of these women deserve more attention (and less paternalistic, middle-class sympathy) in the current feminist recovery of Raj history. The charge that is frequently leveled against the middle- and upper-class women of British India is that they kept a physical and emotional distance between themselves and the Indians. The soldiers' wives were among the few white women in Anglo-Indian society who lived in close contact with the indigenous population of India. The history or histories of their lives might present a different picture of the British/Indian relationship under the conditions of imperialism.

10   It is difficult to gauge Duncan's appraisal of this event in the novel, because the narrator has, until this point, maintained a satirical tone when commenting on Joan and her motives. Joan has been depicted as a woman who is too ardent in her politics and too eager to advocate Indian nationalism without fully understanding the British/Indian relationship. Furthermore, I think that we are expected to regard Joan's response to John's proposal as indicative of her inability to comprehend his deeply felt passion for her. Nevertheless, the narrator has also repeatedly brought to our attention the fact that John has a simplistic approach to politics and to love, one that does not do justice to the complexities of either. Under these conditions, it seems ludicrous to imagine John, with his "simple soul" (47), imposing his convictions on a woman who has been portrayed as more intelligent and more politically astute than he is.

11   A collection of essays, edited by Nupur Chauduri and Margaret Strobel and entitled *Western Women and Imperialism: Complicity and Resistance,* deals with this very issue of empathy between the patriarchally ruled white women who participated in the Empire and the colonized men and women they ruled.

12   Like most events in *The Burnt Offering,* Janaki's, Kristodas's, and Yadava's spiritual withdrawal from the world, which closes the novel, can be interpreted in two, quite contradictory ways. On the one hand, it is a conservative ending. Duncan uses the Indian tradition of *sannyasi* simply to tie up the loose bits, getting rid of those Indian characters whose beliefs have been most challenged and altered by the climactic events of the novel. Duncan's refusal to deal with the ramifications of John's death and Ganendra's conviction in the lives of Janaki and Kristodas seems to be part of her attempt to impose some closure on the text which would demonstrate the ascendancy of imperialism. On the other hand, readers might interpret this ending in a more radical light, seeing it as a criticism of the very imperialism the novel inscribes. The fact that only the politically moderate characters have left the world of British India suggests that this world does not properly accommodate or satisfy them, any more than it accommodates or satisfies the nationalists. One of the narrator's comments would seem to support this reading: "Life not having pleased them,

they have exercised towards it the profound and delicate option which is their inheritance; they have left it in the world" (319). It could be argued that even the moderate Indians in *The Burnt Offering* are not "pleased" with the life available to them under British rule.

13   Kipling's short story "Without Benefit of Clergy" and Leonard Woolf's "A Tale Told By Moonlight" contain examples of this type of interracial relationship. In Kipling's tale, the Indian woman dies of cholera. Woolf has her kill herself out of grief when her British lover leaves her. Both of these stories are reprinted in *More Stories from the Raj and After,* selected by Saros Cowasjee.

14   In Canadian scholarship on Anglo-Indian literature, there is some movement toward incorporating Duncan into the Canadian or Commonwealth canon. I am thinking here of Thomas E. Tausky's *Sara Jeannette Duncan: Novelist of Empire* (1980) and of the publications of *The Burnt Offering* (1978) in the University of Toronto Press, *The Simple Adventures of a Memsahib* in Tecumseh Press (1986), and a collection of her short stories entitled *The Pool in the Desert* in Penguin Books.

3   Liberal Imperialism as a Passage to India

1   When I use the word "myth" I do not mean to suggest that the historical circumstances to which I am referring are untrue. Of course, there was an August 1917 pledge and, of course, Gandhi was an immensely important figure in the Indian nationalist movement. What I wish to highlight with this word are the complex and detailed mythic constructions that inevitably rise up around significant events and people.

2   Schuster and Wint were far from alone among British writers of Indian history in articulating this liberal myth of imperialism. In a much better-known book, *India Old and New,* published some twenty years earlier, closer to the time of Forster's novel, Valentine Chirol constructs an almost identical justification for British rule in India, replete with the insistence that something out of British control (for Chirol this was the French challenge to British authority in the eighteenth century) had given Britain domination over India: "We had gone to India with no purpose of seeking dominion, but circumstances had forced dominion upon us. With dominion had come the recognition of the great responsibilities which it involved, and having imposed upon India our own role of law we imposed it also upon the agencies through which we then exercised dominion—a self-denying ordinance for ourselves, for Indians a pledge of justice" (299–300).

3   See the *Subaltern Studies* volumes and specifically Ranajit Guha's introductory essay, "On Some Aspects of the Historiography of Colonial India" and Gyan Pandey's "Peasant Revolt and Indian Nationalism: The Peasant Movement in Awadh, 1919–1922" in Volume I.

4   In his article "On Some Aspects of Historiography of Colonial India," Guha

identifies four categories of elitist historiography. The first two, colonialist and neo-colonialist, which have been practiced by historians in Britain, India, and in other countries as well, focus on the events that surrounded and involved the British in colonial India. The second two, nationalist and neo-nationalist, find their protagonists among Indian nationalist leaders and the educated elite. Although predominantly an Indian practice, nationalist and neo-nationalist historiography has its imitators outside of India "in the ranks of liberal historians in Britain and elsewhere" (1:1). What these four varieties of historiography share is their tendency to see nationalism primarily or exclusively as an elite movement.

5 Without undermining the genuine emotion that has gone into the creation of this image, it is important that we understand how convenient it is as an explanatory trope. It is convenient because it explains away the Englishman's attraction to India, without making him examine his part in that attraction. Englishmen come because India calls. That there might be some other motive behind the Englishman's residence in India, for instance, that Englishmen stood to gain financially by living in India, is an issue that is suppressed by this romantic trope of India's seductiveness.

6 I am indebted to Jenny Sharpe's article "Figures of Colonial Resistance" for making this connection between the punkah wallah and Orientalism.

7 Throughout this chapter, I have argued that English imperialism manifested two separate and distinct forms in India, the liberal reformative ethic and conservative Orientalism. I am convinced that this bipartite understanding of imperialism accounts for many apparently contradictory events and their accompanying attitudes—such as the social reform movement of the early and middle nineteenth century, with its openness to change, followed by the later reaction to reform after the Mutiny or Indian Revolt of 1857, which enshrined India as unchangeable. It is not enough to interpret imperialism, as Said often does in *Orientalism,* as stable and static, an ethos which simply grew more intractable as the Empire expanded, because such an interpretation ignores the rhythms through which English imperialism in India expressed itself. The one aspect of imperialism which remained constant, however, was the desire of the English to rule the Indians, though that rule was occasionally liberal and at other times conservative in tone. In the pursuit of this desire, the two streams frequently merged or subtly and unresistantly gave way to one another. Liberalism was frequently informed by conservative Orientalism and vice versa. When I say, therefore, that Forster switches camps from the liberal to the conservative through the introduction of the figures of the punkah wallah and temple servitor, I am acknowledging the tendency of English imperialism to move back and forth between these streams.

4   The High-Caste Hindu Woman as a Site of Contest
    in Imperialist/Nationalist India

1   Included in Queen Victoria's 1858 proclamation to her newly acquired Indian
    subjects was the following threat, aimed at those British people in power in
    India: "We do strictly charge and enjoin all those who may be in authority
    under us that they abstain from all interference with the religious belief or
    worship of any of our subjects on pain of our highest displeasure" (quoted in
    Moorhouse 124).

2   Fuller is critical of the government only insofar as it does not do what she
    expects of it, namely pass more legislation to protect Indian women. Neither
    she nor Billington sees the British presence in India as somehow contributing
    to the plight of the Indian woman. For both authors, although the former
    is a liberal imperialist and the latter an Orientalist, the government and the
    English society that upholds it stand outside Indian culture, their only effect
    being one which is dependent on parliaments and law courts. The idea that
    imperialism might have insidious repercussions for the cultures it dominates
    does not enter into either of their texts.

3   For wonderful exceptions to this rule, see *Recasting Women: Essays in Colonial
    History,* edited by Kumkum Sangari and Sudesh Vaid, and Kumari Jayawar-
    dena's *Feminism and Nationalism in the Third World.*

4   At this point, I should mention another fascinating novel written by an Indian
    woman some twenty-five years after Swarnakumari Devi's *An Unfinished Song.*
    Entitled *Purdah and Polygamy* and published by the author herself, Iqbalun-
    nisa Hussain, in 1944, this novel offers a much more scathing attack on Indian
    patriarchy and particularly Muslim patriarchy than is apparent in Swarna-
    kumari's text. Like Swarnakumari, Hussain is interested in the remaking of
    Indian womanhood. However, she does not appear to share her predecessor's
    nationalist leanings.

5   Spivak presents this concept in a number of her essays. "Three Women's Texts
    and a Critique of Imperialism," "Can the Subaltern Speak?", and "The Rani
    of Sirmur" are three in which the notion of the "self-consolidating Other" is
    central.

6   See "Can the Subaltern Speak?"

7   The purpose of this ideal was to create women who were more appropriate
    matches for the emerging westernized class of Hindu men, women who were
    educated, who had renounced purdah and other such customs which these
    men began to regard as backward. The exclusion of the lower caste woman—
    with her continued belief in certain Hindu rituals that the westernized classes
    found contemptible—from this early nationalist discourse was necessary in
    order to produce an image of progress along western lines, which men of
    these classes believed was necessary to the process of social reform concern-
    ing high-caste women. The absence of the working-class or subaltern woman

from the woman's nationalist movement and from associated writing about the movement was a contentious issue as late as 1939, less than ten years before independence, when the renowned Indian feminist/nationalist Kamaladevi Chattopadhyayya wrote, "The women's movement . . . in India as in other countries is in the hands of the few bourgeois women. . . . It is consequently coloured by their own problems and needs and does not correctly reflect the demands or the problems of the large mass of women" (7). An interesting book, entitled *Our Cause: A Symposium by Indian Women,* published in 1936, also identified the movement's irrelevance to the lives of the vast majority of women in India as one of its major defects (see introduction by Shyam Kumari Nehru). The refusal to include the lower caste women in the early nationalist movement resulted in a crisis of conscience, which later feminists were not able to resolve.

Uma Chakravarti and Kumari Jayawardena have each examined the nineteenth-century nationalist construction of the high-caste Hindu woman. I recommend both of their works.

8   In 1891, the nationalist Bal Gangadhar Tilak wrote five editorials in his newspaper *Kesari* criticizing Pandita Ramabai for going to the Christians to procure funds for her school. Such indebtedness to Christian supporters, he suggested, would inevitably lead to a situation in which the school became simply a pretext for missionary activities. From the beginning, however, the Pandita insisted that her school was a place where Hindu child widows could obtain an education without fearing the loss of their religion and caste. In *The High-Caste Hindu Woman* she insists that, in spite of her own conversion, her school remain a refuge only for Hindu girls interested in maintaining their religion. There already existed in India many mission schools for those Hindu women who wanted to become Christian.

9   In her introduction, Bodley quotes Pandita Ramabai as saying that, once educated, the high-caste child widow will one day "redeem India" (xxiv), but how this is to be accomplished is not mentioned. The statement seems to have been made in the interests of the inflated rhetoric of the introduction, rather than with any serious intent or as the basis of a thought-out plan of emancipation for Hindu women in particular and India in general.

10   The question of whether or not *An Unfinished Song* was originally composed in English or translated in 1913 from the Bengali does not seem to matter much to those few people who have written about Swarnakumari Devi's work. G. P. Sarma recognizes *An Unfinished Song* as an English novel when he mentions it in the bibliography to his book, *Nationalism in Indo-Anglian Fiction,* which he insists lists only those novels by Indian writers written originally in English. Bhupal Singh's *A Survey of Anglo-Indian Fiction,* which was first published in 1934, also mentions *An Unfinished Song* and a later novel in English *The Fatal Garland.* The introduction to the 1913 edition of *An Unfinished Song* merely

states that "this is the first time that a book of hers has been brought before the English public" (7). In her 1918 preface to *The Fatal Garland*, Swarnakumari states that *An Unfinished Song* was written "in my own tongue" twenty years before (13). There is evidence, however, in the novel itself that, even if it were originally written in Bengali, it was altered to some degree for an English audience. *An Unfinished Song* is full of statements such as, "This is a custom generally adopted in India in country districts" (21) and "No Westerner can realise what a powerful influence matrimony has upon the life of a Hindu woman" (44–45). These suggest that the author is conscious of writing for a non-Indian audience. My own interest in *An Unfinished Song* lies in the way in which Swarnakumari constructed her idea of the high-caste Hindu woman for both the English-educated Indian elite, of which she was one, and for a readership outside India. The fact that the novel was rendered in English at all is the important detail here.

11 I use the phrase "come to be regarded" because I wish to stress my belief that traditions are always constructed. I think that this particular tradition of the high-caste Hindu woman was a combined construct, involving Victorian notions of femininity, the new ideals of womanhood which the western-educated elite in India were historicizing, and the image of Indian women which was predominant in Anglo-Indian novels. Nina Auerbach's *Woman and the Demon* is one of the many texts on the Victorian conception of the feminine. The Indian endeavor to reconstruct the image of the elite woman is examined in three articles from *Recasting Women: Essays in Colonial History.* These are Uma Chakravarti's "Whatever Happened to the Vedic *Dasi*? Orientalism, Nationalism and a Script for the Past," Sumanta Banerjee's "Marginalization of Women's Popular Culture in Nineteenth-Century Bengal," and "Tracing Savitri's Pedigree: Victorian Racism and the Image of Women in Indo-Anglian Literature" by Susie Tharu. My own article on the representation of India and Indian women in the fiction of Kipling and Duncan covers the third aspect of the construct mentioned above.

12 In this passage, she is taking norms, which before her had been applied primarily to Victorian women, and charting them as Indian. I would argue that this transference is a legitimate effort to resist colonialism, made in the same spirit as that which Gandhi demonstrated in the 1920s, 30s, and 40s. Employing Nandy's terms, we might say that Swarnakumari Devi is protecting her society from the White Sahib by using the Occident—or, more precisely, what the Occident has laid claim to—for her own purposes. Much more than a simple assertion of Indianness, her portrait of the Hindu woman as the only authentic example of traditional femininity is a declaration of the redundance of the West in India.

5   Gandhi, Ambedkar, and *Untouchable*

1   Gandhi coined the word 'harijan,' to counter the prevailing reputation of the untouchables in the earlier part of this century. It was and still is the favored name for untouchables among caste Hindus and especially Congress members. According to D. S. Khare, for untouchables, this name has come to be associated with Hindu guilt. He quotes a Lucknow Chamar: "Harijan means what we can never be allowed to become by the caste Hindu, and what we may not want to be anyway. It was a superficial way for Gandhi to resolve *his* guilt" (120). The imperial government tended to use the term 'depressed classes,' and the post-independence Indian government refers to untouchables as 'scheduled castes,' a term that originated with the implementation of the Government of India Act, 1935, in which those castes entitled to reserved seats were listed in a schedule. In India some contemporary untouchable communities have adopted the term 'dalit' or 'dalita,' which means 'depressed' in Hindi, as a means of empowerment. For a detailed history and analysis of the political business of naming the untouchable, see chapter 1 of Trilok Nath's *Politics of the Depressed Classes*. In his book *The Untouchable as himself,* Khare provides an excellent description of the way in which the Lucknow Chamars manipulate these names (118–22).

2   Many historians who write about the nationalist movement, Bipan Chandra included, tend to represent Gandhi's approach to untouchability as if it were also that of the Congress. But, in fact, there was much more debate about this issue in Congress circles than is generally assumed. In the thirties, Nehru was at odds with Gandhi about untouchability as a feature of the Congress platform. When news reached him in jail that Gandhi had decided to undertake a "fast unto death" in protest against the government's communal 1932 award, Nehru was angry: "I felt annoyed with him for choosing a side issue for his final sacrifice. What would be the result on our freedom movement? Would not the larger issues fade into the background?" (*Toward Freedom* 236). The notion that untouchability was a "side issue," which we see in so many later histories of nationalism, originated with such powerful politicians and influential thinkers as Nehru.

3   Untouchables were, of course, encouraged to join protest movements launched in the interests of other political issues. Only in the matter of their own untouchability did Gandhi expect them to step back and allow caste Hindus to redeem themselves.

4   I do not wish to suggest, however, that Ambedkar was the only untouchable leader. Ambedkar had to compete with a number of other educated untouchables who were winning positions of prominence in their own communities and in the nationalist arena. I am thinking here particularly of M. C. Rajah of Madras, the first untouchable of India to be nominated to a legislative council

and a staunch advocate of separate electorates. But many other untouchable leaders, with positions similar or often opposed to Ambedkar's stance, were working for the improvement of the untouchable standard of living throughout the twenties, thirties, and forties. It is often difficult to find information about them because of the tendency of nationalist histories to absorb the question of untouchability into the overall Congress program. Trilok Nath's *Politics of the Depressed Classes,* however, offers a good examination of untouchable issues raised by untouchable leaders who operated both outside of and in conjunction with Congress policies.

Nor do I want to create the impression that the untouchables of India were entirely homogeneous in insisting that Congress *not* speak for them. There were, of course, many untouchables who joined the Congress and trusted that Gandhi's policies would secure their freedom in Hindu society.

5   Although I use the word 'Hindu' to describe Ambedkar, I recognize that it is problematic. At the time he wrote his speech, in 1936, he was contemplating converting to Buddhism. He eventually did so, but not for a number of years. Perhaps he delayed his conversion because of the unique position his 'Hindu' connection offered him. As an untouchable addressing Hindus, Ambedkar occupied a place that was neither inside nor outside Hinduism. He could critique Hinduism with the confidence of someone who had direct experience and knowledge of it, while at the same time he remained far enough on the margins of Hinduism that non-Hindus could trust his opinions, could believe that he was free of the sorts of allegiances which might color a caste Hindu's assessment of the situation.

6   *Untouchable* is clearly part of a much larger, nationalist body of writing, whose audience comprises the English-educated Indian and the western reader interested in India's independence movement. Although frequently charitable in its motives, this writing tended to depict the participation of the peasant, untouchable, or worker in the nationalist struggle as fundamentally physical. He or she is generally constructed as a body who swells the ranks of the oppressed and whose politicization is in line with the teachings of the mainstream nationalists leaders. Nehru's *The Discovery of India* is a particularly important expression of this narrative delineation.

6   Nostalgia and 1947

1   Before I argue this point any further, I should like to acknowledge those novels, written within the last ten years of the Raj, which are not particularly nostalgic. Specifically, I am referring here to Christine Weston's 1943 *Indigo,* one of the most complex treatments of Indian nationalism to be found among Anglo-Indian pre-independence fiction, and Rumer Godden's *The Lady and the Unicorn* and *Black Narcissus,* published in 1938 and 1939 respectively. Few

literary scholars have written about these two novelists, perhaps because what they have to say about India and Indians represents a significant departure from the attitudes conveyed in such works as Mason's *The Wild Sweet Witch* and even Thompson's trilogy about the shutting down of the Indian Empire. I choose to mention Weston and Godden because their texts constitute exceptions to my argument.

2   This is practically a truism in historiography about Indian nationalism. P. N. Chopra sees the Quit India movement of 1942 as a sign that the Gandhian phase of the struggle was over: "It was clear to discerning eyes that Gandhi's policy of non-violence, non-cooperation had outlived its utility for the achievement of independence and was no longer popular with the Indian nationalists who were convinced that more radical and revolutionary methods were needed . . ." (intro). This is also the tacit assumption of the two penultimate chapters in *India's Struggle for Independence,* delineating the final few years of the Empire in India, and of the last chapter of Sumit Sarkar's *Modern India.*

3   If we compare Tregard's statement here with Orde's general attitude to the "vocal classes" in "The Enlightenments of Pagett, M.P., we realize how great a concession Mason is making here. Tregard recognizes the legitimacy of the same class of educated Indians that Orde so confidently dismisses. Moreover, Tregard's later remark that "the good we can do has to be balanced against the harm to our own lives" (199) suggests that the Anglo-Indian sacrifice, of which Orde is so proud, is by 1938, the period of the last section of the novel, to be replaced by a calculation of self-interest. The rhetoric of the Englishman's civilizing mission had begun to break down during Mason's career in the ICS.

4   For another interpretation of this situation, see Humphrey Trevelyan's history-cum-memoir, *The India We Left,* which paints a much more positive picture of Indian participation in the ICS toward the end of British rule and of Congress politicians.

5   It is significant that nostalgia appears in the novel only in the last two sections, when Upton and Tregard are the deputy commissioners of Garhwal. Both of these men come into power only after Indian nationalism and constitutional reforms have left their impress on the ICS, unlike Bennett whose era in the novel, 1875, figures as a kind of golden age for the district officer, when there were supposedly no encroachments on British power. Nostalgia becomes a feature of the novel only at that moment when ICS control is threatened. Nostalgia and control are inevitably linked in *The Wild Sweet Witch.*

6   Ela Sen's 1944 collection of short stories, *Darkening Days: Being a Narrative of Famine-Stricken Bengal,* paints a similar picture of social and moral breakdown.

7   Over the years, the death rate during the famine has been calculated by various scholars and government officials at anywhere between 1 million to

Greenough's estimate of 3.5 to 3.8 million (see 237). I use Greenough's figures here because his is one of the most recent and comprehensive studies of the famine available. Exactly how many people died in the famine remains unknown. The gathering of mortality statistics grew increasingly difficult as the famine progressed throughout 1943 because the *chowkidars,* who reported the deaths in their respective villages to the external authorities, often died themselves and their replacement often took several weeks, during which many deaths presumably went unrecorded (see Famine Inquiry Commission 108-10).

8   Nehru in *The Discovery of India* comes to much the same conclusion about the effect of British intervention in the allocation of land during the early colonial period in Bengal (218-19). Kabir's views, then, were in keeping with the standard nationalist reconstruction of history, the purpose of which was to develop a nationalist ideology.

9   The fact that the majority of Bengal's peasants were Muslim and that the peasants died in far greater numbers than any other section of the population also leads to the conclusion that the Muslims suffered as much or more loss during the famine than any other community.

10   Both the provincial governments in power during the Bengal famine, however, were Muslim-based, and, according to Bhatia's research, many of the government's officials were corrupt and may have been involved in profit-making at the expense of the starving peasants (see 334-36).

11   All of the above statistics are taken from Sarkar's *Modern India 1885-1947,* pages 432-34.

Bibliography

Ahmad, Aijaz. *In Theory: Classes, Nations, Literatures.* London and New York: Verso, 1992.

Ambedkar, B. R. *What Congress and Gandhi Have Done to the Untouchables.* Bombay: Thacker and Co. Ltd., 1946.

———. *Writings and Speeches.* Vol. 1. comp. Vasant Moon. Bombay: Education Department, Government of Maharashtra, 1989.

The Amrita Bazar Patrika. "Swarnakumari Devi's Death—Bengal's Loss." 5 July 1932: 3. National Library, Calcutta.

———. 7 July 1932: 3. National Library, Calcutta.

Anand, Mulk Raj. *Untouchable.* 1935. New Delhi: Arnold Publishers, 1981.

———. "The Sources of Protest in My Novels." *Contemporary Indian Fiction in English: Proceedings of the National Seminar held at the University of Kerala on the 80th Birthday of Mulk Raj Anand.* Ed. K. Ayyappa Paniker. n.p. and n.d.

Andrews, Judith W. Introduction. *The High-Caste Hindu Woman.* By Pandita Ramabai Sarasvati. 1887. New York, Chicago, and Toronto: Fleming H. Revell, 1901.

Anstey, F. [Thomas Anstey Guthrie]. *A Barnyard for Bengal.* London: Methuen, 1902.

———. *Baboo Hurry Bungshoo Jabberjee, B.A.* London: J. M. Dent, 1897.

Arnold, Edwin. *India Revisited.* 2nd ed. London: Kegan Paul, Trench, Trubner, 1891.

Auerbach, Nina. *Woman and the Demon.* Cambridge: Harvard UP, 1982.

Bald, Suresht Renjen. *Novelists and Political Consciousness: Literary Expression of Indian Nationalism 1919-1947.* Delhi: Chanakya Publications, 1982.

Ballhatchet, Kenneth. *Race, Sex and Class under the Raj: Imperial Attitudes and Policies and their Critics, 1793-1905.* London: Weidenfeld and Nicolson, 1980.

Banerjee, Sumanta. "Marginalization of Women's Popular Culture in Nineteenth-Century Bengal." *Recasting Women: Essays in Colonial History.* Eds. Kumkum Sangari and Sudesh Vaid. New Delhi: kali for women, 1989. 127-79.

Barr, Pat. *The Memsahibs: The Women of Victorian India.* 1976. London: Century, 1989.

Becker, George J., ed. *Documents of Modern Literary Realism.* Princeton: Princeton UP, 1963.

Belsey, Catherine. "Literature, History, Politics." *Literature and History.* 9 (1982): 17-27.

Bhatia, B. M. *Famines in India: A Study in Some Aspects of the Economic History of India (1860-1945)*. London: Asia Publishing House, 1963.

Bhattacharya, Bhabani. *So Many Hungers!* London: Gollancz, 1947.

Billington, Mary Frances. *Women in India*. 1895. New Delhi: Amarko Book Agency, 1973.

Bodley, Rachel L. Introduction. *The High-Caste Hindu Woman*. By Pandita Ramabai Sarasvati. 1887. New Delhi: Inter-India Publications, 1984.

Brantlinger, Patrick. *Rule of Darkness: British Literature and Imperialism, 1830-1914*. Ithaca and London: Cornell UP, 1988.

Chakravarti, Uma. "Whatever Happened to the Vedic *Dasi?* Orientalism, Nationalism and a Script for the Past." *Recasting Woman: Essays in Colonial History*. Eds. Kumkum Sangari and Sudesh Vaid. New Delhi: kali for women, 1989. 27–89.

Chandra, Bipan and Mridula Mukherjee, Aditya Mukherjee, K. N. Panikkar, and Sucheta Mahajan. *India's Struggle for Independence: 1857-1947*. 1988. New Delhi: Penguin, 1989.

Chatterjee, Partha. *Nationalist Thought and the Colonial World: A Derivative Discourse?* London and Delhi: Zed Books, and Oxford UP, 1986.

Chattopadhyayya, Kamaladevi. *The Awakening of Indian Women*. Madras: Everyman's Press, 1939.

Chaudhuri, Nupur and Margaret Strobel, eds. *Western Women and Imperialism: Complicity and Resistance*. Bloomington and Indianapolis: Indiana UP, 1992.

Chirol, Valentine. *India Old and New*. London: Macmillan, 1921.

Chopra, P. N. Introduction. *Quit India Movement: British Secret Documents*. New Delhi: Interprint, 1986.

Cowasjee, Saros, ed. *More Stories from the Raj and After: From Kipling to the Present Day*. London: Graften Books, 1986.

Dangle, Arjun, ed. *No Entry for the New Sun: Translations from Modern Marathi Dalit Poetry*. Bombay: Disha, 1992.

Darling, Sir Malcolm. *Apprentice to Power: India 1904-1908*. London: Hogarth P, 1966.

Das, G. K. *E. M. Forster's India*. London: Macmillan, 1977.

Dobbin, Christine E. *Basic Documents in the Development of Modern India and Pakistan*. London: Van Nostrand Reinhold, 1970.

Duffett, W. E., and A. R. Hicks and G. R. Parkin. *India Today: The Background of Indian Nationalism*. New York: John Day, 1942.

Duncan, Sara Jeannette. *The Burnt Offering*. 1909. Toronto: Toronto UP, 1978.

———. *Set in Authority*. New York: Doubleday, Page & Company, 1906.

———. *The Simple Adventures of a Memsahib*. 1893. Ed. Thomas E. Tausky. Ottawa: Tecumseh, 1986.

Dutt, R. Palme. *India To-Day*. London: Gollancz, 1940.

Dyer, Helen S. *Pandita Ramabai: The Story of Her Life*. London: Morgan and Scott, 1907.

Eliot, George. *Adam Bede*. 1859. Harmondsworth: Penguin, 1983.

Eliot, T. S. "Rudyard Kipling." *A Choice of Kipling's Verse*. 1941. London and Boston: Faber, 1987.

Epstein, Simon. "District Officers in Decline: The Erosion of British Authority in the Bombay Countryside, 1919 to 1947." *Modern Asian Studies* 16.3 (1982): 493–518.

[India] Famine Inquiry Commission. *Report on Bengal*. 1945. New York: Arno, 1976.

Fischer, Louis. *Gandhi: His Life and Message for the World*. New York: New American Library, 1954.

Forster, E. M. *A Passage to India*. 1924. Harmondsworth: Penguin, 1980.

———. "Reflections in India: I—Too Late?" *The Nation and the Athenaeum*. 30 Jan. 1922: 614–15.

Fowler, Marian. *Below the Peacock Fan: First Ladies of the Raj*. 1987. Markham: Penguin Canada, 1988.

———. *Redney: A Life of Sara Jeannette Duncan*. Toronto: Anansi, 1983.

Frankenberg, Ruth. *White Women, Race Matters: The Social Construction of Whiteness*. Minneapolis: U of Minnesota P, 1993.

Fuller, Mrs. Marcus B. (Jenny). *The Wrongs of Indian Womanhood*. 1900. New Delhi: Inter-India Publications, 1984.

Gandhi, M. K. *M. K. Gandhi: Select Writings*. Ed. B. K. Ahluwalia. New Delhi: Sagor Publications, 1970.

Ghosal, Swarnakumari Devi (or Srimati Svarna Kumari Devi). *The Fatal Garland*. 1915. New York: Macmillan, 1918.

———. *Short Stories*. Madras: Ganesh, 1919.

———. *An Unfinished Song*. 1913. New York: Macmillan, 1914.

Gilbert, Elliot L. *The Good Kipling: Studies in the Short Story*. Oberlin: Ohio UP, 1970.

Godden, Rumer. *Black Narcissus*. 1939. Harmondsworth: Penguin, 1979.

———. *The Lady and the Unicorn*. 1938. Harmondsworth: Penguin, 1982.

Golant, William. *The Long Afternoon: British India 1601-1947*. London: Hamish Hamilton, 1975.

Gopal, Ram. *How India Struggled For Freedom: (A Political History)*. Bombay: The Book Centre, 1967.

Greenberger, Allen J. *The British Image of India: A Study in the Literature of Imperialism 1880-1960*. London: Oxford UP, 1969.

Greenough, Paul R. *Prosperity and Misery in Modern Bengal: The Famine of 1943-44*. New York and Oxford: Oxford UP, 1982.

Guha, Ranajit. "On Some Aspects of the Historiography of Colonial India." *Subaltern Studies I: Writings on South Asian History and Society*. Ed. Ranajit Guha. Delhi: Oxford UP, 1982. 1–8.

———, ed. *Subaltern Studies I: Writings on South Asian History and Society*. Delhi: Oxford UP, 1982.

——, ed. *Subaltern Studies II*. Delhi: Oxford UP, 1983.

——, ed. *Subaltern Studies III*. Delhi: Oxford UP, 1984.

——, ed. *Subaltern Studies IV*. Delhi: Oxford UP, 1985.

——, ed. *Subaltern Studies V*. Delhi: Oxford UP, 1987.

——, ed. *Subaltern Studies VI*. Delhi: Oxford UP, 1989.

Heimsath, Charles H. *Indian Nationalism and Hindu Social Reform*. Princeton: Princeton UP, 1964.

Heller, Erich. "The Realistic Fallacy." *Documents of Modern Literary Realism*. George J. Becker, ed. Princeton: Princeton UP, 1963. 591-98.

Howe, Susanne. *Novels of Empire*. 1949. New York: Kraus Reprint, 1971.

Hubel, Teresa. " 'The Bride of His Country': Love, Marriage, and the Imperialist Paradox in the Indian Fiction of Sara Jeannette Duncan and Rudyard Kipling." *Ariel* 21.1 (1990): 3-19.

Hussain, Iqbalunnisa. *Purdah and Polygamy, Life in an Indian Muslim Household*. Bangalore: Hosali, 1944.

Hutchins, Francis G. *The Illusion of Permanence: British Imperialism in India*. Princeton: Princeton UP, 1967.

Jayawardena, Kumari. *Feminism and Nationalism in the Third World*. London: Zed Books, 1986.

Johnson, Gordon. "Partition, Agitation and Congress: Bengal 1904 to 1908." *Locality, Province and Nation: Essays on Indian Politics 1870 to 1940, Reprinted from Modern Asian Studies 1973*. Eds. John Gallagher, Gordon Johnson, and Anil Seal. London: Cambridge UP, 1973. 213-268.

Joshi, Barbara R. *Democracy in Search of Equality: Untouchable Politics and Indian Social Change*. Atlantic Highlands, New Jersey: Humanities P, 1982.

Kabir, Humayun. *Muslim Politics 1906-47 and Other Essays*. Calcutta: Firma K. L. Mukhopadhyay, 1969.

Karaka, D. F. *I've Shed My Tears: A Candid View of Resurgent India*. New York and London: D. Appleton-Century, 1947.

Karlekar, Malavika. *Voices from Within: Early Personal Narratives of Bengali Women*. Delhi: Oxford UP, 1991.

Kaushik, Asha. *Politics, Aesthetics and Culture: A Study of Indo-Anglian Political Novel*. New Delhi: Manohar Publications, 1988.

Kenner, Hugh. "The Making of the Modernist Canon." *Chicago Review* 34.2 (1984): 49-61.

Khare, D. S. *The Untouchable as himself: ideology, identity, and pragmatism among the Lucknow Chamars*. Cambridge: Cambridge UP, 1984.

Kipling, Rudyard. "The Enlightenments of Pagett, M.P." *Many Inventions*. 1893. *The Collected Works of Rudyard Kipling*. Vol. 5. New York: AMS, 1970.

——. "Mandalay." *A Choice of Kipling's Verse*. London: Faber, 1987.

——. "On the City Wall." *Soldier's Three: The Story of the Gadsbys: In Black and White*. 1895. *The Collected Works of Rudyard Kipling*. Vol. 2. New York: AMS, 1970.

——. *Plain Tales from the Hills*. 1888. Harmondsworth: Penguin, 1987.

——. *The Readers' Guide to Rudyard Kipling's Work*. Ed. R. E. Harbord. Kent: Gibs & Sons, 1965/66.

Krupat, Arnold. "Native American Literature and the Canon." *Canons*. Ed. Robert von Hallberg. Chicago: U of Chicago P, 1984. 309–35.

Low, D. A. "Introduction: The Climactic Years 1917–1947." *Congress and the Raj: Facets of the Indian Struggle 1917–47*. London: Heinemann, 1977.

Lukacs, Georg. *Studies in European Realism*. New York: Grosset Dunlap, 1964.

Lyall, Alfred. *The Rise and Expansion of the British Dominion in India*. London: John Murray, 1910.

MacMillan, Margaret. *Women of the Raj*. New York: Thames and Hudson, 1988.

Mani, Lata. "The Production of an Official Discourse on *Sati* in Early Nineteenth-Century Bengal." *Europe and its Others*. Vol. I: Proceedings of the Essex Conference on the Sociology of Literature July 1984. Eds. Francis Barker et al, Colchester: U of Essex, 1985. 107–27.

Mason, Philip. *The Wild Sweet Witch*. 1947. New Delhi: Penguin, 1989.

——. (under the name Philip Woodruff) *The Men Who Ruled India: The Guardians*. New York: Schocken Books, 1954.

Meyers, Jeffrey. *Fiction and the Colonial Experience*. New Jersey: Rowman and Littlefield, 1973.

Mill, John Stuart. *Collected Works of John Stuart Mill: Essays on Politics and Society*. Volume XIX. Ed. J. M. Robson. Toronto: Toronto UP, 1977.

Mohanty, Chandra Talpade. "Under Western Eyes: Feminist Scholarship and Colonial Discourse." *boundary 2* 12.3 (1984): 333–58.

Moore, R.J. *Endgames of Empire: Studies of Britain's Indian Problem*. Delhi: Oxford UP, 1988.

Moorhouse, Geoffrey. *India Britannica*. New York: Harper, 1983.

Morris, James/Jan. *Pax Britannica: The Climax of an Empire*. 1968. Harmondsworth: Penguin, 1979.

Mukherjee, Arun P. "The Exclusions of Postcolonial Theory and Mulk Raj Anand's 'Untouchable': A Case Study." *Ariel* 22.3 (1991): 27–48.

Mukherjee, Meenakshi. *Realism and Reality: The Novel and Society in India*. Delhi: Oxford UP, 1985.

Naipaul, V. S. *India: A Wounded Civilization*. London: Deutsch, 1977.

Nandy, Ashis. *The Intimate Enemy: Loss and Recovery of Self Under Colonialism*. 1983. Delhi: Oxford UP, 1990.

Nath, Trilok. *Politics of the Depressed Classes*. Delhi: Deputy Publications, 1987.

Nehru, Jawaharlal. *The Discovery of India*. 1946. Ed. Robert I. Crane. Garden City: Doubleday, 1960.

——. *Toward Freedom: The Autobiography of Jawaharlal Nehru*. New York: John Day, 1941.

Nehru, Shyam Kumari, ed. *Our Cause: A Symposium by Indian Women*. Allahabad: Kitabistan, 1936.

Newcomb, John Timberman. "Canonical Ahistoricism vs. Histories of Canons: Towards Methodological Dissensus." *South Atlantic Review* 54.4 (1989): 3-20.

O'Hanlon, Rosalind. *Caste, Conflict, and Ideology: Mahatma Jotirao Phule and Low Caste Protest in Nineteenth-Century Western India.* Cambridge: Cambridge UP, 1985.

———. "Recovering the Subject: Subaltern Studies and Histories of Resistance in Colonial South Asia." *Modern Asian Studies* 22.1 (1988): 189-224.

Orwell, George. "Rudyard Kipling." *Decline of the English Murder and Other Essays.* 1942. Harmondsworth: Penguin, 1981. 45-62.

Pandey, Gyan. "Peasant Revolt and Indian Nationalism: The Peasant Movement in Awadh, 1919-22." *Subaltern Studies I: Writings on South Asian History and Society.* Ed. Ranajit Guha. New Delhi: Oxford UP, 1982. 143-97.

Pandey, Gyanendra. "In Defense of the Fragment: Writing About Hindu-Muslim Riots for 'Indian' Pasts?" *Representations* 37.1 (1992): 27-55.

Parry, Benita. *Delusions and Discoveries: Studies on India in the British Imagination: 1880-1930.* Berkeley and Los Angeles: U of California, 1972.

———. "The Politics of Representation in *A Passage to India.*" *A Passage to India: Essays in Interpretation.* Ed. John Beer. London: Macmillan, 1985. 27-43.

Plimpton, George. "Ernest Hemingway." *Writers at Work, Second Series.* New York: The Viking Press, 1965. 217-39.

Prakash, Gyan. "Writing Post-Orientalist Histories of the Third World: Perspectives from Indian Historiography." *Comparative Studies in Society and History* 32 (1990): 383-408.

Ray, Bharati. "Freedom Movement and Women's Awakening in Bengal, 1911-1929." *The Indian Historical Review* 12 (n.y.): 130-63.

———. "*Swadeshi* Movement and Women's Awakening in Bengal, 1903-1910." *The Calcutta Historical Journal* 9.2 (1985): 72-97.

Rosaldo, Renato. "Imperialist Nostalgia." *Representations* 26.1 (1989): 107-22.

Rudolph, Lloyd I. and Susanne Hoeber Rudolph. *The Modernity of Tradition: Political Development in India.* Chicago: U of Chicago P, 1967.

Rushdie, Salman. *Midnight's Children.* 1981. London: Pan, 1982.

Said, Edward W. *Culture and Imperialism.* Knopf: New York, 1993.

———. *Orientalism.* 1978. New York: Vintage, 1979.

———. *The World, the Text, and the Critic.* Cambridge: Harvard UP, 1983.

Sangari, Kumkum and Sudesh Vaid, eds. *Recasting Women: Essays in Colonial History.* New Delhi: kali for women, 1989.

Sarasvati, Pandita Ramabai. *The High-Caste Hindu Woman.* 1887. New Delhi: Inter-India Publications, 1984.

Sarkar, Sumit. *Modern India, 1885-1947.* (1983) London: Macmillan, 1989.

Sarkar, Tanika. "Politics and women in Bengal—the conditions and meaning of participation." *Women in Colonial India: Essays on Survival, Work and the State.* Delhi: Oxford UP, 1989. 231-41.

Sarma, Gobinda Prasad. *Nationalism in Indo-Anglian Fiction*. 1978. New Delhi: Sterling Publishers Private Limited, 1990.

Schuster, George and Guy Wint. *India and Democracy*. London, Macmillan, 1941.

Sen, Ela. *Darkening Days: Being a Narrative of Famine-Stricken Bengal*. Calcutta: Susil Gopta, 1944.

Sen Gupta, Padmini. *Pioneer Woman of India*. Bombay: Thacker, 1944.

Sharpe, Jenny. "Figures of Colonial Resistance." *Modern Fiction Studies* 35.1 (1989): 137–55.

Showalter, Elaine. "*A Passage to India* as 'Marriage Fiction': Forster's Sexual Politics." *Women & Literature* 5.2 (1977): 3–16.

Singh, Bhupal. *A Survey of Anglo-Indian Fiction*. 1934. London and Totowa: Curzon Press and Rowman and Littlefield, 1974.

Singh, Frances B. "*A Passage to India*, the National Movement, and Independence." *Twentieth Century Literature* 31. 2–3 (1985): 265–78.

Singh, Rashna B. *The Imperishable Empire: A Study of British Fiction on India*. Washington: Three Continents P, 1988.

Smith, Barbara Herrnstein. "Contingencies of Value." *Canons*. Ed. Robert von Hallberg. Chicago and London: U of Chicago P, 1984. 5–39.

Smith, Vincent A. *The Oxford History of India*. Ed. Percival Spear. 4th ed. Delhi: Oxford UP, 1958.

Spear, Percival. *A History of India: Volume Two*. 1965. London: Penguin, 1987.

Spivak, Gayatri Chakravorty. "Can the Subaltern Speak?" *Marxism and the Interpretation of Culture*. Eds. Cary Nelson and Lawrence Grossberg. Urbana and Chicago: U of Illinois P, 1988.

———. "Interview with Gayatri Chakravorty Spivak." *Ariel: A Review of English Literature*. By Leon De Kock. 23.3 (1992): 29–47.

———. "A Literary Representation of The Subaltern: A Woman's Text From the Third World." *In Other Worlds: Essays in Cultural Politics*. New York and London: Routledge, 1988. 241–68.

———. *Outside in the Teaching Machine*. New York and London: Routledge, 1993.

———. "Three Women's Texts and a Critique of Imperialism." *Critical Inquiry* 12.1 (1985): 243–61.

———. "The Rani of Sirmur." *Europe and its Others*. Vol. I: Proceedings of the Essex Conference on the Sociology of Literature July 1984. Eds. Francis Barker et al. Colchester: U of Essex, 1985. 128–51.

Suleri, Sara. "The Geography of *A Passage to India*." *Modern Critical Views: E. M. Forster*. Ed. Harold Bloom. New York, New Haven, and Philadelphia: Chelsea House, 1987. 169–75.

———. *The Rhetoric of English India*. Chicago and London: U of Chicago P, 1992.

Tausky, Thomas E. *Sara Jeannette Duncan: Novelist of Empire*. Port Credit: P. D. Meany, 1980.

Thapar, Romila. "Imagined Religious Communities? Ancient History and the

Modern Search for a Hindu Identity." *Modern Asian Studies*. 23.2 (1989): 209–231.

Tharu, Susie. "Tracing Savitri's Pedigree: Victorian Racism and the Image of Women in Indo-Anglian Literature." *Recasting Women: Essays in Colonial History*. Eds. Kumkum Sangari and Sudesh Vaid. New Delhi: kali for women, 1989. 254–68.

Thompson, Edward. *An End of the Hours*. London: Macmillan, 1938.

———. *A Farewell to India*. London: Ernest Benn, 1931.

———. *An Indian Day*. 1927. Harmondsworth: Penguin, 1938.

——— and G. T. Garratt. *Rise and Fulfilment of British Rule in India*. 1934. New York: AMS, 1971.

Tokarczyk, Michelle M. and Elizabeth A. Fay, eds. *Working-Class Women in the Academy: Laborers in the Knowledge Factory*. Amherst: U of Massachusetts P, 1993.

Trevelyan, Humphrey. *The India We Left: Charles Trevelyan 1826–65, Humphrey Trevelyan 1929–47*. London and Basingstoke: Macmillan London, 1972.

Trilling, Lionel. "Kipling." 1943. *The Liberal Imagination: Essays on Literature and Society*. Garden City: Doubleday, 1954. 120–29.

Viswanathan, Gauri. "The Beginnings of English Literary Study in British India." *The Oxford Literary Review* 9.1–2 (1987): 2–25.

Vivekananda, Swami. *Women of India*. Madras: Sri Ramakrishna Math, n.d.

Watt, Ian. *The Rise of the Novel: Studies in Defoe, Richardson and Fielding*. 1957. London: Hogarth P, 1987.

Weston, Christine. *Indigo*. New York: Scribner's, 1943.

White, Hayden. *Tropics of Discourse: Essays in Cultural Criticism*. 1978. Baltimore and London: Johns Hopkins UP, 1987.

Whitman, Walt. "Passage to India." 1871. *The Norton Anthology of American Literature*. Volume I. New York and London: Norton, 1979. 2061–68.

Index

Ambedkar, B. R., 8, 9, 148–50, 154,
155, 157–62, 172, 176, 177–78
Anand, Mulk Raj, 122, 208; *Untouchable*, 7, 9, 85, 150–51, 161–77
Anglo-India: attitudes toward middle-
class Indians, 49–50; attitudes
toward nationalism, 45–46, 189–91;
defensiveness of, 27; and Duncan,
46–47, 49–60; in Forster, 99; and
Kipling, 8, 24, 27–37, 43–44; and
retirement, 181–82, 192–93. *See
also* British women in India; Indian
women; Literature; Marriage; Memsahibs

Bhattacharya, Bhabani, 208; *So Many
Hungers!*, 10, 183–84, 196–207
Billington, Mary Frances (journalist),
111–15, 116, 117, 127, 128, 133, 139,
141
British imperialism, 1–3, 14, 45, 70,
72; absentmindedness, myth of, 75–
76; in Bhattacharya, 196–97, 200–
201; civilizing mission, 111, 118, 135;
connection to nationalism, 79–82,
131–34, 136–37; divide-and-rule, 78,
149; and Duncan, 46–51, 62–65,
69, 70; and Forster, 86–87; Indian
Civil Service (ICS), 27, 29–30, 58,
62, 68, 98, 108, 182–95; and Indian
peasants, 29–30, 49–50, 85, 184–
86, 194, 198; justification of, 35–36,
47–48, 71, 90, 219 n.2; and Kipling,
23, 24, 27–44; liberal imperialism,
73–76, 89–94, 138, 185–87, 213 n.2,
214 n.7; and Mason, 185–95; mis-

sionaries, ties to, 115; nostalgia for,
9–10, 179–82, 192–95, 220 n.5; as
permanent, 111–13; policy of non-
interference, 110–11, 215 n.1; as
psychological colonization, 123–24;
and realism, 168–70; and transfer
of power, 179–84, 187–89, 192–95;
and untouchables, 150, 162. *See also*
Orientalism
British women in India, 47; as activists
for women's rights, 109–10; as emblems of stability, 52–57; as *femme
fatales*, 55–56; in Forster, 95; praise
of, 53–54; as subordinate to men, 51;
as voices of imperialism, 53, 98–99,
111–18, 127, 133, 135, 193; work of,
20, 36–37, 53, 111–18; from working
classes, 57, 211–12 n.9; as writers,
24, 46, 57, 70. *See also* Memsahibs

Canons: analysis of, 6–8, 69, 86–
88, 95, 121–22, 163; of history, 5;
Kipling and, 23–25
Class: analysis of, 10–12; conflict between classes, 80–84, 85, 149–50,
153–61, 164–66, 170–73, 175, 177–
78, 197–202; in postcolonial theory,
10–12, 176; and realism, 167–70
Congress. *See* Indian National Congress

Devi, Swarnakumari, 7, 121, 122, 126,
137–39, 208; *The Fatal Garland*, 140;
An Unfinished Song, 9, 121, 123, 137,
140–46, 161
Duncan, Sara Jeannette, 45–46, 181;

Teresa Hubel is a visiting scholar
at the University of Western Ontario.

Library of Congress Cataloging-in-Publication Data
Hubel, Teresa.
Whose India? : the independence struggle in British and Indian fiction and history /
Teresa Hubel.
   p.   cm.
Includes bibliographical references and index.
ISBN 0-8223-1708-7 (alk. paper). — ISBN 0-8223-1718-4 (pbk. : alk. paper)
1. Anglo-Indian fiction—History and criticism. 2. India—History—Autonomy and
independence movements—Historiography. 3. Kipling, Rudyard, 1865–1936—
Knowledge—India. 4. Indic fiction (English)—History and criticism. 5. English
fiction—Indic influences. 6. India—In literature. I. Title.
PR9492.5.H83   1996
823.009'3254—dc20

                                                                95-30470

DATE DUE